Max Weber and Postmodern Theory

Max Weber and Postmodern Theory:

Rationalization versus Re-enchantment

Nicholas Gane

First published 2002 by
PALGRAVE
Houndmills, Basingstoke, Hampshire RG21 6XS and
175 Fifth Avenue, New York, N.Y. 10010
Companies and representatives throughout the world

PALGRAVE is the new global academic imprint of
St. Martin's Press LLC Scholarly and Reference Division and
Palgrave Publishers Ltd (formerly Macmillan Press Ltd).

ISBN 0–333–93058–4

This book is printed on paper suitable for recycling and
made from fully managed and sustained forest sources.

A catalogue record for this book is available
from the British Library.

Library of Congress Cataloging-in-Publication Data

Gane, Nicholas, 1971–
Max Weber and postmodern theory: rationalisation versus
re-enchantment/Nicholas Gane.
    p. cm.
Includes bibliographical references and index.
    ISBN 0–333–93058–4
1. Weber, Max, 1864–1920. 2. Postmodernism – Social aspects. 3. Culture.
4. Civilization, Modern. I. Title.

HM449.G36 2002
306–dc21

                                                        2001056111

10 9 8 7 6 5 4 3 2 1
11 10 09 08 07 06 05 04 03 02

Printed and bound in Great Britain by
Antony Rowe Ltd, Chippenham, Wiltshire

Contents

Acknowledgements   ix

1   **Introduction**   1
    Reading Weber   4
    Towards the postmodern   10

**PART I – Max Weber's theory and critique
of rationalization**   **13**

2   **Rationalization and disenchantment, I: from
the origins of religion to the death of God**   15
    Magical religiosity: naturalism, symbolism and beyond   16
    Universal religion: from ancient Judaism to the
    Protestant ethic   17
    The death of God: towards cultural nihilism   19
    From cultural to societal rationalization:
    towards bureaucratic domination   23
    Conclusion   26

3   **Rationalization and disenchantment, II: the
differentiation and de-differentiation of
modern culture**   28
    Rationalization and the differentiation of culture   29
    The 'Intermediate Reflection'   30
    The question of value-incommensurability   34
    Cultural de-differentiation: the tragedy of rationalization   41
    Conclusion   44

4   **The value of instrumental reason: 'Science as
a Vocation'**   45
    The scientific calling   46
    From Plato to Newton: the historical values of science   49
    Weber, Nietzsche and the 'last men'   51
    Weber and Tolstoy: exhuming the presuppositions of science   55
    The value of practical reason   59
    Conclusion   62

5   The ethical irrationality of the world:
     'Politics as a Vocation'   64
     The ideal-types of political action   65
     Towards a reconciliation of conviction and responsibility   69
     The immediacy of political judgement   73
     Weber and Kant: from autonomy to heteronomy   76
     Conclusion   78

PART II – Weber and postmodern theory:
Lyotard, Foucault and Baudrillard   81

6   Intermediate reflection   83

7   Weber, Lyotard and the aesthetic sphere   89
     Postmodern science   89
     *Cultural differentiation and the collapse of the
     grand narrative*   94
     The later Lyotard   102
     Art, figure and the aesthetic sphere   103
     Conclusion   112

8   Weber, Foucault and the political sphere   113
     Foucault's genealogical practice   114
     Foucault's use of genealogy   117
     Cultural science and genealogical history   120
     The political ethics of legislative and interpretive practice 124
     Conclusion   129

9   Weber, Baudrillard and the erotic sphere   131
     Symbolic exchange and the law of value   132
     Baudrillard's genealogy of value: the transition to modernity 135
     The erotic sphere and seduction   142
     Possibilities for re-enchantment   146
     Conclusion   149

10   Conclusion   151

     Notes   157

     Bibliography   179

     Index   190

Acknowledgements

This project was funded initially by a research studentship from London Guildhall University. Chapter 5 has been published in revised form as 'Max Weber on the Ethical Irrationality of Political Leadership', *Sociology*, 31, 3, August 1997, pp. 549–64. Special thanks are due to Howard Caygill, Howard Dyke ('Das *Wahre* ist die *Wahrheit!*'), Thomas M. Kemple, Chris Rhodes, Scott Lash and Sam Whimster for reading, commenting on and criticizing various sections of this work. Above all, however, I would like to thank my mother and father for their inspiration, encouragement and advice, without which this book would not have been possible.

1
Introduction

> European and American social and economic life is 'rationalized'
> in a specific way and in a specific sense. The explanation of this
> rationalization and the analysis of related phenomena is one of the
> chief tasks of our disciplines.
>
> Weber (1949, 34).

There is currently a resurgence of interest in the work of Max Weber, and this is, I believe, for three main reasons.[1] First, the collapse of communism in the late 1980s and early 1990s effectively marked the decline of Marxism as a dominant paradigm of social theory.[2] This sharp collapse of the Marxist orthodoxy vindicated Weber's analysis of modernity, and, in particular, his critique of Marx. Here, one may recall Weber's critique of historical materialism (Weber, 1949, 68), his critique of historical 'progress' (Weber, 1970, 134–56), his argument for the force of beliefs and ideas – or, more generally, *culture*–in shaping history (Weber, 1992), his thesis that socialism could not escape the progressive bureaucratization of the world (Weber, 1994, 272–302), and his perceptive critique of the political means employed by revolutionary movements (Weber, 1970, 115–28).[3] Each of these lines of criticism has to some extent proved justified, and, because of this, Weber's intellectual status has risen in the post-Marxist world.

Weber's work is currently of interest because, secondly, it establishes a theory and critique of the nature, rise and trajectory of modern culture. In spite of this, Weber has never received serious attention from the disciplines of cultural studies and cultural theory, for these disciplines have been inspired by Marx since their inception (somewhat ironic given the Marxist attack on Weber for privileging the cultural over the economic), and today, rather one-sidedly, continue to

1

treat Weber as a social rather than cultural theorist. On the side of social theory, however, there has been considerable interest in Weber's cultural sociology and sociology of culture (see Scaff, 1991; Schroeder, 1992; Owen, 1994; Maffesoli, 1996; Ritzer, 1999). This interest has ranged across Weber's vast sociology of religion (*Religionssoziologie*) (Schluchter, 1989, 1996) to his experiences of, and reflections on, the 'culture of anarchy' (Whimster, 1999), but has centred on one main theme: his theory and critique of *modernity* (see Gane, 2000). This theory remains of great contemporary significance for it views the development and trajectory of Western rationalism with a degree of pessimism, and connects the process of *rationalization* (the 'secularization, intellectualization, and the systematization of the everyday world' (Holton and Turner, 1989, 68)) to the loss of authentic meaning in modern life.

The work of Weber, like that of Nietzsche, identifies in the general process of enlightenment a movement towards nihilism (the devaluation of ultimate values) in the West, and holds scientific rationalization to be not a cure but a key contributory factor to this process. For with the onset of the rationalization of culture, ultimate meanings or values are *disenchanted*, or, in Nietzschean terms, which Weber adopts, *devalued*, and are replaced increasingly by the means – ends pursuit of material interests (see Chapter 2). This process, affecting the entire structure of Western culture, involves the subordination of value-rationality (*Wertrationalität*) to instrumental rationality (*Zweckrationalität*), and the reduction of religious ethics and ultimate beliefs to rational calculation and routinized *this-worldly* action.[4] Here, Weber stands against the (Enlightenment) view that technical or scientific progress and human 'progress' are one, and hence against Emile Durkheim's belief in the moral nature of science (Durkheim, 1984, 13–14) and the possibility of moving in a single analytic from questions of fact (is) to those of value (ought) (established by the scientific distinction of the normal from the pathological; Durkheim, 1982, 85–107).[5] Weber's distance from Durkheim on the question of whether 'progress' occurs through science has provoked much interest in the current climate of counter-Enlightenment critique, in the light of critiques which either question the legitimacy of expert (intellectual) knowledge (Foucault, 1980; Lyotard, 1984b) or which posit a connection between instrumental reason and the capacity for domination (Bauman, 1989; Adorno and Horkheimer, 1992). And in this respect, the basic questions asked by Weber of the nature, value and fate of Western rationalism remain central to the concerns of social and cultural theory today.

Weber's work, thirdly, continues to be of interest because of its decisive influence on two of the main strands of contemporary cultural and social critique: Frankfurt school critical theory and postmodern theory. Weber's influence on the former has been the subject of much discussion, and has been well documented (Wilson, 1976; McCarthy, 1984; Bernstein, 1995; B. Turner, 1996). By contrast, the connection of his work to postmodern theory or postmodernism, while arousing some interest (Holton and Turner, 1989a, 68–102; Lassman and Velody 1989b, 169–73; C. Turner, 1990; Diggins, 1996, 274–8), remains, by comparison, under-examined. This is somewhat surprising given the volume of research addressing the relation of Nietzsche and Weber (see, for example, Eden, 1983; Schroeder, 1987; Stauth and Turner, 1988; Hennis 1988, 146–61; Albrow, 1990; Scaff, 1991, 127–33; Warren, 1994; Kemple, 1998; Szakolczai, 1998). This literature however, has rarely moved beyond a comparative reconstruction of respective ideas and influences, and has not addressed or questioned, at a more general level, the trajectory of counter-Enlightenment thought which runs from Nietzsche through to Weber, and to which postmodern social theory offers a response.

There are two notable exceptions. First, the work of Jürgen Habermas (1987), which sees Nietzsche as opening two paths into postmodernity: the one pursued by Heidegger (the overcoming of metaphysics through an ontology of Being), the other by Bataille (the opening up of subject-centred reason to its other through the concept of sovereignty). Weber is important in this context, for his work, in particular his sociology of religion, underpins that of Bataille (see Habermas, 1987, 230–2), which, in turn, exerted a great influence over post-structuralist thinkers such as Derrida and Foucault. Habermas however fails to examine this Nietesche-Weber–Bataille connection in any detail, and beyond this, or perhaps in line with this, neglects the wider question of Weber's connection to, and influence on, postmodern thought more generally.[6] Second, the work of David Owen (1994), which, *contra* Habermas, traces the emergence of the philosophical discourse of modernity to Nietzsche's (rather than Hegel's) critique of Kant. This work locates Weber within an intellectual trajectory of post-Enlightenment critique running from Nietzsche through to Foucault, but, rather disappointingly, stops short of an analysis of the extension of this trajectory into postmodern theory (see Gane, 1998b). And this is also the case with existing works which read directly 'between' Weber and Foucault (Gordon, 1987; O'Neill, 1995; Whimster, 1995; Szakolczai, 1998) and Weber and Lyotard (Turner, 1990), which, while important in their own right, only hint at the wider theoretical connections between Weber and postmodern or post-structuralist thought.

The present work focuses on these surprisingly neglected connections. It seeks to establish the ways in which postmodern theory, in particular the writings of three prominent postmodern theorists, namely Jean-François Lyotard, Michel Foucault and Jean Baudrillard, develop and respond to the work of Weber. It will be argued that there exists an *implicit* dialogue between postmodern theory and Weber, one concerning the trajectory of Western culture, and, more specifically, the cultural crisis that has resulted from the rationalization and disenchantment of the world. The aim is to bring this dialogue to centre stage through examination of the ways in which postmodern theory develops Weber's analysis and critique of modern culture, and offers a response, through an appeal to a Nietzschean *revaluation* of all values, to ongoing processes of rationalization and disenchantment. There are three main parts of this project: to establish, first, the nature of Weber's analysis and critique of the nihilism of modern (Western) culture (Chapters 2 and 3); to examine, second, the ascetic, *this-worldly* modes of resistance to rationalization and disenchantment which may be developed from Weber's work (Chapters 4 and 5); and finally, to read between the work of Weber and that of Lyotard, Foucault and Baudrillard, focusing on their respective analyses of, and responses to, the rise, logic and trajectory of Western culture (Chapters 7, 8 and 9).[7]

Reading Weber

In pursuing this project, one is presented with an immediate challenge: how to read Weber's work? Weber's oeuvre is not only daunting in scope and magnitude (the Max Weber *Gesamtausgabe* is projected to run to thirty-three volumes) but is in many respects fragmentary and incomplete. Wilhelm Hennis (1988) reminds us that

> In his lifetime Weber published only two 'proper' books, and these were the dissertation and *Habilitationsschrift* indispensable for an academic career. The entirety of the remaining work consists of survey reports and essays that were, for the most part, hurriedly composed. It was only after his death that these appeared as collections in book form: the collected writings on methodology, on sociology and social policy, on the sociology of religion, on social and economic history constructed from student's notes, the political writings, and finally *Economy and Society*. (p. 24–5)

This, coupled with the inaccuracies of existing translations of key texts (a famous example is discussed by Kent, 1983), and the fact that much of his vast personal correspondence has yet to be collected in print, means that reading Weber, especially in English, is itself a difficult and problematic exercise.

Indeed any attempt at reading Weber's work as a whole, as a unified statement or position, can only proceed through a reconstruction of key ideas from a wide range of different (often seemingly disparate) research interests and texts. This question of reconstruction, and of the theme or question around which it should proceed, has been the subject of fierce debate within recent Weber scholarship (see Schroeder, 1992, 3–6). The earliest (and most traditional) view on this matter is that Weber's central interest is rationality, and, by extension, the historical process of rationalization, and that this interest provides the key to the entirety of his work. This position was dominant in the 1920s (see Habermas, 1984, 143, 1984, 428), and is to be found at the centre of Karl Löwith's 1932 essay on Max Weber and Karl Marx:

> the fundamental and entire theme of Weber's investigations is the character of the reality surrounding us and into which we have been placed. The basic *motif* of his 'scientific' inquiry turns out to be the trend towards secularity. Weber summed up the particular problematic of this reality of ours in the concept of 'rationality'. He attempted to make intelligible this general process of the rationalization of our whole existence precisely because the rationality which emerges from this process is something specifically irrational and incomprehensible. (Löwith, 1993, 62)

In the late 1930s Talcott Parsons challenged this position, positing the concept of social action rather than rationality as the central theme of Weber's work,[8] but in the 1960s Weber scholarship broadly reaffirmed *rationality* as *the* interest of his work (Bendix, 1966; Freund 1968).[9] This reaffirmation has been forcefully elaborated by Friedrich Tenbruck in his 1975 essay on the problem of thematic unity in Weber's work,[10] and by Rogers Brubaker (1984), who, like Schluchter (1981), argues:

> The idea of rationality is a great unifying theme in Max Weber's work. Weber's seemingly disparate empirical studies converge on one underlying aim: to characterize and explain the development of the 'specific and peculiar rationalism' that distinguishes modern

Western civilization from every other. His methodological investigations emphasize the universal capacity of men to act rationally and the consequent power of social science to understand as well as to explain action. His political writings are punctuated by passionate warnings about the threat posed by unchecked bureaucratic rationalization to human freedom. And his moral reflections build on an understanding of the truly human life as one guided by reason. Rationality, then, is an *idée-maîtresse* in Weber's work, one that links his empirical and methodological investigations with his political and moral reflections. (p. 1984, 1)

This reconstruction of Weber's work around the concepts of rationality or rationalization, however, has recently been placed under scrutiny. Lawrence Scaff, for example, has argued that rationality or rationalization can only be taken as the central themes of Weber's work if one ignores the significance of his early writings. On this basis he disputes the conventional view of the central concept of Weber's work, arguing that while 'Concepts like rationalization, bureaucratization, and domination come to mind ... another concept seems an attractive candidate: *Arbeitsverfassung* [labour relations], the key theoretical term in Weber's major writings from 1892 to 1894' (Scaff, 1989, 25). And this argument against using rationality or rationalization as the key to Weber's work is supported and extended by Wilhelm Hennis (1988), who asks:

> does the process of rationalization help us understand *Economy and Society*, its introductory chapter or the body of the text? Does it help to explain the methodology, the planned and completed surveys, the early economic works, the political options? Certainly not. Does it make the sociology of religion intelligible? That I doubt as well. (p. 23)

Hennis argues that while it is not wrong to read rationalization as a fundamental theme in Weber's later work, it is 'misleading to read everything in its terms and to see it everywhere' (ibid., 24). Questions of rationality and rationalization, he argues, must be placed in a much wider context, and be read in relation to Weber's interest in the development of *Menschentum* ('humanness'). And to do this, Hennis proposes that Weber's work must be reconstructed in the light of the contemporary controversies of its time, one such controversy being the storm caused by the publication of *The Protestant Ethic and the Spirit of Capitalism* (ibid., 24–46; see Weber, 1992, 1978c).

The reading I wish to develop in the course of this work concurs with, but also departs from, Hennis's argument. Hennis is to be commended for treating the concepts of rationality and rationalization not as the ends of Weber's work, but as conceptual means that enable us to gain an understanding of the modern (and perhaps even the postmodern) condition. This said, I do not believe *Menschentum*, any more than rationality or rationalization, to be the central interest or theme that provides the key to the entirety of Weber's thought. The question of *Menschentum* is one interest rather than the *central* interest of Weber's work. It is an interest which, although of considerable importance, in no way unlocks all of Weber's detailed studies of economics, politics, labour relations, law, religion and methodology.[11] For here, as Wolfgang Mommsen suggests (1974, 1, Mommsen and Osterhammel 1987, 6), there is no one Weber, and no single theme which dominates all his writings.

As a consequence, rather than impose an artificial unity on Weber's work, I propose one should accept and affirm its conceptual and substantive diversity. This approach immediately renders the question of Weber's central interest redundant, but raises a further question of how to read his diverse oeuvre. The answer to this problem lies, I believe, in a more active engagement with Weber's published texts, for too often Weber scholarship has failed to advance beyond mere reconstruction and clarification of his work (for example, Schluchter, 1996; see Gane, 1998a). This same frustration with theory 'bound simply to the exegetical study of texts' was expressed over ten years ago by Robert Holton and Bryan Turner in their study of Weber (Holton and Turner, 1989, 13), and still applies today. The answer, as Holton and Turner themselves suggested, is that theory, especially Weberian theory (which has too often simply lost itself in the complexities of Weber's own work), needs to be fired by a strong *evaluative* interest. Endless searching for 'master keys' and 'central interests' must thus be replaced by more active concerns. And in this regard, I suggest the following questions: in what senses do elements of Weber's work remain relevant to the present, and how may these be *used* to develop a critical understanding of the social and cultural phenomena of *our* time?

In attempting to answer these questions, the present work will have little more to say about the overriding or 'true' interests of Weber's own writings. Rather it will pursue a reading of Weber (and postmodern theory) in accordance with its own present-relevant evaluative interest, namely: what is the nature and trajectory of modern and postmodern culture, and, beyond this, how may we (as modern individuals and as social scientists or cultural theorists) develop a response to the ongoing rationalization and disenchantment of the world?

In line with these evaluative interests, the first half of the present work analyses Weber's position on the nature and fate of modern (Western) culture. Chapter 2 examines Weber's rationalization thesis, and focuses in particular on his account both of the rise of Western rationalism and of the accompanying descent of Western culture into nihilism, as certain ultimate values succumb to a logic of *self*-disenchantment or devaluation. This descent, which will be traced through Weber's analysis of the transition from primitive religion to universal religion, and from universal religion to the 'death of God' in modernity, will be theorized in relation to a series of connected developments – in particular, the subordination of value-rationality to instrumental reason, and the shift from charismatic or traditional to bureaucratic forms of domination and discipline.

Chapter 3 extends this analysis through a study of the processes of cultural differentiation and de-differentiation outlined by Weber (1970) in his essay 'The Religious Rejections of the World and their Directions' (the *'Zwischenbetrachtung'* or 'Intermediate Reflection', pp. 323–59). Weber argues in this essay that with the disenchantment of religious legitimation a number of autonomous life-orders, each with their own value-spheres, separate out and enter into conflict with one another: the religious, economic, political, aesthetic, erotic and intellectual. This process of differentiation, or *Eigengeseztlichkeit*, leads to a world torn by endless value-conflicts, for while, following the 'death' of God, modern value-spheres contain the basis of their own legitimacy, value-conflicts, for Weber, cannot be resolved scientifically and can no longer be arbitrated through natural right or natural law or any resort to a single 'spiritual authority'. Here, as Holton and Turner (1989) have argued, Weber's rationalization thesis seems to contain a postmodern moment, for it points to the emergence of 'an incoherent, unstable, and meaningless world of polytheistic values and nihilism' (p. 88). Alongside this, however, Weber observes that Western culture is not simply fragmented in the transition to modernity, for value-spheres are also subject to a logic of rationalization, and thereby join in a contradictory way in a process of *de-differentiation*. This is a tragic and distinctly *modern* process, for at this point each value-sphere is seduced by the force of instrumental reason, with the effect that the pursuit of values is one which becomes ruled by rational purpose rather than ultimate convictions, leading in turn to the constriction of the types (and perhaps even range) of values it is possible to pursue, and hence to the general homogenization of Western culture.

Chapters 4 and 5 turn to Weber's response to the rationalization and disenchantment of the world. In the light of the above pessimistic vision of Western history, Chapter 4 analyses Weber's position on the value of science and enlightenment. This position is more complex than it may at first seem, for on the one hand Weber appears committed to the scientific vocation, to the preservation of individual freedom through reason, while on the other, he is critical of the scientific rationalization of the world, and of world-mastery through the reduction of value-rationality to instrumental reason. The aim of this chapter, given the apparent ambivalence of Weber's position, is to reassess the argument of the lecture 'Science as a Vocation', his most explicit statement on science and enlightenment. It is argued that in this lecture Weber forges a position against that of Tolstoy (who argues for the ethical rejection of the modern world) and of Nietzsche (who advocates the revaluation of all values), for he remains critical of the devaluation of ultimate values which accompanies the rationalization of the world, and of the idea of progress which legitimizes this process, but at the same time defends the scientific vocation in so far as it can clarify and therefore inform value-judgements (which themselves lie outside of the realm of science). The concluding chapter of this work (Chapter 10) returns to this point to suggest that Weber's position here is ultimately unsatisfactory, for although it seeks to confine scientific activity within strict limits, it endorses a form of interpretative sociology which risks intensifying, rather than overcoming, further processes of rationalization and disenchantment.

Chapter 5 analyses the possibility of resisting the rationalization and disenchantment of life through the vocation of politics. The political ethics of conviction (*Gesinnungsethik*) and responsibility (*Verantwortungsethik*) outlined by Weber (1970) in his lecture 'Politics as a Vocation' (pp. 77–128) are treated as ideal-typical forms of value- and instrumentally-rational action. It is proposed that Weber's theory of the political vocation calls for the overcoming of this formal opposition. The political leader, for Weber, should pursue achievable ends and take responsibility for the consequences of this action, thereby avoiding the possible sacrifice of political means to ultimate ends, while at the same time resisting the eradication of ultimate values by the rational (means–ends) pursuit of mundane ends (or what could be termed the process of 'instrumentalization' (*Instrumentierung*)). Ultimately, this endeavour works within but also against the rationalization of the world, for it demands not only an acute sense of realism, but also calls upon the individual to 'take a stand' and with this confer the value and legitimacy of ultimate values.

Towards the postmodern

The second part of this work explores thematic parallels between Max Weber's theory of the rationalization and disenchantment of the modern world and the critiques of contemporary culture advanced by three 'postmodern' theorists: Jean-François Lyotard, Michel Foucault and Jean Baudrillard. This second part is framed by an intermediate reflection (Chapter 6) which addresses the definition of the term 'post-modern' to be employed in this work, then the way in which Lyotard, Foucault and Baudrillard can be termed postmodern theorists, and finally, the basis upon which it is possible to read between the work of these three theorists and that of Weber. Three main theses are developed here. First, that the postmodern is that which works to expose and transgress the limits of the modern order through the aporetic resuscitation of forms of difference or otherness which are repressed by, or concealed within, this order. Second, that on the basis of this definition, the work of Lyotard, Foucault and Baudrillard can be read as *postmodern* in nature. And third, that it is possible to read between Weber and these three postmodern theorists through an analysis of their respective accounts of the nature, rise and trajectory of Western culture, and their different (*ascetic* or *transgressive*) responses to the problems of rationalization and disenchantment.

Thus, in developing these ideas in detail, Chapter 7 explores parallels between the work of Weber and Lyotard. This chapter opens with an analysis of Lyotard's postmodern science before drawing a comparison between Lyotard and Weber's respective accounts of the differentiation of Western culture. It is argued that Lyotard (at least in his work up to and including *The Postmodern Condition*), unlike Weber, celebrates this process as a movement towards freedom, but does so only by neglecting the overriding movement of rationalization, which, for Weber, progressively subordinates value-rationality to instrumental rationality in each life-order and value-sphere. The final section of this chapter examines the thesis that there remains the possibility of escaping this rationalization process through work within the aesthetic sphere; a sphere which, on the surface, would seem to resist and perhaps even threaten the instrumental rationalism which is intrinsic to modern culture.

Chapter 8 analyses Foucault's counter-historical attack on the modern order. This chapter opens with an analysis of the form and uses of 'genealogy' before questioning the ethics of this historical practice, which, Foucault claims, proceeds without pre-established rules, and leaves the ends of political work undefined. It is argued that Foucault's genealogical history is in fact not as radical as it may at first seem, for not only does it remain tied to the construction of presentist metanarratives, it also, while claiming to be free from presuppositions or a particular telos, conceals the value and direction of its own enterprise, and therefore the normative basis which it formally claims to avoid.

Chapter 9 is a reading of Baudrillard's work on symbolic exchange as an argument for the possibility of re-enchantment. Baudrillard argues that modernity is unable to free itself from the archaic or *symbolic* order that it seeks to eradicate, and that in view of this the elements for a reversal of modern 'progress' are always present. This chapter examines Weber and Baudrillard's respective positions on this possibility of re-enchantment through analysis of their work on the erotic sphere and seduction. It is argued that whereas Weber refuses to place faith in the possibility of the re-enchantment of the world, Baudrillard works to affirm this possibility, but in doing so perhaps underestimates the capacity of Western culture to resist the threat of forms that are other to itself.

Finally, Chapter 10 reflects on the ways in which Lyotard, Foucault and Baudrillard develop Weber's rationalization thesis but offer differing responses to the rationalization and disenchantment of the world. A contrast is drawn between Weber's commitment to vocational work (work within but against the limits of the modern world) and the affirmative and transgressive strategies forwarded by Lyotard, Foucault and Baudrillard (which seek to expose and overcome the limits of the modern order). The key difficulties of Weber's rationalist response to rationalization, on the one hand, and of the postmodern belief in the potentiality of a rational or irrational forms, on the other, are elucidated, before it is suggested, by way of conclusion, that the strengths of these two approaches may be clarified and developed to form a possible basis for future work in the social and cultural sciences.

Part I

Max Weber's Theory and Critique of Rationalization

2
Rationalization and Disenchantment, I: From the Origins of Religion to the Death of God

> What does nihilism mean? That the highest values devalue [*entwerten*] themselves.
>
> Nietzsche (1970, 14)[1]

Max Weber's sociology of religion contains an account of the emergence and development of modern Western culture. This account reads the history of the West in terms of two interconnected processes: the rise and spread of Occidental (instrumental) rationalism (the process of *rationalization*) and the accompanying *dis-enchantment* (*Entzauberung*) of religious superstition and myth.[2] More precisely, it treats Western culture as the product of two key developmental transitions (Schroeder, 1987, 207; Owen, 1994, 101): the elimination of prehistoric forms of magical religiosity with the rise of universal religion, and the subsequent disenchantment of universal religion with the emergence of modern 'rational' science and the advanced capitalist order. The present chapter will examine the logic of these two transitions, and with this analyse Weber's position on the rise, trajectory and logic of modern culture.[3] It will be argued that, for Weber, the transition to modernity is driven by a process of cultural rationalization, one in which ultimate values rationalize and *devalue themselves*, and are replaced increasingly by the pursuit of materialistic, mundane ends. This process of devaluation or *disenchantment*, gives rise to a condition of cultural nihilism in which the intrinsic value or meaning of values or actions are subordinated increasingly to a 'rational' quest for efficiency and control. The outcome of this rationalization process will be examined at the level of the 'social' through analysis of Weber's theory of the modern, bureaucratic state.

Magical religiosity: naturalism, symbolism and beyond

Weber's *Sociology of Religion* (1978a, 399–634) opens with an account of the historical origins of religious activity, and then proceeds to trace the displacement of naturalistic forms of magical action by universal, monotheistic forms of religious belief. This account states that the earliest types of religious behaviour were everyday forms of *this-worldly* activity that were guided by rules learned from day-to-day experience. Weber observes that such activity tended not to follow a means–end (instrumentally rational) course, for its effects were, in the main, 'magical' rather than the result of 'rational' calculation or understanding. He states: 'Rubbing will elicit sparks from pieces of wood, and in like fashion the mimetical actions of a magician will evoke rain from the heavens. The sparks resulting from twirling the wooden sticks are as much a "magical" effect as the rain evoked by the manipulations of the rainmaker' (ibid., 400).[4] The powers to evoke such magical effects were not universal, for the capacity to do so required *charismatic* power, which could either be naturally endowed or artificially produced through extraordinary means. This power rested in turn upon a belief in a 'spirit' or essence that lay within or behind the physical appearance of concrete objects (artefacts, animals or persons). And, for Weber, this '"spirit" is neither soul, demon, nor god, but something indeterminate, material yet invisible, non-personal and yet somehow endowed with volition' (ibid., 401), meaning that in these early forms of religious belief, gods and demons tended to be neither personal nor enduring, and often had no names of their own.

Over time, however, not only did concrete things and events which actually existed play a role in life, but experiences that *signified* something assumed meaning. This is an important development, for at this point magic is transformed from a practice that proceeds through the direct manipulation of forces into a *symbolic* activity. This transformation is tied to the development of a realm of souls, demons and gods which has a transcendental rather than concrete existence, and which can only be accessed and coerced through the mediation of symbols and meanings. Weber (1978a) suggests that: 'More and more, things and events assumed meanings beyond the potencies that actually or presumably inhered in them, and efforts were made to achieve real effects by means of symbolically significant action' (p. 405). This development signals the increasing predominance of worship through representation and analogy, and with this the decline of pre-animistic forms of naturalism. And this process is of particular sociological interest, for this displacement of naturalism depended on the degree to which the 'professional masters' of symbolism could find support for their beliefs and hence gain *power* within the community (see ibid., p. 404).[5]

This transition from naturalism to religious symbolism based upon analogy, which, for Weber, is only replaced in modern times by the syllogistic construction of rational concepts, is accompanied by the personification and characterization of different gods. With this the forms of the gods become secure, and ideas regarding the nature of these forms are increasingly systematized, a process which tends, in turn, to result in the emergence of a pantheon:

> as a rule there is a tendency for a pantheon to evolve once systematic thinking concerning religious practice and the rationalization of life generally, with its increasing demands upon the gods, have reached a certain level, the details of which may differ greatly from case to case. The emergence of a pantheon entails the specialization and characterization of the various gods as well as the allocation of constant attributes and the differentiation of their jurisdictions. (Weber, 1978a, 407)

This rationalization of religious belief, which entails the functional specialization of the gods, is connected to the economic demands of a people and to the progressive delimitation of political jurisdictions. For with the pursuit of shared economic goals and the demarcation of political territory, particular gods are called upon to secure a group's economic and political success. Indeed, Weber proposes that 'it is a universal phenomenon that the formation of a political association entails subordination to its corresponding god ... every permanent political association had a special god who guaranteed the success of the political action of the group' (ibid., 413).

Universal religion: from ancient Judaism to the Protestant ethic

This process, whereby a group subordinates itself to a particular god in pursuit of economic and political gain or territorial security, marks the earliest stage of the developmental transition from religious polytheism to monotheistic universal religion. For this act of subordination suggests the rise of single god to a position of domination over the pantheon, and this, possibly as a result of *this-worldly* political or military conquest (see Weber, 1978a, 413), may in turn lead to the establishment of a universal deity. Weber illustrates this transition from magical religiosity to universal religion through reference to ancient Judaism (see Weber, 1967a; Schroeder, 1992, 72–84; Owen, 1994, 102–7). He argues that the early tribal confederation of the Jews, the result of an alliance of the Jews and the Midianites, found integration under a common god: Yahweh. This god presided over the confederation but was not simply a functional or local god, for he was seen to rule over all spheres of life, and his promise of salvation was open to all (see Schroeder, 1992, 73). Yahweh was thus a universal god, and the Israelites accepted him under oath, entering a contractual relationship that demanded his commandments be satisfied.[6] This said, Yahweh's will was always changeable, with the consequence that the believer could never be sure that these demands had actually been met (a condition later reproduced in ascetic Protestantism), which led in turn both to the progressive systematization of conduct and to the pursuit of an ordered understanding of Yahweh's demands and purpose. This gap between Yahweh, as a transcendent god who could not be represented through symbolism, and the imperfection of the human world drove the pursuit of rational knowledge, and with this the rationalization of everyday life. And in view of this the foundations of Western rationalism lie within the religious ethics of ancient Judaism: 'In considering the condition of the Jewry's evolution, we stand at the turning point of the whole cultural development of the West and the Middle East' (Weber, 1967a, 5).

While ancient Judaism played a key role in the development of Western rationalism, a stronger affinity exists between the religious ethics of ascetic Protestantism and the 'specific and peculiar' rationalism of modern Western culture. Weber holds that Protestantism is similar to Judaism in one key respect: its worldview centres around the idea of a transcendent God, a God separated from the imperfect human world and whose demands and purpose can never fully be known. In view of this, David Owen, developing the work of Nietzsche,[7] rightly proposes that 'Protestantism is in fact the "logical conclusion" of the process initiated by Judaism simply because it rules out *any* mediation between God and the world' (Owen, 1994, 109). But at the same time, there are also key differences between Protestantism and Judaism. First, whereas ancient Judaism is founded upon an ethical contract which calls Yahweh to intervene in history, Protestantism rests, at least initially, on faith alone and conceives the whole of history as preordained in the moment of creation. Second, it is a central tenet of Protestant theodicy that not everyone will be saved, and in this regard God's will is not open to human influence.

This belief finds its strongest expression in the Calvinist doctrine of predestination:

> The Father in heaven of the New Testament, so human and under-standing, who rejoices over the repentance of a sinner as a woman over the lost piece of silver she has found, is gone. His place has been taken by a transcendental being, beyond the reach of human under-standing, who with His quite incomprehensible decrees has decided the fate of every individual and regulated the tiniest details of the cosmos from eternity. God's grace is, since His decrees cannot change, as impossible for those to whom He has granted it to lose as it is unat-tainable for those whom He has denied it. (Weber, 1992, 103–4)

This doctrine of predestination is a crucial influence on the develop-ment of Western rationalism, for while one would assume it would engender an ethic of resignation, Weber argues that in fact it leads to an increasingly rational engagement in worldly activity. For while believers can never know whether or not they are of the elect, it remains their duty to believe that they have been chosen, and to work for the utmost glory of God through their allotted vocation. This belief, which is not found in Catholicism, is manifested in the form of the Protestant 'calling', and demands that believers fulfil their duties within *this* world. While for Luther this calling remained traditionalis-tic, in so far as the calling was not seen to be *the* task set by God, fol-lowers of Calvin increasingly saw worldly activity as the means to attaining God's favour. And this shift contributed to the progressive rationalization of all spheres of life. For on one level, it led to the inter-nal transformation of personality, to the systematization of thought and conduct. Weber observes: 'A man without a calling ... lacks the systematic, methodical character which is ... demanded by worldly asceticism' (ibid., 161). On another, it had a profound impact on all aspects of external life, for it led to the emergence of 'rational' labour, and, in view of the fact that one engaged in this labour on an ascetic basis (for the glory of god rather than private gain), to a radical ethic of investment and accumulation.

The death of God: towards cultural nihilism

Weber's thesis is that ascetic Protestantism, in particular Calvinism, contained an ethic or 'spirit' which, albeit indirectly, enabled and legit-imated the rise of capitalism in the West. Further to this, he posits a more general connection between Protestantism and the rise of Occidental rationalism.[8] There is a connection, first, between the Protestant 'calling' and the progressive systematization of life, in particular the emergence of 'rational' (capitalist) labour. Weber (1992) observes: 'rational conduct on the basis of the idea of calling, was born ... from the spirit of Christian asceticism' (p. 180). Second, there is a connection between the systematization of life (in the attempt to understand and fulfil God's demands) and the pursuit and accumulation of 'rational' knowledge. This latter tendency is part of a process of *cultural rationalization* whereby ideas and beliefs *themselves* become ever more intellectualized and thus more 'rational' in nature (see Weber, 1970, 330). This process may be observed in the sphere of theology: 'All theology represents an intellectual *rationalization* of the possession of sacred values ... Every theology, including for instance Hinduist theology, presupposes that the world must have a *meaning*, and the question is how to interpret this meaning so that it is intellectually conceivable' (ibid., 153). And this process, whereby religious beliefs and values are lent an almost scientific validity, reaches its pinnacle with Calvinist Protestantism: 'That great historic process in the development of religions, the elimination of magic from the world, which had begun with the old Hebrew prophets and, in conjunction with Hellenistic scientific thought, had repudiated all magical means to salvation as superstition and sin, came here to its logical conclusion' (Weber, 1992, 105).

The important point here is that in two senses Protestantism works towards an unforeseen and ironic end. First, while there exists an affinity between the Protestant spirit and rise of capitalism, capitalism itself engenders the decline of religious (ultimate) values, for once fully established it obeys its own formal logic of production, accumulation and exchange, and no longer requires any form of spiritual legitimation. At the conclusion of the *Protestant Ethic and the Spirit of Capitalism* Weber (1992) writes:

> Since asceticism undertook to remodel the world and to work out its ideals in the world, material goods have gained an increasing and finally an inexorable power over the lives of men as at no previous period in history. Today the spirit of religious asceticism – whether finally, who knows? – has escaped from the cage. But victorious capitalism, since it rests on mechanical foundations, needs its support no longer. (pp. 1992, 181–2).

Second, just as advanced capitalism no longer requires the spiritual support of Protestantism, rational thought (science) too breaks free from the constraints of religious narrative, and, like capitalism, turns against and attacks the very basis of all forms of religious legitimation. With this, science becomes a secular end in itself (see Chapter 4), and proceeds to denude all religious beliefs (including those of Protestantism), denigrating them as irrational forms of superstition or myth regardless of their intrinsic rationality or value.

Weber, in depicting this movement from the pursuit of God through the use of science to the disenchantment of religious forms through scientific means (see Chapter 4), adheres to a Nietzschean thesis: that with the transition to modernity 'the highest values devalue themselves' (Nietzsche, 1968, 9).[9] This is so because, says Weber, a logic of rationalization and disenchantment is to be found at the core of Protestantism, which devalues itself through its unintentional and unforeseen contribution to the rise of Western rationalism. He analyses this process of self-disenchantment as follows:

> The rational knowledge to which ethical religiosity had itself appealed followed its own autonomous and innerworldly norms. It fashioned a cosmos of truths which no longer had anything to do with the systematic postulates of a rational religious ethic – postulates to the effect that the world as a cosmos must satisfy the demands of this ethic or evince some 'meaning' or other. On the contrary, rational knowledge had to reject this claim in principle. (Weber, quoted in Habermas, 1984, 229)

The argument here is that Protestantism, in its quest for 'rational knowledge' of God's purpose and for an understanding of *this world*, engendered its own demise, for it lent legitimacy to a secular science that in turn rejected and *devalued* all religious values. And in this respect, Protestantism effectively *devalued* or *disenchanted* itself, for in its attempt to prove its own intrinsic rationality through non-religious means it affirmed the value of science, and with this laid itself open to the charge of irrationalism and to attack from the outside from 'rational', secular forms of this-worldly legitimation.

This process of self-devaluation is part of a movement towards a modern condition of nihilism in which the majority of time-honoured, ultimate values are disenchanted by the force of instrumental reason. With this, cultural values are set free from the bounds of a religious narrative and are tied instead to a scientific call for infinite progress and perfection (see Chapter 4). Salvation religion, in turn, can respond only by devaluing *this-worldly* rationalism and by becoming at the same time increasingly *other-worldly* in its orientation. In a key passage, Weber (1970) writes:

> The advancement of cultural values appears the more meaningless the more it is made a holy task, a 'calling'. Culture becomes ever more senseless as a locus of imperfection, of injustice, of suffering, of sin, of futility. For it is necessarily burdened with guilt, and its deployment and differentiation thus necessarily become ever more meaningless. Viewed from a purely ethical point of view, the world has to appear fragmentary and devalued in all those instances when judged in the light of the religious postulate of a divine 'meaning' of existence ... The need for 'salvation' responds to this devaluation by becoming more other-worldly, more alienated from all structured forms of life, and, in exact parallel, by confining itself to the specific religious essence. This reaction is stronger the more systematic the thinking about the 'meaning' of the universe becomes, the more the external organization of the world is rationalized, and the more the conscious experience of the world's irrational content is subli- mated. And not only theoretical thought, disenchanting the world, led to this course, but also the very attempt of religious ethics prac- tically and ethically to rationalize the world. (p. 357)

This passage suggests that with the rationalization of the world, worldly values break free of all religious constraints and begin to follow their own relatively autonomous logics (see Chapter 3). The result of this is that culture itself becomes 'ever more senseless', for the reli- gious, 'organically prescribed' cycle of life is at this point broken, and cultural values proliferate within their own secular cosmos and 'progress indefinitely' (see Weber, 1970, 356). This, in turn, means that modern culture, measured against its own secular (scientific) standard of self-perfection, appears more and more meaningless (see Chapter 4), for it can never reach a final point of completion and hence can never escape the guilt or *bad conscience* of its own imperfection. Such imper- fection is especially prominent when the world is seen from a 'purely ethical' (religious) point of view, for from this standpoint modern culture appears to consist of nothing more than a meaningless (*de- valued*) and fragmented array of 'worthless', 'self-contradictory' and 'mutually antagonistic' ends. Traditional religious ethics here enter into fundamental conflict with the 'rationality' of the modern world, and turn away from this world through the pursuit of a fundamental 'religious essence'. The irony of this development, however, as stated above and at the conclusion of the above passage, is that these very ethics gave rise, through the practical and ethical rationalization of the world, to the inauguration of 'rational' (scientific) culture, which in turn takes its revenge through the devaluation and debasement of all religious values (including those from which it itself was born).

This process of devaluation or *disenchantment*, which underlies the shift from a traditional world ordered by ultimate (religious) values to a world dominated by impersonal capitalist relations and the concepts of 'rational' science, is accompanied by a change in the basis of societal rationality and legitimation. With the rationalization of culture, and the corresponding disenchantment of religious ideas and beliefs, the modern world is ordered increasingly upon instrumentally rational grounds, and hence organizes itself less and less according to value-rational principles. This leads in turn to a world in which social action is separated increasingly from the sphere of (ethical) meaning, as particular (often technical) means are employed to realize specific ends regardless of the ethical significance or meaning of such action.

Rationalization, then, may be understood as a general movement towards a condition of cultural nihilism, for it proceeds through the devaluation of ultimate values, and with this the reduction of questions of meaning and value, which define the scope for creative action, to scientific (instrumental) questions of technique and purpose, the value of which tend to be presupposed (see Chapter 4). This reduction of the pursuit of ultimate values to the rational pursuit of secular ends leads, by its logical conclusion, to an impersonal social world – exemplified by capitalism and the power politics of the bureaucratic state (see below). In this world, individuals are treated not as ends in themselves but as the instrumental means to a particular end. And With this modern life becomes dominated by a principle of impersonal rationalism, a principle that, finally, is far removed from the Protestant ethic that is found at its historical roots. Weber (1970) reflects: 'The intellect, like all cultural values, has created an aristocracy based on the possession of rational culture and independent of all personal ethical qualities of man. The aristocracy of intellect is hence an unbrotherly aristocracy' (p. 355).

From cultural to societal rationalization: towards bureaucratic domination

The sociological logic of Weber's thesis is relentless: processes of *cultural* rationalization influence and sometimes even revolutionize the organization and nature of *social* life. Indeed, this is the central message of the *Protestant Ethic*: that shifts in the ideas, values and beliefs (or *culture*) of a population, when coupled with favourable material circumstances, can engender profound changes in the nature of societal organization (for example, the rise of modern capitalist structures). This, as Habermas (1987) observes, suggests in turn an intimate connection between cultural *and* social rationalization: 'What Weber depicted was not only the secularization of Western *culture*, but also and especially the development of modern *societies* from the viewpoint of rationalization' (p. 1). Whereas, for Habermas, however, cultural and social rationalization are separate and distinct entities, these processes are, for Weber, inextricably bound together. This is so in Weber's account of the rise of Western capitalism (see above), and also in regard to his theory of modern (monocratic) bureaucracy.[10] For ascetic Protestantism not only provided the 'spirit' which enabled the development of advanced capitalism in the West, but also contributed, albeit indirectly, to the 'rational' forms of ordering life which lie at the centre of the 'godless' new world (modernity).

Weber's thesis suggests then that while Protestantism exerted a decisive influence over the development of Occidental (instrumental) rationalism (see above), and thus gave rise in turn to new legal-rational forms of domination, modern bureaucracies, like the advanced capitalist relations to which they are tied,[11] now need no spiritual support or legitimation. Indeed, as Ralph Schroeder (1987) notes: 'The striving for mastery over the world continues to dominate modern life, yet it is nowadays completely devoid of its former religious and ethical significance' (p. 211). This is particularly the case with that 'coldest of all cold monsters' (Nietzsche, 1969, 75): the modern bureaucratic state, which, for Weber, has become the institutional embodiment of instrumental reason. This type of state legitimates itself on rational grounds, and rests upon a complex order of formal rights, rules and duties that together constitute a whole new realm of expert knowledge (officialdom): 'Bureaucratic administration means fundamentally domination through knowledge. This is the feature of it which makes it specifically rational' (Weber, 1978a, 225). This type of legal–rational domination is an impersonal form of rule based upon the objective pragmatism of the nation-state and the principle of formal equality before the law. It gives rise to an impersonal order of social relations or 'external life' in which personal or ultimate values and beliefs are subordinated increasingly to the rational consideration of worldly conduct: 'It is decisive for the modern loyalty to an office that, in the pure type, it does not establish a relationship to a *person*, like the vassal's or disciple's faith under feudal or patrimonial authority, but rather is devoted to *impersonal* and *functional* purposes' (ibid., 959). And this rationalization of societal organization, has a tragic outcome, for it not only strips the world of its ultimate values, but subordinates creative action to the rational consideration of means and ends, in the process draining social life of its vitality and 'humanness' (*Menschentum*). Weber summarizes this process as follows: 'Bureaucracy develops the more perfectly, the more it is "dehumanized", the more completely it succeeds in eliminating from official business love, hatred, and all purely personal, irrational, and emotional elements which escape calculation' (ibid., 975).

In these respects bureaucratic domination, guided by instrumental reason, lies in stark contrast to pre-modern forms of legitimate authority. The pre-modern world is characterized by a combination of traditional and charismatic, rather than bureaucratic authority (Weber, 1978a, 245). Weber defines these two types of authority as forms of legitimate domination which confer the validity of rule either on 'Traditional grounds – resting on an established belief in the sanctity of immemorial traditions and the legitimacy of those exercising authority under them (traditional authority)' or 'Charismatic grounds – resting on devotion to the exceptional sanctity, heroism or exemplary character of an individual person, and of the normative patterns or order revealed or ordained by him (charismatic authority)' (ibid., 215). Both these types of domination are personal rather than impersonal forms of rule, and neither is grounded upon a system of rational law. On the one hand, traditional authority, which includes gerontocracy, primary patriarchalism, patrimonialism and, in extreme cases, sultanism, demands 'obedience to the master' and 'personal loyalty', and proceeds 'by virtue of age-old rules and powers' (ibid., 226) through a form of traditional rationality that is determined by 'ingrained habituation' (ibid., 25).[12] On the other, charismatic authority, while based on personal devotion to the leader or hero (prophet), is foreign to rules and proceeds through the repudiation of past authority. This repudiation of history is exemplified by the earliest forms of Christian faith, which, for example, marked the authority of Christ with a new narrative of time – anno Domini ('in the year of our Lord', or, colloquially, 'advancing age'). This type of authority is characterized by value-rational (*wertrational*) rather than instrumentally rational social action. That is, it is 'determined by a conscious belief in the value for its own sake of some ethical, aesthetic, religious, or other form of behaviour, independently of its prospects of success', and also by affectual action 'determined by the actor's specific affects and feeling states' (ibid., 24–5).

Weber's thesis here is well-known with the rationalization of the world, traditional and charismatic authority – both of which are orders of personal authority that demand unlimited personal obligation, the former ruling through a personal master with a traditional status, the latter through an individual personality who is treated as if 'endowed with supernatural, superhuman, or at least specifically exceptional powers or qualities' (Weber, 1978a, 241) – tend to be replaced by the impersonal rule of the modern (capitalist) bureaucratic state.[13] Pre-modern forms of authority, based predominantly upon value-rationality and natural law, are here succeeded by legal–rational forms of domination and by the rule of instrumental reason. With this, religious beliefs and ultimate ideals gradually recede from (public) life as they are disenchanted by the claims of 'rational' science and are replaced increasingly by the idealized pursuit of secular, material ends. This leads to a world in which questions of meaning and value disappear from the public arena, and in which the scope for creative action and for the pursuit of ultimate values becomes increasingly restricted. And in this regard, the twin processes of cultural and social rationalization lead to the same end: to a condition of nihilism in which the highest 'ultimate' values are devalued, or devalue themselves, and hence, for the most part, are no longer able to guide social action, which itself becomes, in turn, increasingly routinized and mundane.

Conclusion

Processes of rationalization and disenchantment engender a shift from a social order founded upon value-rational beliefs and governed through charismatic and traditional forms of authority, to an order ruled by the force of instrumental reason and dominated by new forms of institutional bureaucracy. This movement results in the depersonalization of the social world: instrumental calculation steadily suppresses the passionate pursuit of ultimate values, and bureaucracy reduces the scope for individual initiative and personal fulfilment. The rationalization of the world can on these grounds be seen as engendering a general movement towards nihilism, in which ultimate values are devalued, or, as demonstrated by the developmental transition to universal religion and beyond to the 'death of God', *devalue themselves*, and in the process become subordinated to a means–ends rationality based on questions of technique and calculation. This shift towards instrumental reason and its institutional embodiment, bureaucracy, may, in these terms, be seen as a tragic development, for while it renders social relations more predictable it does so by restricting the basis for creative and meaningful value-rational social action. 'Human' progress and rationalization are, for Weber, therefore not necessarily one, for the rise of instrumental reason, which underlies the modern drive for 'rational' order, is not only tied to the devaluation or disenchantment of the highest and most sublime values and ideals, but places important limits on the scope for individual autonomy and freedom in the modern world.

3
Rationalization and Disenchantment, II: the Differentiation and De-differentiation of Modern Culture

> We live as did the ancients when their world was not yet disenchanted of its gods and demons, only we live in a different sense. As Hellenic man at times sacrificed to Aphrodite and at other times to Apollo, and, above all, as everybody sacrificed to the gods of his city, so do we still nowadays, only the bearing of man has been disenchanted and denuded of its mystical but inwardly genuine plasticity.
>
> Weber, (1970, 148)

A crucial aspect of the rationalization and disenchantment of the world is the differentiation of modern culture. For Weber, this process accompanies the general movement of nihilism in the West (see Chapter 2), for with the 'death' of God worldly values proliferate, separate out and are drawn into endless conflict with one another. This process leads to the formation of a world torn by an infinite number of value-conflicts, for 'rational' (scientific) knowledge, which, for Weber, is limited to questions of fact rather than value, is unable to resolve the crisis of values that it itself inaugurated. Weber argues, however, that the differentiation of culture into irreconcilable value-positions is accompanied at the same time by the overarching de-differentiation of values within each modern life-order. This process takes the form of the rationalization of value-positions, and this in turn leads to the increasing homogenization of all cultural forms. The rationalization process is, therefore, deeply tragic in nature, for, while seeming to contain a heterogeneous or *postmodern* moment (Holton and Turner, 1989), it in fact intensifies the underlying sameness of culture, and with this contributes to the increasing sameness of modern life itself.

Rationalization and the differentiation of culture

There are, for Weber, two main consequences of the rationalization and disenchantment of modern culture. The first, as analysed in the previous chapter, is the rise of what Holton and Turner (1989, 88) term 'a world of stable calculations'; a world characterized by the devaluation of ultimate values and by the predominance of new impersonal forms of political domination. The second is the emergence of a polytheistic and disordered world of competing values and ideals. For with the rise of modern scientific (or 'rational') knowledge religion is, for the first time, challenged by the disparate claims of other life-orders (*Lebensordnungen*), the economic, political, aesthetic, erotic and intellectual,[1] which, with the onset of modernity, separate out into relatively autonomous realms (the process of *Eigengeseztlichkeit*) with their own value-spheres (*Wertsphären*). This process leads, in turn, to the progressive differentiation of culture: these orders, once emancipated from a binding religious narrative, develop according to their own internal logics, and give rise to a proliferation of worldly (predominantly secular) beliefs and values. And with this, a new form of absolute polytheism is born, for religion itself is reduced to one life-order among many, meaning that there no longer exists an overarching (transcendental) viewpoint from which the world can either be understood or legitimated, and as a consequence, values are free to circulate within their own self-referential spheres.

Weber's central proposition is that this form mirrors the ancient order of polytheism in appearance but not in reality. His thesis is that the whole fabric of life and therefore 'culture' has changed with the transition to the modern world, for we now live in a *different sense* from the ancients, whose lives were, and in some cases may still be, conducted according to charismatic powers. Weber (1970) proclaims: 'Today the routines of everyday life challenge religion. Many old gods ascend from their graves; they are disenchanted and hence take the form of impersonal forces. They strive to gain power over our lives and again they resume their eternal struggle with one another' (p. 149).

Charles Turner (1992) puts forward a Hegelian reading of this passage: 'When he [Weber] refers to the old *gods* having ascended from their graves he refers to their (charismatic) power to generate forms of community based on the alleged universal validity of values, not simply to modern institutional differentiation' (p. 124). The key point, however, which Turner misses, is that, in the West at least, the gods are now *disenchanted*, with the implication that they have been stripped of their charismatic power and thus reduced to *impersonal forces*. This means that their power to generate new forms of community *has been lost*, and with this the struggle of the gods resumes and continues ad infinitum, not, however, in its traditional form but in the guise of a new conflict between different life-orders and opposing value-positions.[2] This is not to say, however, that the formation of a worldview from a particular value stance is not possible, for there are, in practice, grounds upon which conflicts between values may be resolved. Indeed, Weber (1970) notes: 'The theoretically constructed types of conflicts between "life orders" merely signify that at certain points these internal conflicts are *possible* and "adequate", but not that there is no standpoint from which they could be held to be resolved in a higher synthesis' (p. 323, translation corrected by Charles Turner, 1992, 87). This passage is not to be read, as a call for Hegelian synthesis and totality but as a neo-Kantian argument that stresses the divide between ideal-typical constructs (the life-orders and their value-spheres) and empirical reality. For while there can be no scientific resolution of conflicts between value-spheres (see the following section) there must exist practical grounds for compromise or reconciliation between opposing parties for day-to-day life to be possible. Such reconciliation though is always likely to be difficult, for the legitimacy of a value can only be conferred through the fundamental rejection of an opposing belief: 'It is really a question not only of alternatives between values but of an irreconcilable death-struggle, like that between "God" and the "Devil". Between these, neither relativization nor compromise is possible. At least, not in the true sense' (Weber, 1949, 17–18).[3] And this means, by consequence, that modern life places an enormous burden on the individual, for it calls upon one to select and uphold ultimate values ('to take a stand'), but at the same time renders this a possibility only in the face of constant, and often fierce, opposition from others.

The 'Intermediate Reflection'

Weber addresses the irreconcilable nature of the modern life-orders and their value-spheres in his essay 'Religious Rejections of the World and Their Directions' (pp. 323–59) (or, to use its actual title, *'Zwischenbetrachtung'* or 'Intermediate Reflection'; see Whimster's note to Tenbruck, 1989, 58).[4] This essay, located in the first volume of his collected writings on the sociology of religion (*Gesammelte Aufsätze zur*

Religionssoziologie) between Weber's studies of Confucianism and Taoism – *Konfuzianismus und Taoismus* (Weber, 1922, 276–536) – and Hinduism and Buddhism – *Hinduismus und Buddhismus* (Weber, 1923, 1–378) – analyses the conflict of the different spheres of modern culture from the viewpoint of a Protestant ethic of brotherliness. Charles Turner has explained this approach by arguing that Weber, following Rickert and Windelband, is here working within the broad tradition of neo-Kantian value-philosophy, which tends to grant religion an exceptional analytical status in its analysis of social phenomena (see C. Turner, 1992, 88–91). This is indeed the case, but there are more fundamental reasons for Weber's approach. On a basic level, Weber addresses the conflict between life-orders from the perspective of the religious sphere because this analysis is itself an 'intermediate reflection' (*Zwischenbetrachtung*) on the *Religionssoziologie* project. In addition, the 'Intermediate Reflection' privileges the religious sphere for it was written, at least in part, as a response to Georg Lukács and Ernest Bloch (key figures in the Weber circle), who espoused 'eschatological hopes' for '"salvation from the world" through creation of a new "socialist society founded upon an ethic of brotherliness"' (Scaff, 1991, 93; see also Marianne Weber, 1975, 466). Most importantly, however, religion is granted an 'exceptional status' because it is precisely through the rationalization and accompanying disenchantment of religious belief that the modern conflict between value-spheres was inaugurated. In a key passage, Weber (1970) reflects:

> the further the rationalization and sublimation of the external and internal possession of – in the widest sense – "things worldly" has progressed, the stronger has the tension on the part of religion become. For the rationalization and the conscious sublimation of man's relations to the various spheres of values, external and internal, as well as religious and secular, have then pressed towards making conscious the *internal and lawful autonomy* of the individual spheres; thereby letting them drift into those tensions which remain hidden to the originally naive relation with the external world. This results quite generally from the development of inner- and otherworldly values towards rationality, towards conscious endeavour, and towards sublimation by *knowledge*. (p. 328)

Weber draws out this tension between 'things-worldly' and religious values through analysis of the process by which the modern life-orders (the economic, political, intellectual, aesthetic and erotic) freed themselves from traditional religious narratives and developed into relatively autonomous, secular realms in their own right.[5] This analysis proceeds from the perspective of salvation religion (the religion of 'brotherliness'), an approach which not only reasserts the dynamic tension between Protestantism and rationalism, but which places the emerging conflict between religious belief and personal autonomy centre stage. Hence, as Weber himself states, the *'Zwischenbetrachtung'* is more than simply an intermediate reflection on the *Sociology of Religion* or an analysis of 'religious rejections of the world and their directions', but a contribution 'to the typology and sociology of rationalism' (ibid., 324). More importantly, however, this work contains a highly nuanced account of the rise and trajectory of modernity, and with this a powerful diagnosis of the nature of modern culture following the disenchantment and eventual 'death' of God.

This analysis starts with the economic sphere: the sphere in which the 'tension between brotherly religion and the world has been most obvious' (Weber, 1970, 331). Weber observes that in early forms of religious belief there existed no conflict between religious and economic interest, for 'All the primeval magical or mystagogic ways of influencing spirits and deities have pursued special interests. They have striven for wealth, as well as long life, health, honour, progeny and, possibly, the improvement of one's fate in the hereafter' (ibid.). This relation changed radically, however, with the modern sublimation of salvation religion and the accompanying rationalization of the economic sphere, for with the rise of 'rational' capitalism a fundamental tension emerged between the impersonal economic sphere and the personal religious ethics of brotherliness. The irony of this development is that the Protestant calling contributed, albeit indirectly, to the creation of this new impersonal world; the asceticism of salvation religion created precisely the material wealth which in principle it rejected, and with this helped found a capitalist order which, once established, obeyed its own formal logic (see Chapter 2). And in view of this paradox, Weber concludes that no religion of salvation has, in practice, ultimately overcome 'the tension between their religiosity and rational economy'. This said, he proposes that there have been two ways of dealing with this conflict 'in a principled and consistent manner': either through dedication to a Puritan vocation which accepts, works within, and ultimately contributes to the rationalization of the economic world, or through the pursuit of a mysticism which seeks to escape this world through an objectless devotion to anybody 'for devotion's sake'.

The relation of religious ethics to the political orders of the world follows a parallel course of historical development. Weber claims that originally there existed no tension between early forms of magical religiosity or functional deities and the political sphere, for the ancient gods of locality, tribe and polity protected the 'undoubted values' of everyday routine. A tension arose, however, 'when these barriers of locality, tribe and polity were shattered by universalist religions, by a religion with a unified God of the entire world. And the problem arose in full strength only when this God was a God of "love"' (Weber, 1970, 333). This tension comes to the fore in the modern world as politics begins to follow its own laws and becomes an autonomous value-sphere in its own right, for with this a fundamental conflict arises between political power, which rests on the threat of violence (see Chapter 5), and an ethic of brotherliness, which pursues an 'ethical right' through 'love'. This tension is accentuated with the rationalization of the political sphere. It becomes particularly acute with the development of the modern state, which is bureaucratic and impersonal in nature, and which stands therefore against the personal values of brotherliness (see Chapter 2, penultimate section). Weber comments:

> The bureaucratic state apparatus, and the rational *homo politicus* integrated into the state, manage affairs, including the punishment of evil, when they discharge business in the most ideal sense, according to the rational rules of the state order. In this, the political man acts just like the economic man, in a matter-of-fact manner 'without regard to the person', *sine ira et studio*, without hate and therefore without love. (ibid., 333–4)

In view of this, the ethics of salvation religion and the legal-rational power politics of the modern world lie in radical opposition. According to Weber, there have been only two consistent ways of resolving this fundamental conflict: the Puritan attempt to interpret God's will through the means of this world (violence), and the radical anti-political attitude of mysticism, which 'resists no evil' and 'withdraws from the pragma of violence which no political action can escape' (ibid., 336).

Following this analysis, Weber (1970) also examines the connection between the 'intellectual' sphere and redemption religion, observing at the outset that 'the self-conscious tension of religion is greatest and most principled where religion faces the sphere of intellectual knowledge' (p. 350). His argument here is that these two orders are unified in all magical approaches to the world, and that there exists a 'far-going and mutual recognition' between religion and metaphysical speculation. This unity is shattered, however, the moment science becomes a 'rational' sphere in its own right and proceeds to systematically rationalize and disenchant the world. At this point, the religious and intellectual life-orders are drawn into direct conflict: 'The tension between religion and intellectual knowledge definitely comes to the fore wherever rational, empirical knowledge has consistently worked through to the disenchantment of the world and its transformation into a causal mechanism' (ibid.).

The irony of this development is that salvation religion, like all universal religion, itself lent force to this process through its affirmation of doctrine over magic, which embraced increasingly scientific attempts to order, understand and interpret the world (see Chapter 2, third section). With this, a fundamental tension between intellectual rationalism and religion was born, for science gradually emancipated itself from all spiritual ties to become a sphere in its own right. In this process, it condemned magic and religion as nothing more than irrational follies, and the opposition between the intellectual and religious spheres became strikingly apparent. For whereas modern ('rational') science attacks all ideas of a 'God-ordained' and meaningful cosmos, religious doctrines remain tied to some form of inner- or other-worldly legitimation and at some point demand 'the *credo non quod, sed quia absurdum* – the "sacrifice of the intellect"' (Weber, 1970, 352). This relentless demand drives these two spheres apart, as does the increasingly cool, impersonal nature of intellectual labour, which finally breaks the unity between the intellectual vocation and ethical religiosity: 'The intellect, like all cultural values, has created an aristocracy based on the possession of rational culture and independent of all personal ethical qualities of man. The aristocracy of intellect is hence an unbrotherly aristocracy' (ibid., 355).

The question of value-incommensurability

Weber's analysis of the connection between religion, in particular salvation religion, and the economic, political and intellectual spheres suggests that with the rationalization of the world the *unity* of pre-modern culture is shattered, for, with the decline of religious or spiritual authority, worldly values proliferate and are drawn into a violent and irreconcilable conflict with one another. The transition to modernity is thus a paradoxical one, for it brings new 'rational' means for controlling and systematising life (see Chapter 2) while at the same time inaugurating an endless struggle between (and within) opposing value-spheres. In the absence of a divine, transcendental authority there no longer exist ultimate grounds upon which value-conflicts may be resolved, meaning in turn that modern culture is necessarily conflict-ridden. I will illustrate why this is the case through reference to three models of legitimacy that attempt, but ultimately fail, to bring some degree of unity to the world: science, natural right and natural law.

Weber holds that there can be no reconciliation of modern values through recourse to scientific knowledge: science disenchants the traditional (religious) basis upon which values have been legitimated but itself provides no grounds upon which questions of value may finally be resolved. Rather, questions of value and meaning lie outside of the realm of science for they demand a subjective preference, the rightness of which cannot be proven through scientific means:

> Even such simple questions as the extent to which an end should sanction unavoidable means, or the extent to which undesired repercussions should be taken into consideration, or how conflicts between several concretely conflicting ends are to be arbitrated, are entirely matters of choice or compromise. There is no (rational or empirical) scientific procedure of any kind whatsoever which can provide us with a decision here. (Weber, 1949, 18–19)

The irony of this is that scientific knowledge is unable consequently to resolve the very crisis it inaugurated. It set into play the modern conflict between different value-spheres through the progressive devaluation of religious 'truths', but is itself unable to resolve this conflict through the founding of a new value-standard. This is because science, in Weber's view, should be concerned strictly with what 'is' and not what 'ought' to be, and may clarify but not *answer* questions of ultimate meaning or value. In view of this, he concludes that the endless value-conflicts of modern culture are, in the last instance, without resolution: '"Scientific" pleading is meaningless in principle because the various value spheres of the world stand in irreconcilable conflict with each other' (Weber 1970, 147).

This position is firmly at odds with positivist thinkers who claim that scientific methods may be employed to derive ethical norms from objective social facts. Durkheim, for example, proposes that this very possibility justifies the existence of science itself, for the practical value of this enterprise lies, he claims, in its ability to assist us in the creation of value-standards, or norms. This practice of obtaining knowledge of what ought to be through the use of science rests, for Durkheim, on the biological distinction between the *normal*, the state of health, and the *pathological*, the state of abnormality (see Durkheim, 1982, 85–107):

> For societies, as for individuals, health is good and desirable; sickness, on the other hand, is bad and must be avoided. If therefore we find an objective criterion, inherent in the facts themselves, to allow us to distinguish scientifically health from sickness in the various orders of social phenomena, science will be in a position to throw light on practical matters while remaining true to its own method. (ibid., 86)

Durkheim's position holds that health is the norm that is to serve as the basis for practical reasoning, and that this norm may be derived from phenomena that are generalized throughout the species at a given point in the evolution of a particular social structure. He proposes that it is the purpose of the life sciences to define and explain this norm or generality, and to distinguish it from the condition of pathology, which is characterized by social forms that are exceptional and thus encountered as minority cases. This distinction between the normal and the pathological, it is argued, enables science to regulate action and thought, for it verifies and legitimates the ways in which health, which is always desirable and thus normal, may be established and maintained. Durkheim illustrates this claim through reference to the realm of politics: 'The duty of the statesman is no longer to propel societies violently towards an ideal which appears attractive to him. His role is rather that of the doctor: he forestalls the outbreak of sickness by maintaining good hygiene, or when it does break out, seeks to cure it' (ibid., 104). The key point of this argument is that science can be used to explain the existing state of health, in the form of the generality of social facts, and on this basis can tell us what *ought* to be and how we *should* act. And in view of this, science, for Durkheim, can be prescriptive in nature, for it can affirm 'ought' on the basis of what is, and hence proffer a standard upon which the legitimacy of ideal values may be evaluated and judged, and thus value-conflicts be resolved.

Weber is deeply critical of this position. He insists, *contra* Durkheim, that one should not attempt to use science to derive value (ought) from fact (is) as there is no purely logical basis for determining the former from the latter. Indeed, he believes the deduction of a value-judgement, an ought, from a statement of fact to be *inadmissible* (Weber, 1949, 46), and proposes instead that value-judgements should neither condition nor result from scientific work (the ideal of value-freedom, *Wertfreiheit*). The reason for this is twofold: first, it is not possible, says Weber, to confer the objective validity of facts on the basis of a value-judgement; and second, it is not possible to judge the value of values through the use of scientific reason. This leads him to maintain a distinction between science and ethics, the former dealing with questions of fact, the latter with questions of value. And this separation distinguishes Weber's work from that of Durkheim and Marx, for, contrary to the belief of Zygmunt Bauman (1987), it divorces science from norm-making, or *legislative* activity. Weber (1949) is keen to emphasize this point: 'it can never be the task of an empirical science to provide binding norms and ideals from which directives for immediate practical activity can be derived' (p. 1949, 52).

This argument against the normative capacity of science is accompanied by an outline of the legitimate uses of scientific reason (see Chapter 4). Weber thinks, for example, that while a distinction is to be upheld between 'is' and 'ought', values and value-judgements are not to be withdrawn from scientific discussion, for science may be employed to understand and 'empathetically analyse' (*nacherleben*) the *meanings* of value-positions. In addition, scientific methods can be used to provide a *critical* assessment of the ideals that underlie value-judgements since they can yield 'a formal logical judgement of historically given value-judgements and ideas, a testing of the ideals according to the postulate of the internal *consistency* of the desired end' (Weber, 1949, 54). This in turn, Weber claims, may aid practical activity because it facilitates clarification of the axioms and means which underpin the pursuit of particular ends (see Weber, 1970, 151). He is quick to add, however, that such clarification is to remain strictly at the level of formal or logical explanation, and is not to be used to prescribe particular forms of practical conduct: 'An empirical science cannot tell anyone what he *should* do – but rather what he *can* do – and under certain circumstances what he wishes to do' (Weber, 1949, 54). Weber here upholds a neo-Kantian distinction between 'is' and 'ought', science and ethics, for he limits science to the clarification of existing conditions and possible value-choices rather than seeking, like Durkheim, to resolve conflicts between competing alternatives through the imposition of a regulative norm. Weber suggests that science may clarify, or at least offer the conceptual tools to clarify, the empirical basis of value-choices and value-incommensurability, but is ultimately unable to reconcile conflicts of interest through the hierarchical ranking of ideal values.

This argument for the incommensurability of values and against the possibility of reconciling value-spheres through (scientific) reason also places Weber in radical opposition to natural right theorists such as Leo Strauss. Strauss, whose work has tended to be overlooked by Weber scholars (with the notable exception of Bendix and Roth, 1971, 62–4, and Charles Turner, 1992, 17–19) and by social scientists more generally (Eden, 1987), is deeply critical of Weber for proposing that values cannot be evaluated and ranked through the use of scientific reason. Strauss develops this critique, however, in a different direction to Durkheim, arguing that Weber's neo-Kantian distinction between fact and value shifts values themselves into the realm of the *non-rational*, thereby depriving us of *genuine* knowledge of what 'ought to be' (see Strauss, 1953, 41). This move, for Strauss, plunges Weber's work into philosophical relativism and beyond into nihilism, for it treats all values, at least from the perspective of reason, as having an equal claim to legitimacy. He states: 'Weber assumed as a matter of course that there is no hierarchy of values: all values are of the same rank' (ibid., 66). And this, for Strauss, effectively devalues both science and ultimate values, for it implies that the former cannot be employed to confer human 'right', and that the latter, as irrational forms, are equivalent to all other values before the tribunal of reason.

Against this position, Strauss insists that the faculty of human reason may be used, if only by a select few, to discover the principles of justice upon which social and political forms are to be based. This is what Strauss terms 'natural right': the right of the wise (the philosopher) to use the highest form of human knowledge (philosophy/science) to discover the natural and superior form of right or good for 'man'. He explains:

> Natural right in its classic form is connected with a teleological view of the universe. All natural beings have a natural end, a natural destiny, which determines what kind of operation is good for them. In the case of man, reason is required for discerning these operations: reason determines what is by nature right with ultimate regard to man's natural end. (Strauss, 1953, 7)

The crux of this argument is that the philosopher is to use reason to establish the 'natural' order of things, including the natural, hierarchical order of values, and on this basis legislate what *ought* to be. In this respect, science, for Strauss, as for Durkheim, is to be prescriptive, for it is to be used to confer 'ought' on the basis of what 'is', by nature, 'right'. This places Strauss in direct opposition to Weber, for he proposes that science is to be used to discover and enact the ideal values that lie within our 'natural end' or 'destiny'. Hence, reason, suggests Strauss, is never to be value-free, for it is to be employed to establish a 'natural' value-standard according to which values may be ranked, and disputes between opposing value positions resolved.

This natural right critique of Weber's commitment to value-free social science is, problematic in a number of respects. In particular, Strauss criticizes Weber for arguing that conflicts between values cannot be resolved through the use of science, but gives little indication himself of the means or *methods* to be employed, in practice, to resolve value-disputes. Indeed, Strauss, while deeply critical of Weber's commitment to value-freedom (*Wertfreiheit*), completely ignores his examples of specific value-conflicts that cannot be resolved through the use of scientific reason. Weber asks, for example, how science might settle the value-conflict between a Catholic and a Freemason, or a dispute over the value of French and German culture (see Weber, 1970, 146–48). Strauss provides no answer to these questions. Instead, he dismisses Weber's neo-Kantian distinction between facts and values on the grounds that it places questions of value beyond the limits of scientific reason. Strauss argues instead simply that ideal values, in particular principles of 'right' and 'good', may be derived from the intrinsic properties or nature of things. But this argument, in turn, is abstract and utopian in character, and, more worryingly, lies open to systematic abuse. For, as Weber suggests, once science is employed to justify and enact ideal values, especially through the actions of an elite few (the academy), particular values, in this case the idea of what is 'natural', are cast into an objectively valid and *legitimate* form, and thus appear as being beyond critique. And at this point Weber rightly warns that science, contrary to Durkheim's belief, is not both cognitive and moral in nature, for it rests upon a designation of authority, and may, especially if used beyond its own limits, give rise to new means of domination.

Strauss, moreover, neglects the connection between Weber's idea of value-pluralism and his theory of the rationalization and disenchantment of the world. This connection, however, is pivotal for it suggests that science, contrary to the claims of Strauss and Durkheim, is more

likely to inaugurate than resolve value-conflicts, for it disenchants traditional (religious) forms of legitimation and with this sets into motion
new conflicts between opposing value-spheres (see above). Strauss fails
to address this point, and with this also overlooks the following. First,
that there exists a connection between Weber's historical analysis of
disenchantment and his commitment to value-free methodology, for
Weber employs a neo-Kantian method in order to clarify the nature of
modern values and value-conflicts; this is an approach which does not
in itself posit the equivalency of all values but does point to the limits
of science in dealing with the question of value itself. Second, that, for
Weber, the differentiation of culture into competing life-orders and
value-spheres is a tragic condition (see below), one that, ironically,
scientific reason contributes to but is unable to resolve. In view of both
these points, contrary to Strauss's belief, Weber is not a nihilist. Rather,
like Nietzsche, he is a critic of nihilism, and attacks the processes of
rationalization and disenchantment on the grounds that they reduce
ultimate values to mere instrumental means (see Chapter 2). He is thus
critical of the presupposition which underlies Strauss's position,
namely that scientific reason is *necessarily* of value, and argues instead
that the very 'progress' of such reason subordinates value itself to questions of technique or purpose (see Chapter 4). Contrary to Strauss and
also Durkheim, Weber insists that the value of science is always to be
questioned and not simply presupposed, for not only are advances in
scientific knowledge likely to produce new value-conflicts which
cannot in turn be resolved through the use of science (the recent
debate over the value of genetically modified crops, or genetic engi-
neering more generally, is an example), they are also inherently problematic for they risk contributing to the further rationalization and
disenchantment of the world.

Finally, the conflict between modern value-spheres cannot be
resolved through reference to a *natural law*, a law which Strauss rejects
for resting on divine will and not natural human reason (Strauss, 1953,
vii). This is so because the rationalization process engenders a shift
from natural law to positive right (typified by legal positivism) through
the disenchantment of the traditional basis of law itself. The effect of
this process is as follows:

> The disappearance of the old natural law conceptions has destroyed
> all possibility of providing the law with a metaphysical dignity by
> virtue of its immanent qualities. In the great majority of its most
> important provisions, it has been unmasked all too visibly, indeed,

as the product or the technical means of a compromise between conflicting interests. (Weber, 1978a, 874–5; see also 1975, 71)

This process of disenchantment reduces law from a divine standard that is 'legitimated by God's will' to a technical, this-worldly means of settling questions of positive right.[6] Jürgen Habermas (1984) neatly summarizes this process: 'From the perspective of a formal ethic based on general principles, legal norms (as well as the creation and application of laws) that appeal to magic, sacred traditions, revelation and the like are devalued. Norms now count as mere conventions that can be considered hypothetically and enacted positively' (pp. 162–3). Weber argues that there can be no foreseeable reversal of this process and hence no return to a world governed by natural law. The possibility of such a return, of reunifying the differentiated life-orders through reference to a religious narrative (thereby reversing the process of *Eigengeseztlichkeit*), rests on the re-enchantment of the world and with this a 'sacrifice of the intellect', a possibility which remains open but which Weber rejects as nothing more than a fantastical form of world-flight (*Weltflucht*).

Cultural de-differentiation: the tragedy of rationalization

There is then, in Weber's theory, no clear solution to the conflict between the value-spheres of the modern world, for with the decline of religious legitimation there no longer exists a transcendental standpoint from which it is possible to resolve value-conflicts and thus restore unity to the world. Holton and Turner (1989) detect a latent Nietzscheanism in this position: 'Weber was forced to digest a good deal of Nietzsche's message: the security which had been provided by an absolute authority (God) had disappeared, leaving behind a world of endless value conflict, and no new absolute basis for knowledge (the working class, society, or history) could fill the gap which had been opened up by God's death' (p. 10). This, they claim, constitutes the pessimistic or *postmodern* side of Weber's rationalization thesis, for here Weber not only asserts the limits of reason in dealing with the question of value, but also emphasizes the 'arbitrariness of rational thought' and with this the nihilism of modern culture. But in contradiction to this, Holton and Turner also argue that there is a more positive, and distinctly modern, side to Weber's thought, one which draws from the Enlightenment tradition of Kant and which welcomes the modern world of 'stable calculations'. In this guise, they argue,

Weber 'was more optimistic in calmly accepting the inevitability of rationalization, secularization, and the spread of bureaucratic management with the increasing democratization of culture and politics' (ibid., 100).

Holton and Turner are right to emphasize the two seemingly conflicting outcomes of the rationalization process: the emergence of an unstable world of competing values on the one hand (the differentiation of culture), and of a stable, instrumentally rational order of calculable action on the other (the movement towards *de*-differentiation). They are also right to argue that Weber's position is highly ambivalent, for it identifies the costs *as well as* the gains associated with the rise of modernity. Less convincing, however, is their demarcation of the positive (modern) and negative (postmodern) sides of Weber's rationalization thesis. On one side, the movement towards a world of 'stable calculations' is, for Weber, by no means simply a 'positive' tendency: it also has many 'negative' consequences, the devaluation of ultimate values and the bureaucratic paralysis of individual action being the most prominent (see Chapter 2). On the other, postmodern readings of the differentiation of culture tend not to greet this process with pessimism but rather *affirm* the differences intrinsic to a polytheistic (dis)order of values (this point is addressed at length in Chapter 7).

The problem here is twofold. First, Holton and Turner fail to recognize the Nietzschean influence on both sides of Weber's rationalization thesis, for it is not simply the differentiation of culture into competing value-spheres that induces cultural nihilism, but also, and perhaps more fundamentally, the transition to a world in which 'stable', calculable action predominates. It is with this shift, as argued in the previous chapter, that the world, at least in theory, becomes ever more 'rational' until life itself is stripped of its ultimate meanings. Second, it is wrong to disengage these two sides of the rationalization process (the differentiation and de-differentiation of culture), because in Weber's conception they are intimately connected. This is so not simply because the rationalization of the world inaugurates the irreconcilable tension between competing value-spheres, but because in turn, especially in the case of the economic, political and intellectual orders (see above), these spheres themselves tend towards rationalization.

It may be argued then that, for Weber, *contrary* to the postmodern position (see Chapter 7), the differentiation of modern culture is not accompanied by a movement towards a greater freedom, but is in fact part of the wider extension of instrumental rationalism through all spheres of life. In this respect, the process of differentiation is at the same time accompanied by a process of *de-differentiation* (Featherstone, 1995, 49), for while the claims of the different value-spheres remain mutually irreconcilable, the rationalization process tends to reduce or restrict the range of values and the number of valued ends offered by each sphere. This means that while the rationalization of the world appears to diversify culture through the differentiation of value-spheres, to some extent it engenders the opposite, namely the progressive homogenization of culture within all spheres of life (a process identified and attacked by a number of postmodern theorists, in particular Foucault and Baudrillard; see Chapters 7 and 8). Two possible exceptions to this process are the aesthetic (see Chapter 7) and the erotic (Chapter 9) spheres. These spheres, whose 'fundamental essences are "a-rational" or "antirational"', would appear to lie outside of the course of rationalization, and with this seem to offer the possibility of escape from modern (instrumental) rationalism (see Scaff, 1991, 101–2). This possibility is addressed in detail in the second half of the present work, but for now we may note that, for Weber, even these spheres are likely to tend toward rationalization if pursued with any rational intent: 'the spheres of the irrational, the only spheres that intellectualism has not yet touched, are ... raised into consciousness and put under its lens ... This method of emancipation from intellectualism may well bring about the very opposite of what those who take to it conceive as its goal' (Weber, 1970, 143).

Weber's thesis is that all value-spheres, even those that appear to be a-rational in nature, submit to an equivalent logic of rationalization. This is a process that constricts the range of values contained within each life-order (as ultimate values are reduced to mundane, materialistic means and ends), and leads in turn to the increasing sameness of modern culture. In spite of this, however, the individual is still obliged to confer the legitimacy of mutually antagonistic values, for even though the array of ultimate values may contract with the rationalization of the world, one is never relieved from the existential burden of choice ('taking a stand'). And in this respect, the rationalization process is of a tragic nature. On the one hand, the scope for individual action is curtailed by the rise of instrumental reason, and by the predominance of new forms of bureaucratic domination. As Wolfgang Mommsen suggests: 'Weber thought that the free societies of the West were undergoing a process of routinization and rationalization of all aspects of social life which would slowly but steadily lead to a paralysis of all individual initiative' (Mommsen, 1989, 34–5). On the other hand, the modern individual is, for Weber, to exercise his or her subjectivity in conferring the legitimacy of values from an array of competing life-orders and value-spheres which themselves tend towards rationalization. The individual is thus torn in opposite directions by the same process. With the transition to modernity the individual gains the autonomy to affirm particular values but is at the same time subject to the restrictions instrumental reason imposes on this freedom. For while we are now able to pursue and legitimate particular values at will, such action is dominated increasingly by the demands of the 'rational', bureaucratic world, which, in its drive for efficiency and calculability, seeks, in sum, to rid itself of the formal irrationality of everything individual or 'human' (see Chapter 2). And this means, by consequence, that modern life is always experienced as a struggle: to impose one's individuality on the world one has to work against the fabric of modern culture itself and uphold ultimate values in the face of purely instrumental and ever more 'rational' forces (see Chapter 5).

Conclusion

Weber's account of the transition to modernity may be read, in the light of the above two chapters, as a theory of the descent rather than progress of Western culture. The promises of Western rationalism – universal freedom, personal autonomy – have, in capitalist modernity, turned into their opposites, and been supplanted by new forms of 'rational' discipline and formal domination, and by an infinitely 'polytheistic' culture characterized, paradoxically, by structural sameness. In view of this, one is left with the following question: how is it possible to work against the instrumentalism of modern culture, and with this resist the further rationalization and disenchantment of the world? The second half of the present work examines three postmodern responses to this question. For Weber, however, there are only two choices: withdrawal into the 'acosmic brotherliness' of Christian mysticism (a form of *Weltflucht*), or devotion to the inner-worldly asceticism of the Protestant ethic of vocation. Weber chooses the latter of these two options, committing himself to work within *this* world,[7] and it is to this vocational ethic, this 'this-worldly' form of resistance to the rationalization of the world, that we now turn.

4
The Value of Instrumental Reason: 'Science as a Vocation'

Reason, that highest faculty of man, essential for his life, which gives him ... the means of existence and enjoyment: this same faculty poisons his life.

Tolstoy (1934, 7)

Reason commands us much more imperiously than a master. If we disobey a master we are unhappy, but if we defy reason we are fools.

Pascal (1961, 101)

The rationalization and disenchantment of the world, as outlined in the previous two chapters, is accompanied by the rise of new instrumentally rational forms of *this-worldly* legitimation (for example, monocratic bureaucracy), and by the differentiation and de-differentiation of modern culture, manifested in the emergence and rationalization of autonomous and conflicting life-orders. The outcome of this movement, is a form of cultural nihilism, for with the rationalization of the world ultimate values are progressively disenchanted by the claims of 'rational' science, or even devalue and disenchant themselves through a process of self-rationalization that is spurred by the (unintended) cultivation of new forms of instrumental reason. In view of this, the present chapter analyses Weber's position on science, and questions the value of this enterprise given, first, its role in disenchanting the world, and second, its apparent inability to fill the void left by the death of God. This chapter will focus on the lecture 'Science as a Vocation', Weber's most explicit statement on science, and will pay particular attention to its allusions to the work of Tolstoy and Nietzsche. It will be argued that Weber, in forging a position against that of Tolstoy (the rejection of this world) and Nietzsche (the revaluation of all values), offers us a guide to how we may employ instrumental reason while remaining sensitive to the further rationalization and disenchantment of the world.

The scientific calling

Weber's 'Science as a Vocation' is concerned, above all, with the fate of science (what is termed 'the *inward* calling of science'), and with the bearing of this fate on the nature of modern life. A key point of this concern is the impact of specialization on the vocation of scientific work. Modern science, like all areas of modern culture, has become a highly specialized field, and this, Weber (1970) predicts, will 'forever remain the case' (p. 134). This process of specialization has had important effects on the nature of scientific activity, for now it is normal for the scientist to remain isolated within the confines of his or her specialized vocation (as in the Protestant *Beruf*). Beyond this scientific work is itself rendered partial and incomplete in so far as it offers only one viewpoint on a limited field of inquiry. Hence, Weber argues that 'One's own work must inevitably remain highly imperfect' (ibid., 135), for 'definitive' and 'enduring' accomplishments today tend not only to be highly specialized in nature but to assume a *general* significance in so far as they raise questions in other specialized fields. Scientists have to work with the 'resigned realization' that their knowledge is likely to constitute a 'specialized point of view' (a *perspective*) and nothing more. And, in view of this, to pursue science as a vocation one must be passionately devoted to life confined within a specialism, and hence be able to work in a highly rationalized field yet not be disenchanted.

Beyond this, there is, for Weber, a further and perhaps more problematic sense in which modern scientific activity remains imperfect: it strives for the accumulation and perfection of knowledge, and in this respect is tied to a model (and ideal) of *progress*. The vocation of science rests on the presupposition that knowledge itself remains open to future refutation or further refinement, and hence that the need for further scientific work never ends. This affirmation of the constant progress of ideas, which stands in direct opposition to the Comtean ideal of the unification and completion of the sciences, has, in the Weberian perspective, a tragic consequence, for it removes, by implication, the possibility of definitive or absolute knowledge. Weber illustrates this point by comparing the fate of science to that of art. He argues that a work of art that brings 'genuine fulfilment' can never be antiquated, for in spite of advances in technique such a work can never be *qualitatively* surpassed. Hence, as Löwith (1989) observes, 'Homer was not supplanted by Dante, nor Dante by Shakespeare' (p. 138). Scientific work, for Weber, is by its very nature different, for each accomplishment in the realm of science raises new questions and thus asks to be transcended. He states:

> In science, each of us knows that what he has accomplished will be antiquated in ten, twenty, fifty years. That is the fate to which science is subjected; it is the very *meaning* of scientific work, to which it is devoted in a quite specific sense, as compared with other spheres of culture for which in general the same holds. Every scientific 'fulfilment' raises new 'questions'; it *asks* to be 'surpassed' and outdated. Whoever wishes to serve science has to resign himself to this fact. Scientific works certainly can last as 'gratifications' because of their artistic quality, or they may remain important as a means of training. Yet they will be surpassed scientifically ... for it is our common fate and, more, our common goal. We cannot work without hoping that others will advance further than we have. In principle, this progress goes on *ad infinitum*. (Weber, 1970, 138)

This passage raises an important question regarding the value of the vocation of science. If scientific work is imperfect, in so far as it is highly specialized and calls to be surpassed, then why, as Weber asks, 'engage in doing something that in reality never comes, and never can come, to an end?' (ibid.). Here lies the central problem of the scientific vocation: why indeed should one want to commit one's life to the production of knowledge, which will soon become redundant? This problem, for Weber, is not confined simply to the vocation of science: it is symptomatic of life in general within the rationalized world, for where do we, as individuals, stand before the infinite 'progress' of technical means and ideas, before what Simmel (1997, 73) aptly termed the 'unlimited capacity of accomplishment'? Weber's analysis here raises questions far beyond those pertaining simply to the nature or vocation of science. It questions the position of the vocation of science within 'the total life of humanity', and on this basis proceeds to question the bearing of the rationalization of culture on the life of the individual.

The key concern here is the *meaning* of science, the meaning of an enterprise which, for Weber, *contra* Durkheim, can give no *legitimate* guidance as regards the leading of life, and which disenchants the

world by subordinating questions of meaning or value to predominantly quantitative concerns which, at least in theory, can be resolved
through calculation. This concern raises a broader question regarding
the meaning of life itself in the disenchanted world, a question Weber
answers through reference to the work of Tolstoy.[1] He argues:

> for civilized man death has no meaning. It is has none because the
> individual life of civilized man, placed into an infinite 'progress',
> according to its own imminent meaning should never come to an
> end; for there is always a further step ahead of one who stands in
> the march of progress. And no man who comes to die stands upon
> the peak which lies in infinity ... civilized man, placed in the midst
> of the continuous enrichment of culture by ideas, knowledge, and
> problems, may become 'tired of life' but not 'satiated with life'. He
> catches only the most minute part of what the life of the spirit
> brings forth ever anew, and what he seizes is always something pro-
> visional and not definitive, and therefore death for him is a mean-
> ingless occurrence. And because death is meaningless, civilized life
> as such is meaningless; by its very 'progressiveness' it gives death
> the imprint of meaninglessness. Throughout his late novels one
> meets with this thought as the keynote of the Tolstoyan art. (Weber,
> 1970, 139–40; see also 356–7).

This meaninglessness of modern life follows from the disenchantment
or *devaluation* of ultimate values which accompanies the rationalization of the world (what might be termed the descent into cultural
nihilism; see Chapters 2 and 3), and from the fact that the modern
individual is today placed before an infinite number of ever-changing
ideas that can never be grasped in their totality. This is what Simmel,
Weber's contemporary, termed the 'tragedy of culture', for at this point
the 'objectified spirit' of culture begins to obey its own accumulative
logic, with the effect that so many 'cultural elements' or ideas enter circulation they can never be fully assimilated by the individual, which in
turn renders the very existence of these elements superfluous (see
Simmel, 1997, 71–5, and Featherstone, 1995, 40–1).
  For Weber, while this is true, the tragedy of modern culture, also has
a further dimension: that science, while diminishing the importance of
life itself by placing the individual before an infinite realm of technical
progress and disenchanting all values, cannot and thus should not be
used to *create* or *legitimate* new ultimate values. It is for this very reason
that modern culture is nihilistic in nature, for, contrary to Durkheim

and Strauss, he argues that there exists no rational or scientific grounds upon which a new value-standard may be founded or new values created (see Chapter 3). As a result, as the above passage suggests, we remain stranded in a meaningless world, one scarred by conflicts between an ever-increasing number of mundane values and liable to further rationalization and disenchantment. And it is because of this that Weber, unlike the philosophers of the Enlightenment, places little faith in the qualitative effects of scientific 'progress', and refuses to defend the pursuit of science for science's sake. Rather, following Nietzsche (1998, 112; 1956, 3–15) he questions the *meaning* of the vocation of science, and asks: 'What is the value of science?' (Weber, 1970, 140).

From Plato to Newton: the historical values of science

Weber, as one would expect, addresses this question historically, and draws out the 'tremendous' differences that exist between past and present values of science (see Weber, 1970, 140–3). Weber cites Plato's vision of science as the path to true being as an example, and recalls the simile of the cave in part seven of *The Republic*, in which men who are held in chains and deprived of light (reason) break free of their fetters, ascend into the sunlight (truth, enlightenment), and see the world for the first time as it really is (reality) (see Plato, 1987, 316–25). Weber argues that Socrates' distinction of reality (true being) from appearance (abstraction) is of particular importance for it marks the first conscious discovery of 'one of the great tools of scientific knowledge': the *concept*. This tool of knowledge, for Weber, explains Plato's 'passionate enthusiasm' in *The Republic*, as it enabled one to pursue the true substance of life. Weber (1970) states: 'if one only found the right concept of the beautiful, the good, or, for instance, of bravery, of the soul ... then one could also grasp its true being' (p. 141).[2] This pursuit of true being, however, was also tied to the pursuit of ethical life: it opened the way for knowing the 'good' or the 'right' in life, and on this basis also indicated how to act as a citizen of the state. Science thus was of ethical and political value, and on the basis of this, Weber argues, one engaged in scientific activity. But, Weber asks, clearly overlooking the claims of Marx and Durkheim, 'who today views science in such a manner?' (ibid., 140). He concludes that today conceptual abstractions are no longer seen as the means to true being or experience, and argues that in fact quite the reverse is now seen to be true, in so far as it is believed that 'the intellectual constructions of science constitute an unreal realm of artificial abstractions, which with their bony hands seek to grasp the blood-and-the-sap of true life without ever catching up with it' (ibid., 140–1). And as for science constituting the path to an ethical or a political good, arguments positing the connection of instrumental (scientific) rationality and political domination (see Bauman, 1989; Adorno and Horkheimer, 1992), and renewed calls for greater accountability of scientific knowledge (see O'Neill, 1995), indicate that this again is a value which is rarely held to be true today.

The second value of science analysed by Weber comes from the Renaissance, and is connected to the emergence of the rational experiment. Weber reminds us that the experiment, as a means of 'reliably controlling experience', existed both in India and in Hellenic antiquity, but only became a principle of research in the West during the Renaissance. More specifically, this principle of experimentation came from the sphere of art, where pioneers such as Leonardo saw science as the path to true art, and who argued that art itself should be raised to the rank of a science (see da Vinci, 1989, 11–46). From this sphere, the experiment entered science through Galileo, and theory through Bacon, and in the process science acquired a further value: it became the path to knowledge of true nature. Weber (1970) treats this as a third example of the historical value of science: 'To artistic experimenters of the type of Leonardo and the musical innovators, science meant the path to *true* art, and that meant the path to true *nature*' (p. 142). Weber argues, however, that today precisely the reverse is again seen to be true: redemption from the intellect is held as the prerequisite for a return to true nature. And as for science being the path to true art, he rightly states: 'Here no criticism is even needed' (ibid.).

Weber's fourth example of the differing historical values of science is the belief prevalent among early modern scientists that their work marked the path to 'true' knowledge of God. This value, which Nietzsche (1974) terms the first error of science (p. 105), is summarized neatly by Karl Löwith (1989): 'Copernicus, Kepler, Galileo, and Newton were all equally convinced that God had ordained the world mathematically and that they could come to know Him by reading from what, by analogy with the Bible, they termed the "book" of nature' (p. 142). Weber thinks, however, that this belief in science as a path to God waned as scientific reason gradually rationalized and then disenchanted the claims of theology, and he jests (provocatively) that today only a few 'big children' still believe that natural science (astronomy, biology, physics, chemistry) can teach us anything about the *meaning* of the world (see Weber, 1970, 142). Indeed, for Weber, quite the opposite is more likely to be the case, for science is today a fundamentally *irreligious* power which contributes to the disenchantment of the world through the rationalization of all ultimate values (see Chapter 2), while scientific reason, in subordinating value to instrumental purpose, itself drains the world of its meaning. And here, once again, Weber develops the view that the value of science has changed dramatically from times past, for the pursuit of God now rests, in general, on the revocation of, rather than engagement in, scientific activity.[3] Indeed, today, 'Redemption from the rationalism and intellectualism of science is the fundamental presupposition of living in union with the divine' (ibid.).

Weber, Nietzsche and the 'last men'

Weber's critique of the Enlightenment (and Utilitarian) belief that science presents the means to true happiness, presents a stiffer challenge to modern presuppositions regarding the value of scientific activity. Weber's analysis of this (fifth) historical value is intriguing, for he does not outline the ideological basis of Enlightenment philosophy or his critique of it in any detail, but rather lets his comments regarding the fate of the individual before the rationalization of the world stand (see above and Chapter 2), and beyond this refers his audience to the work of Nietzsche:

> After Nietzsche's devastating criticism of those 'last men' who 'invented happiness', I may leave aside altogether the naive optimism in which science – that is the technique of mastering life which rests upon science – has been celebrated as the way to happiness. Who believes in this? – aside from a few big children in university chairs or editorial offices. (Weber, 1970, 143)

This passage refers to the fifth section of Zarathustra's prologue, in which Nietzsche is highly critical of the 'last men' who sacrifice their future for the sake of the present. This section of *Zarathustra*, which Weber (1992) also refers to at the conclusion of the *Protestant Ethic* (p. 182),[4] reads as follows:

> Alas! The time is coming when man will give birth to no more stars. Alas! The time of the most contemptible man is coming, the man who can no longer despise himself. Behold! I shall show you the

> *Last Man* ... The earth has become small, and upon it hops the Last
> Man, who makes everything small ... 'We have discovered happi-
> ness', say the Last Men [*letzten Menschen*], and blink. (Nietzsche,
> 1969, 46)[5]

Weber's interest in this complex passage lies, I believe, in the following: first, Zarathustra's belief that the rise of modern science has made
the world small, both in terms of its increasing ability to understand
and control nature, and in terms of the outcome of this process,
namely the progressive devaluation of ultimate values and the accompanying descent of modern European culture into nihilism. Second,
the suggestion that this process is accompanied by the concurrent
decline of charismatic authority. Third, Zarathustra's critique of the
modern belief that the outcome of scientific 'progress' is happiness and
not tragedy (Weber makes reference to precisely this point), and
finally, his mocking both of the 'naive optimism' of this belief and of
the unreflective and unquestioning nature of the modern individual
(the blinking of the 'last men'), and with this Nietzsche's call for 'the
modern mind to stare into the abyss [the Godless world] without blinking' (Diggins, 1996, 152).

This said, Weber himself gives little indication of exactly why he sees
Nietzsche's critique of the 'last men' to be so 'devastating', and passes
over the idea, which is present in his own work, that science may be of
value because it enables self-determination and thereby enhances the
possibility of human freedom. This apparent hiatus has been addresses
by Thomas Kemple, who argues, in line with the text of 'Science as a
Vocation', that Weber's 'silence' on this question may be understood,
in part, as a recommendation to read Nietzsche on the question of
enlightenment (see Kemple, 1998, 4). Further to this, Kemple, following the lead of Frederic Jameson, draws a comparison between the narrative strategies of 'Science as a Vocation' and *Thus Spoke Zarathustra*,
arguing that Weber, following Nietzsche, sought 'not to preach directly
to the passions and prejudices of his listeners but to argue allusively by
way of citation, comparison, and analogy' (ibid., 5).

This explanation, which is highly plausible, is lent weight by the
recent work of Wolfgang Schluchter (1996; see Gane, 1998a), who
argues that the content of 'Science as a Vocation' is framed by the
specific context of the lecture and by the nature of the audience
addressed. More specifically, Schluchter argues that the lecture is to be
understood within the broad context of Weber's return to university
teaching, and within the narrower context of his relationship to the

youth and student movements of the time. He here follows Heinrich Rickert's advice: 'It must first be borne in mind that an academic teacher is addressing students here, so that *pedagogic* considerations are at work' (Rickert, 1989, 80). This is an important point, for, as Schluchter himself reminds us, 'Science as a Vocation' was a lecture in a series planned by the Munich Free Students in response to Franz Schwab's essay 'Vocation and Youth'. Weber's lecture thus has a historical context, and must be read, at least in part, as a reply to German student movements craving both 'experience' and leadership (see Weber, 1970, 143 and 149). This context may explain Weber's silence on the value of the Enlightenment and his refusal to discuss Nietzsche's position at any length, for, as Schluchter (1996) argues, Weber was keen to convey a particular message to the Free Students: that of 'an insistence on an ascetic basis of action' (p. 36). And in view of this, 'Science as a Vocation' clearly was not the place for an extended analysis of Nietzsche's critique of the Enlightenment.

For these reasons, Weber is keen to 'resume his argument' without further comment. He does so by returning to his initial question of the present value of science and asking what the *meaning* of the scientific vocation is, now that the five 'former illusions' (science as the path to true being, art, nature, God, happiness) have been dispelled. Weber makes the following observation: that the scientific rationalization of the world, while in principle making all objects and relations in life calculable, is not *necessarily* of practical value, for it does not engender a general understanding of the concrete conditions of life. Weber (1970) argues, for example:

> When we spend money today I bet that even if there are colleagues of political economy here in the hall, almost every one of them will hold a different answer in readiness to the question: How does it happen that one can buy something for money – sometimes more and sometimes less? The savage knows what he does in order to get his daily food and which institutions serve him in this pursuit. The increasing intellectualization and rationalization do not, therefore, indicate an increased and general knowledge of the conditions under which one lives. (p. 139)

This passage is an allusion to the second epilogue of *War and Peace*, in which Tolstoy gives the following example of the completeness of the mythical existence of the peasant, as opposed to the partial, specialized knowledge of the modern individual: 'A locomotive is moving. Some one asks: What moves it? A peasant says the devil moves it. Another man says the locomotive moves because its wheels go round. A third asserts the cause of the movement lies in the smoke which the wind carries away. The peasant is irrefutable. He has devised a complete explanation' (Tolstoy, 1993, 972). The key point of this passage, at least for the purpose of the present work, is that technical and human progress are not necessarily one, for the rationalization of the world shatters the symbolic order that lent pre-modern or peasant life unity, leaving us with a 'rational' but partial understanding of the world in which we live (see Chapter 8).

Here, for Weber, there is a further reason to question the meaningfulness of the vocation of science: while science disenchants the world through the calculation of all forces, it cannot and should not tell us how to lead our lives. There are, Weber tells us, two reasons for this. First, while science may be employed to understand and 'empathetically analyse' (*nacherleben*) the *meanings* of different value-positions and even to provide a *critical* assessment of the ideals which underlie value-judgements, it cannot and thus should not be used to legislate what *ought* to be, as such acts of legislation rest upon value-judgements and hence can never be truly scientific. Weber (1949) hence adopts a position that is diametrically opposed to that of Durkheim: 'it can never be the task of an empirical science to provide binding norms and ideals from which directives for immediate practical activity can be derived' (p. 52). Second, just as natural science can teach us nothing about the *meaning* of the world (Weber, 1970, 42) it can teach us nothing about the meaning of our lives, and in fact, as argued above, contributes to the destruction of meaning itself through the reduction of ultimate beliefs and values to mundane means and ends. In view of these two points, Weber argues that science, now that its former illusions or values have been dispelled, is itself an enterprise which is stripped of meaning. He reflects, again drawing on the work of Tolstoy (1934, 261; 1937, 178–9):

> Tolstoi has given the simplest answer, with the words: 'Science is meaningless because it gives no answer to our question, the only question important for us: "What shall we do and how shall we live?"' That science does not give an answer to this is indisputable. The only question that remains is the sense in which science gives 'no' answer, and whether or not science might yet be of use to the one who puts the question correctly. (Weber, 1970, 143)

This is precisely the challenge Weber sets himself (and us): to formulate a science which, while unable to address or resolve the question of *Lebensführung*, is of value in a practical sense, and which thereby restores a degree of meaningfulness to the scientific vocation. This task lies at the very centre of the lecture 'Science as a Vocation', and perhaps still lies at the core of (social) science today.

Weber and Tolstoy: exhuming the presuppositions of science

Weber (1970) responds to Tolstoy's challenge by examining the existing presuppositions of scientific activity (p. 143). There are, in Weber's view, two main presuppositions buried within science itself: first, that its rules of logic and method are valid, and second, that what is yielded by this enterprise is 'worth being known'. These two presuppositions are bound together and both lend science its legitimacy, but Weber, again following Tolstoy, professes to be more interested in the latter of these assumptions: in the *value* of scientific activity (see ibid.). In particular, Weber is interested in the way in which science fails or is unable to question the meaning of its own enterprise, and, perhaps as a result, presents itself as an activity that is valuable in its own right (see Weber, 1975, 116). This presupposition of value is, for Weber, a fundamental point of concern, for it lends scientific activity its legitimacy and at the same time removes questions regarding the bearing of scientific rationalization on life itself. Weber (1970) expresses this problem as follows: 'Natural science gives us an answer to the question of what we must do if we wish to master life technically. It leaves quite aside, or assumes for its own purposes, whether we should and do wish to master life technically and whether it ultimately makes sense to do so' (p. 144). Weber argues, however, that science not only conceals its assumption of self-value, but that as an activity which both proceeds for its own sake and destroys meaning by placing life within an infinite progress of ideas (see above), it effectively removes the grounds upon which the validity of its enterprise may be questioned. And this idea that science avoids the fundamental question of its own meaning or value may again be found in the writings of Tolstoy, for whom modern scientific investigations, by their very nature, 'evade the essential question calling for an answer' (Tolstoy, 1934, 257).

Weber illustrates this problem by giving a number of examples of rational value-spheres that presuppose their own value while also concealing the value of their presuppositions. The first of these is the sphere of aesthetics, which, he argues, presupposes that works of art actually exist, and on this basis enquires into the conditions of art itself. Weber claims that Lukács, among others, follows this (Kantian) practice. He explains: 'The modern aestheticians (actually or expressly, as for instance, G. v. Lukács) proceed from the presupposition that "works of art exist", and then ask: "How is their existence meaningful and possible?"' (Weber, 1970, 154).[6] This practice of taking the existence of art as given, however, means that the question of whether there *should* be works of art is never asked, and, following this, it is simply presupposed that aesthetics itself is a legitimate subject of inquiry.

Weber makes a similar criticism of jurisprudence. He argues that this discipline

> establishes what is valid according to the rules of juristic thought, which is partly bound by logically compelling and partly by conventionally given schemata. Juridical thought holds when certain legal rules and certain methods of interpretations are recognised as binding. Whether there should be law and whether one should establish just these rules – such questions jurisprudence does not answer. It can only state: If one wishes this result, according to the norms of our legal thought, this legal rule is the appropriate means of attaining it. (Weber, 1970, 144–5)

Jurisprudence, like aesthetics, is thus a discipline which proceeds on the basis of two concealed preconditions: that its object of analysis (law, art) is valid and, following this, that the analysis itself (the discipline of jurisprudence, aesthetics) is of value. These spheres accept a priori that their respective objects of study exist, that they are natural and hence unquestionable, and in doing so reproduce what, for Weber, is the flawed logic of Kantian metaphysics, namely the movement from a presupposition, that 'Scientific truth exists and it is valid', to a critical inquiry: 'Under which presuppositions of thought is truth possible and meaningful?' (ibid., 154; see Kant, 1993, 73–5). As a consequence, the rightness of an object or the value of analysis is not or perhaps even cannot be questioned from *within* disciplines such as aesthetics or jurisprudence, for these questions are repressed from the outset by the presuppositions of the discipline itself. The legitimacy of a rational discipline is, in view of this, derived and perpetuated through the removal of the possibility of self-reflection, ontological critique, and the question of 'ought', for just as aesthetics does not question whether there *should* be works of art, jurisprudence does not question whether there *should* be law. And this problem is further compounded by the fact that such disciplines claim to be ethical on the basis of this formal separation of facts from values. Jurisprudence, for example, claims not to judge the rightness of law itself, but employs a model of instrumental rationality to proceed through legal means in order to realise particular ends. This conceals the fact, however, that this negation of values, which grounds every rational science, is founded upon an affirmation of an initial value (a presupposition), in this case the valid existence of law, and it is on this basis that the discipline derives its own legitimacy. Weber (1970) firmly reminds us of this point: 'No science is absolutely free from presuppositions, and no science can prove its fundamental value to the man who rejects these presuppositions' (p. 153).

The historical and cultural sciences offer further proof of this. These disciplines seek to reach an understanding of political, artistic, literary, and social phenomena, but, following the example of the natural sciences, do not question whether these phenomena have been, or are presently, of *value*. This question of value is excluded from enquiry through the initial presupposition that these historical and cultural phenomena are of interest and are thus worth knowing. But, as Weber (1970) notes, these sciences 'cannot prove "scientifically" that this is the case; and that they presuppose this interest by no means proves that it goes without saying. In fact it is not at all self-evident' (p. 145). This concealed presupposition of interest, however, is crucial, for it constitutes a double act of legitimation: it affirms the value of the phenomena under study and confers the legitimacy of the study itself.

In the light of this, Weber (1970) considers the disciplines closest to him: 'sociology, history, economics, and political science, and those types of cultural philosophy that make it their task to interpret these sciences' (p. 145). His analysis of these disciplines is, however, quite different to his consideration of aesthetics, jurisprudence and historical and cultural science, for Weber does not seek to expose the presuppositions concealed within sociology, history or political science (which perhaps for his audience go without saying), but instead argues that these disciplines should be *value-free*, or, in other words, *free from* (or at the very least reflect upon and be aware of) presuppositions. Weber hence does not ask whether these disciplines are of value in themselves; rather, he reflects on the nature and limits of their enquiry, and in doing so forwards a response to Tolstoy regarding the form and value of science itself.

First, there is a practical or, more specifically, an *ethical* reason for the disciplines of sociology, history, economics and political science proceeding without presuppositions: these disciplines, as academic pursuits that claim to establish and clarify objective facts, should not be biased at any point either by concealed or declared value-judgements. These disciplines, as sciences, are, Weber argues, to proceed on the basis of logical or formal analysis and, beyond an initial valuation of a research interest (the doctrine of value-relevance, *Wertbeziehung*; see Weber, 1949, 21–2), are not to be corrupted by subjective preferences. This position is accompanied by a staunch commitment to academic probity. Weber (1970) states, for example:

> One can only demand of a teacher that he have the intellectual integrity to see that it is one thing to state facts, to determine mathematical or logical relations or the internal structure of cultural values, while it is another thing to answer questions of the *value* of culture and its individual contents and the question of how one should act in the cultural community and in political associations. (p. 146)

This position, which reflects Weber's neo-Kantian separation of facts and values ('is' and 'ought'), asserts that science is not to be used to answer questions of value, and places a demand on the teacher not to imprint his or her personal views on academic work (see ibid., p. 145). Science may be used to clarify and understand values *as empirical facts* but is not to be used to confer the validity of values themselves. It is only through this rigid separation of 'is' from 'ought', Weber argues, that an objective understanding of historical or cultural phenomena may be achieved. Indeed, he argues: 'I am ready to prove from the works of our historians that whenever the man of science introduces his personal value judgement, a full understanding of the facts *ceases*' (ibid., 146).

There is, however, a further argument for the pursuit of a value-free (presuppositionless) science, even if this goal can never be fully realized (see Weber, 1970, 153): science should not be used to arbitrate between values precisely because it cannot do so.[7] It would be impossible, for example, for science to judge the values held by a Catholic or a Freemason, or to decide the value of French or German culture (ibid., 148; see Chapter 3). Science could be used to elucidate the form and logic of these values, and at best analyse them critically, but beyond this, *judgement* of their *validity* 'is a matter of faith' (see Weber, 1949, 55). The key point here is that questions of value cannot be answered through scientific means for there exist no *objective* criteria upon which values may be ranked or judged, and on this basis, Weber, unlike Durkheim, argues that it is not the task of science to rank values or produce binding norms (see ibid., p. 52). The irony of this is that consequently science is unable to resolve the crisis of values it helped initiate (see Chapter 3), for it can neither answer questions of ultimate value nor resolve conflicts between values which are formally irreconcilable. The legitimacy of values is thus left to the subjective preference of the individual, and calls for a judgement of faith ('taking a stand') rather than the detached use of scientific reason. The tragedy of this position though, as analysed in the previous chapter, is that the rationalization of the world promotes instrumental reason at the cost of value-rationality, and in doing so restricts the very capacity of the individual to take such a stand.

The value of practical reason

The inability of science either to answer questions of ultimate value, including those relating to the leading of life (*Lebensführung*), or to create new values or norms returns us to Tolstoy's question regarding the *value* of science. This question is difficult for Weber to answer directly, for it demands a subjective evaluation of culture, and such evaluation would contravene his commitment to a principle of value-freedom (*Wertfreiheit*) in academic work. Weber is thus cautious in his approach to the value of science as a vocation. He argues: 'Whether ... science is a worthwhile "vocation" for somebody, and whether science itself has an objectively valuable "vocation" are ... valuable judgements about which nothing can be said in the lecture-room' (Weber, 1970, 152).

In spite of this formal declaration, Weber in practice does draw a number of conclusions regarding the value of science within the modern world. He claims, for example, that science, within its true limits, is of *practical* value. He argues that there are three ways in which science contributes positively to practical and personal life (Weber, 1970, 150–1). First, it enables the control of life, at least in theory, through the calculation of external objects and 'man's' activities. This point is, of course, double-edged, for control over life, as Weber himself suggests, can only be achieved at a cost, namely the routinization and ossification of all social relations (see Chapters 2 and 3). Second, following Aristotle, science offers rational methods of thinking and 'the tools and the training for thought', and third, through the use of these tools it enables us to gain clarity about the world in which we live. It is this latter contribution that Weber holds to be the most important objective of science. It is the task of the vocational scientist to provide clarity about the empirical world, thereby enabling informed value-choices and responsible social action. Furthermore, science is to be used to raise points of difficulty within the current realm of knowledge, and to present the individual with 'inconvenient facts' and the necessity of making value-choices. In this respect, Siegfried Landshut, a prominent critic of 'Science as a Vocation', is quite wrong to claim that 'The lecture ends, having said nothing concrete about the task of science itself' (Landshut, 1989, 100). Science is not to exist simply as an end in itself, but rather is to be employed to delineate the scope of facts and values in order to help meet the demands of this world. And this calls for the scientist in particular, and the modern individual more generally, to mediate his or her fate *actively*; for us to refuse to tarry for new prophets that may not exist or mourn for the organic totality of times past (Tönnies, 1955; Simmel, 1997), and affirm instead a practical ethic of vocational work. Weber (1970) proclaims: 'we want to draw the lesson that nothing is gained by yearning and tarrying alone, and we shall act differently. We shall set to work and "meet the demands of the day", in human relations as well as in our vocation' (p. 156).

This is an important statement for it indicates that Weber's position on the value of the vocation of science rests, *contra* Tolstoy, on the belief that there can be no redemption from the rationalism of the modern world. Here, Weber stands against all forms of intellectual Romanticism, a point confirmed by the critical distance he kept from the Stefan George circle (see Lepenies, 1988, 279–96) and by his own commitment to a *this-worldly* vocation. Weber argues that knowledge of the world, once realized, is irrevocable, and, following this, that there is no possibility of a return to the naive (enchanted) state of pre-modern times. Hence: 'the fate of our times is characterized by rationalization and intellectualization and, above all, by the "disenchantment of the world"' (Weber, 1970, 155). On the basis of this Weber, unlike Baudrillard (see Chapter 8), neither seeks to abandon the use of reason nor argues that reason itself can be abandoned. Rather, he argues that scientific knowledge, as an irrevocable fact of modern life, should be employed to clarify the existence of facts and values in the world, and to aid thereby the selection of the means through which values may be pursued. In this respect, the use of scientific reason may enhance the possibility of individual autonomy, and Weber works broadly within the spirit of the Enlightenment project. But at the same time, this path to individual freedom always remains limited (contrary to the arguments of Marcuse, 1968), as science itself rests on the subordination of ultimate values to the calculative rule of instrumental reason (see Chapter 2), and with this engenders the possibility of new forms of domination (Bauman, 1989).

From this, Weber draws a number of conclusions regarding the use and value of science. The first and most important of these is that science may be of value only if it remains within its 'true' limits. Science, while of value in so far as it can be used to address and even answer logical or technical questions, cannot and thus should not be used to create new (ultimate) values or provide a final judgement on the legitimacy of values themselves. Weber argues that it is the duty of the vocational scientist to recognize this, and to avoid at all costs presenting academic prophecies in the guise of value-free science (see Weber, 1970, 155). This calls not simply for the vocation of science to be imbued with a sense of ethical responsibility, but for science itself to be a *self-reflective* practice, one that identifies and calls into question its own presuppositions. In this respect, Weber, like Nietzsche (1983, 121), argues that 'science requires superintendence and supervision', for it is to proceed within strictly defined limits, and beyond this is to remain accountable for its own presuppositions or *values*.[8] And it is on this basis that science may assume an objective form, and with this become, paradoxically, a practice that is valuable, if not necessarily meaningful, in its own right.

Beyond this, there is, an additional sense in which science requires supervision: it is, in general, to serve life and not vice versa (in general because life itself may become a vocation). This means that science is neither to be pursued simply as an end in itself (which confers its own value), nor is to be used to create values or properties which may in turn guide our lives; rather it is to be confined to the realm of fact not value. But this 'ascetic ideal' itself creates a further problem: it calls for commitment to a vocation that demands value-freedom, and in this respect asks us to be 'inhuman'. The danger here is not simply that value-judgements may be made in the guise of value-free science, but conversely that the ascetic ideal of science may spread to culture more generally, and in doing so may preclude the critical (re)valuation of existing values and ideals. This problem is raised by Nietzsche (1983):

Science is related to wisdom as virtuousness is related to holiness: it is cold and dry, it has not love and knows nothing of self-dissatisfaction and longing. It is as useful to itself as it is harmful to its servants, in so far as it transfers its own character to them and thereby ossifies their humanity. (p. 169).

Weber is equally critical of this 'sacrifice of mankind to science' (ibid., 132). In his famous conclusion to the *Protestant Ethic* he calls into question the presupposition that science engenders human 'progress' or the qualitative advancement of life, and argues instead that modern culture is characterized by sterility and passionlessness: 'for of the "*last men*" of this cultural development, it might well be truly said: "Specialists without spirit, sensualists without heart; this nullity imagines that it has attained a level of civilization never before achieved"' (Weber, 1992, 182).[9] In response, Weber does not call for the abandonment of the scientific vocation, and, unlike Nietzsche, refuses to flee from the fate of modernity, arguing that there can be no return to the 'infancy of thought' (Lyotard; see Chapter 7) and no foreseeable advancement to a Utopian state (Comte, Marx and perhaps Durkheim). Rather, he argues that we should employ science to help tackle the practical and technical problems of our day, so that science *serves us* in the leading of our lives and not vice versa. Weber thus argues that an ascetic ideal of science need not engender the further ossification of humanity, for if it is used responsibly science may act as *our* servant. Indeed, he argues that while science cannot tell us what 'ought' to be, it may be employed to clarify, and perhaps even critically assess (see Weber, 1949, 54), the existing order of things, and on this basis may even be used to awake the modern individual from the slumber of his or her 'routinized daily existence' (see ibid., p. 18). And in this respect Weber's theory of science works within but also against the fabric of modern culture, for it confronts us with the necessity of choice between opposing value-positions – a choice which through clarification of the empirical world science can aid but not resolve – and with this affirms the necessity of an active mediation of fate, of *taking a stand*.

Conclusion

Weber proposes that the real value of (social) science lies in its capacity to clarify and inform value-choices, and to confront us with, rather than relieve us from, the 'burden of decision' (see Lassman and Velody,

1989b, 204). Weber, unlike Tolstoy, recognizes the inescapable need for the further accumulation of knowledge in the modern world, and, unlike Nietzsche, the need for the individual to make *responsible* and thus reasoned value choices. At the same time, however, Weber remains sceptical towards the Enlightenment ideal of progress through science, leading him to distinguish between qualitative or human progress and the formal progress of scientific or technical ideas, and, beyond this, to call for science to operate within strict limits. In doing so, Weber, *contra* Tolstoy and Nietzsche, does not attempt to flee the modern condition or revoke the irrevocable; rather he works within but against modernity, and it is on this basis that he affirms the value of science as a vocation. The value of this vocation, he argues, lies not in its ability to free us from the world in which we live, but in its ability to clarify the nature of this world, and to thereby delineate the scope for value-choices and future action. In this respect, Weber works within the constraints of modernity but against the totalising tendency of modern science, for he argues that the vocation of science, while seeking to establish the realm of the possible, must be subordinated to an ethic of responsibility and confined within strict limits: it should not seek to confer the legitimacy of values, arbitrate within value conflicts, or be used to create new values or norms. This position is part of a practical project that seeks to establish the limits and uses of scientific reason, a project which seeks to protect values and beliefs from the encroachment of instrumental rationality, and which thereby offers a possible, although limited, form of resistance to the further rationalization and disenchantment of the world.

5
The Ethical Irrationality of the World: 'Politics as a Vocation'

> In all commanding there appeared to me to be an experiment and a risk: and the living creature always risks himself when he commands.
>
> Nietzsche (1969, 137)

Max Weber's vision of the disenchantment of the world is a powerful reminder of the tragic disjunction of scientific 'progress' and political freedom. This vision reminds us that the rationalization of the world is not accompanied by a movement towards human happiness, 'progress', and freedom, but may in fact preclude the realization of these ideals. The previous chapter analysed one possible route of resistance to this process, namely the pursuit of science as a vocation, which lends itself not only to the making of informed and thus responsible value-judgements, but also to the protection of the realm of ultimate values through the identification of the limits of scientific rationalism. The present chapter analyses a further possible means of resistance to the rationalization of the world, that of vocational politics. This analysis focuses on the possibility of resisting the modern denigration of ultimate values through engagement in value-orientated but responsible political work. This analysis proceeds as follows. First, Weber's ideal-typical ethics of responsibility (*Verantwortungsethik*) and conviction (*Gesinnungsethik*), which have been the subject of much contemporary debate, are examined in detail, and are analysed in connection to the ideal-types of rational action outlined in *Economy and Society*. Second, it is argued that Weber's theory of the political vocation calls for a practical reconciliation of these two opposing ethics. Third, following a reading of Weber's ethics against those of Aristotle and Kant, it is argued that this reconciliation may proceed through the responsible pursuit of ultimate values. It is argued in the conclusion to the chapter that Weber's analysis of the vocation of politics here offers a model for passionate yet rational human action, action that works within but also against the fabric of the rationalized world.[1]

The ideal-types of political action

Political leadership, for Weber, entails an active rather then passive mediation of fate. The political leader, like the vocational scientist, must neither live in passive acceptance or bitterness of disenchantment nor flee from reality, but instead measure up 'to the world as it is in its daily routine' (Weber, 1970, 128). This demand above all requires the political leader to face the ethical irrationality of the world and take responsibility for its bearing on political action. This ethical irrationality is manifested, in the sphere of politics, in the fact that all political action is ultimately sanctioned by the exercise of force, a fact which places the struggle for political success in fundamental opposition to the pursuit of an ethical good, for it precludes the possibility of a purely ethical correspondence of political means and ends. Weber states:

> No ethics in the world can dodge the fact that in numerous instances the attainment of 'good' ends is bound to the fact that one must be willing to pay the price of using morally dubious means or at least dangerous ones – and facing the possibility or even the probability of evil ramifications. From no ethics in the world can it be concluded when and to what extent the ethically good purpose 'justifies' the ethically dangerous means and ramifications. (ibid., 121)

Politics is thus, by definition, neither an ethical nor an exact science: it involves dangerous means, and demands both calculation *and* risk. It is an unpredictable enterprise that operates within a sphere of human conduct, and thus retains an element of irrationality. This is demonstrated by the fact that political means, ends and consequences very often do not either correspond as intended or ethically justify one another (a point which is addressed further through analysis of Foucault's work, in Chapter 8). It is the task of the political leader to face up to this fact, and to strive both for the successful pursuit of ultimate values and for an ethical correspondence of political means and ends, purposes and consequences. This form of realistic but ambitious political leadership, which calls for a combination of value-rational and instrumentally rational action, can only be achieved through the reconciliation of two opposing political ethics: an ethic of responsibility (*Verantwortungsethik*) and an ethic of conviction (*Gesinnungsethik*).[2]

These two political ethics are themselves ideal-types of political action that correspond to the ideal-types of rational action outlined by Weber in chapter 1 of *Economy and Society*. Karl Löwith (1993), following the initiative of Eric Voegelin (1925), expresses this connection as follows:

> Weber contrasts the ethic of responsibility with the 'ethic of conviction', which he regards as an ethic of 'irrational conduct' because of its indifference to 'consequences'; in comparison to purposive-rational action, the ethic of conviction has a 'value-rational' orientation. The ethic of responsibility, by contrast, takes account of the prospects and consequences of action on the basis of available means. It is a relative, not an absolute, ethic because it is related to the knowledge, attained through this weighing of means, of the prospects and consequences of pursuing one's aims. If one opts for the ethic of responsibility one also decides in favour of rationality as means – ends rationality. (p. 68)

There is, as Löwith suggests, a strong link between instrumentally rational social action and the *Verantwortungsethik*, and value-rational social action and *Gesinnungsethik*. Conduct comprising the ideal-type of the *Verantwortungsethik* is, for example, instrumental action of the following type:

> Action is instrumentally rational (*zweckrational*) when the end, the means, and the secondary results are all rationally taken into account and weighed. This involves rational consideration of alternative means to the end, of relations of the end to secondary consequences, and finally of the relative importance of different possible ends. Determination of action either in affectual or in traditional terms is thus incompatible with this type. (Weber, 1978a, 26)

This ethic is characterized by a form of Realpolitik in which the relation of the purposes, means and ends of political action are rationally evaluated, *and* 'the responsibility for the predictable consequences of the action ... taken into consideration' (Weber, 1949, 16).

Counterpoised to this ethic of responsibility is an ideal-type of value-rational action and a corresponding *Gesinnungsethik*. Weber details this type of rationality as follows:

Examples of pure value-rational orientation would be the actions of persons who, regardless of possible cost to themselves, act to put into practice their convictions of what seems to them to be required by duty, honour, the pursuit of beauty, a religious call, personal loyalty, or the importance of some 'cause' no matter in what it consists. In our terminology, value-rational action always involves 'commands' or 'demands' which, in the actor's opinion, are always binding on him. It is only in cases where human action is motivated by the fulfilment of such un- conditional demands that it will be called value-rational. (Weber, 1978a, 25)

This type of pure value-rational orientation gives rise to a conviction ethic of ultimate ends, one in which values are pursued uncondi- tionally, regardless of the consequences. Wolfgang Schluchter sug- gests that this conviction ethic may be divided into religious and secular conviction, thereby establishing three political ethics rather than two. He argues, following Weber's distinction in the 'Intermediate Reflection' (the '*Zwischenbetrachtung*') between these two types of conviction, that we should 'distinguish between reli- gious and non-religious ethic of conviction and put both, together with the ethic of responsibility, in an historical model of develop- ment' (Roth and Schluchter, 1979, 89).[3] While Schluchter is right to note that these two types of conviction rest upon differing types of political legitimation, one must also note that they share the same political ethic: an ethic of conviction based upon the religious commitment to values which, whether secular or non-secular, pre- cludes the rational consideration of the consequences of action. The important point here is thus not the religiosity of conviction itself but that the *Gesinnungsethik*, whether secular or religious, demands that conviction overrides all concern for the relation of the means and ends of one's actions, and that this unconditional commitment precludes personal responsibility for the consequences. This convic- tion ethic gives rise to a fundamentalist ethic of political action, one in which devotion to a cause replaces concern both for the chances of realising a particular value and for the cost of such an enterprise. This ethic is present in all cases where the means and consequences of action are subordinated to the demands of the political cause, including 'all radical revolutionary political attitudes, particularly revolutionary "syndicalism"' (Weber, 1949, 16).

The formal opposition of Weber's *two* political ethics is thus clear. Weber (1970) himself observes that

> there is an abysmal contrast between conduct that follows the maxim of an ethic of ultimate ends – that is, in religious terms, 'The Christian does rightly and leaves the results with the Lord' – and conduct that follows an ethic of responsibility, in which case one has to give an account of the foreseeable results of one's actions. (p. 120)

The exact relation of these two ethics to Weber's ideal-types of rational social action is, however, a point of contemporary dispute.[4] Rogers Brubaker, for example, questions the direct correspondence of the ethic of responsibility and instrumental rationality, and the ethic of conviction and value rationality. He argues instead that the ethic of responsibility is in fact a synthesis of value and instrumental rationality:

> the ethic of responsibility is *not* identical with pure *Zweckrationalität*. For pure *Zweckrationalität* ... precludes any reference to ultimate value commitments: ends are determined by the urgency of an individual's 'given subjective wants' and by the ease of satisfying them, not by their 'worth' from the point of view of a system of ultimate values. The ethic of responsibility, on the other hand, is not merely compatible with a commitment to ultimate values, but demands just such a commitment. For responsibility is empty to some 'substantive purpose' unless it is informed by 'passionate devotion to a "cause"'. Far from being identical with pure *Zweckrationalität*, the ethic of responsibility can best be understood as an attempt by Weber to integrate *Wertrationalität* and *Zweckrationalität*, the passionate commitment to ultimate values with the dispassionate analysis of alternative means of pursuing them. (Brubaker, 1984, 108)

Weber does indeed attempt to integrate passionate commitment to ultimate values with detached analysis of political means and ends. This integration, though, does not in itself constitute the *Verantwortungsethik*, for if it did Weber would have no reason to argue for a synthesis of an ethic of conviction and an ethic of responsibility.

For Weber, however, the possibility of synthesising these two ethics is the central problem of modern political leadership: 'an ethic of ultimate ends and an ethic of responsibility are not absolute contrasts but rather supplements, which only in unison constitute a genuine man – a man who *can* have the "calling for politics"' (Weber, 1970, 127). The point here is that neither an ethic of conviction nor an ethic of responsibility can alone guide the leader who wishes to pursue politics as a vocation. The ethic of responsibility is thus not, as Brubaker suggests, the integration of *Wertrationalität* and *Zweckrationalität* but an ideal-type of *Zweckrationalität* that promotes responsibility but precludes commitment to ultimate values, and this is why Weber demands that it be integrated with the value-rationality of the *Gesinnungsethik*. It is precisely the form of this integration of value and instrumental rationality, of an ethic of responsibility and an ethic of conviction, which Weber addresses in his 1919 lecture 'Politics as a Vocation',[5] and which, moreover, gives an indication of how resistance to the rationalization of the world, to the progressive reduction of value-rational to instrumentally rational social action, may proceed.

Towards a reconciliation of conviction and responsibility

It is clear that some kind of practical reconciliation must take place between the *Gesinnungsethik* and the *Verantwortungsethik* and their corresponding rationalities, as neither an ethic of conviction nor an ethic of responsibility can alone guide political leadership that is both passionate and responsible. The passionate conviction of the *Gesinnungsethik*, for example, cannot drive ambitious yet responsible political action, for it 'cannot stand up under the ethical irrationality of the world' (Weber, 1970, 122). This conviction ethic is unconcerned with the violent means of power,[6] and thus the consequences of political action. If anything, the passionate conviction demanded by the *Gesinnungsethik* is likely to deprive the leader of the distance that a sense of political objectivity requires, leading perhaps to power regardless of consequences and even to personal vanity and 'power for power's sake'. The destructive nature of this rule by conviction without responsibility is disturbing, for the value-rationality underlying all passionate commitment to ultimate values is unconditional, and shows no bounds. This is a fact observed by Emile Durkheim: 'Passion leads to violence and tends to break all that hampers or stands in its way' (Durkheim, 1992, 117). In view of this, the political leader must constantly appraise and reappraise the means through which 'he can hope to do justice to the responsibility that power imposes upon him' while at the same time pursuing political values with conviction (Weber, 1970, 115).

In contrast, the ethic of responsibility, despite giving rational consideration to the means, ends and consequences of social action, lacks the passionate involvement that vitalizes politics, and eliminates the risk of striving for success that is not readily attainable.[7] This, for Weber, is clearly a problem, as he notes: 'To take a stand, to be passionate – *ira et studium* – is the politician's element, and above all the element of the political leader' (Weber, 1970, 95). The ethic of responsibility, as an ideal-typical form of instrumentally rational social action that is characteristic of the rationalized world, ultimately eradicates this passion through rigid calculation of the chances and costs of political success. The *Verantwortungsethik* may thus be characterized as a realistic political ethic that, unlike the *Gesinnungsethik*, is able to recognize and take account of the 'ethical irrationality' of the world. Indeed, Wolfgang Schluchter states:

> As a political ethic the ethic of responsibility is, in the first instance, critical in so far as it not only takes account of the ethical irrationality in the world but also recognizes that the peculiar dilemma of realising values in politics consists in using power and force as means and therefore in leading to 'a pact with diabolical powers'. In a specific sense the ethic of responsibility is realistic. (Roth and Schluchter, 1979, 89)

While this *Verantwortungsethik* is realistic in so far as it takes account of the relation of political purposes and consequences, means and ends, it is too formal, too calculating to engender the passionate pursuit of ultimate values. In this respect, it, like the *Gesinnungsethik*, may also be unable to cope with the irrationality of the world, for although it takes account of and responsibility for the consequences of this irrationality, it can never fully master its bearing on political life. For as Weber (1970) states:

> the early Christians knew full well the world is governed by demons and that he who lets himself in for politics, that is for power and force as means, contracts with diabolical powers and for his action it is *not true* that good can only follow from good and evil only from evil, but that often the opposite is true. Anyone who fails to see this is, indeed, a political infant. (p. 123)

Politics thus demands conviction as well as responsibility, for, as J. P. Mayer argues, 'Politics ... without belief (*Glauben*) is impossible' (Mayer, 1950, 115). Faith must here accompany instrumental reason, not least because ethics is a sphere of value-judgements, and therefore cannot be determined or prescribed by science (see Weber, 1949, 1–47).

Faith in the rightness of one's values and actions, and, beyond this, passionate commitment to these values (Kronman, 1983, 179; Diggins, 1996, 61), must thus be combined with a calculated vision of the means, ends and consequences of politics.[8] Weber hence argues: 'Surely, politics is made with the head, but it is certainly not made with the head alone. In this the proponents of an ethic of ultimate ends are right' (p. 127). The correlate of this statement is that, against the fabric of the rationalized world, value-rationality is to accompany instrumental rationality in the political sphere. Indeed, Weber proclaims: 'I, for my part, will not try to dissuade the nation from the view that actions are to be judged not merely by their instrumental value but by their intrinsic value as well' (p. 24). The answer seems clear: that passionate conviction and personal responsibility must clearly be brought to bear on each other, and must coexist within the personality of the political leader.

In view of this, it is thus wrong to argue that between the ethic of responsibility and ethic of conviction 'We must simply choose: there is no rationally justified middle path between these alternatives' (Turner and Factor, 1984, 32), for these two political ethics are ideal-types that in reality demand an ethical reconciliation.[9] Stephen Turner and Regis Factor argue for the incommensurability of these political ethics by recalling Weber's famous statement: 'It is really a question not only of alternatives between values, but of an irreconcilable death-struggle, like that between "God" and "Devil"' (Weber, 1949, 17).[10] There are, however, two key points of difficulty in this argument. First, Weber's political ethics are ideal-types of social action that in reality do not exist in pure form. In reality, there is no strict either/or between the *Gesinnungsethik* and *Verantwortungsethik*, for, as Weber shows, neither of these two ethics can or does exist without the presence of the other. Second, within the struggle between God and the Devil, between the different value-spheres, there exist innumerable points of compromise which make everyday life possible, and it is precisely these points, and in particular those between ethics and politics, that the political leader must pursue in order to be both responsible and successful. Weber states: 'There are, of course, as everyone realizes in the course of his life, compromises, both in fact and appearance, and at every point. In almost every important attitudes of real human beings, the value-spheres cross and interpenetrate' (ibid., 18).

The difficulty then lies not in making a choice between an ethic of responsibility and an ethic of conviction, but in establishing how these ethics can be reconciled in practice. Weber in 'Politics as a Vocation' addresses this question at length:

> how can warm passion and cool judgement be forged together in one and the same soul? Politics is made with the head, not with other parts of the body or soul. And yet devotion to politics, if it is not to be frivolous intellectual play but genuinely human conduct, can be born and nourished from passion alone. (Weber, 1970, 115)

The political leader must combine passion and responsibility in order to pursue politics as a vocation, and this very often may involve a compromize. The exact form that this compromize should take depends largely on the value to be pursued and the particular historical conditions faced by the political leader. In view of this, the form of leadership must be the focus of constant reappraisal. Weber states, for example: 'Each new fact may necessitate the re-adjustment of the relations between end and indispensable means, between desired goals and unavoidable subsidiary consequences' (Weber, 1949, 23).[11] This process of re-adjustment is ultimately without resolution, for the political and ethical value-spheres are not only in constant opposition but also in permanent flux. It is the task of the politician to negotiate this value conflict and to be decisive as to the value to be pursued and the means to be employed. Weber (1970) says: 'the ultimately possible attitudes toward life are irreconcilable, and hence their struggle can never be brought to a final conclusion. Thus it is necessary to make a decisive choice' (p. 152). It is the right but also, and perhaps more importantly, the duty of the political leader to make this choice, and to be personally responsible for the consequences. It is this double responsibility that defines Weber's distinction between political leadership and *Beamtenherrschaft* ('civil-service rule'): 'The honour of the political leader, of the leading statesman ... lies precisely in an exclusive *personal* responsibility for what he does, a responsibility he cannot and must not reject or transfer' (ibid., 1970, 95).

The success of political leadership thus depends on the responsible judgement of the political leader, and his or her ability not only to seek a practical reconciliation between politics and ethics but also to actively take a stand for a particular ultimate value. This impossible demand entails a life of constant struggle, and Weber (1970) warns us that 'He who is inwardly defenceless and unable to find the proper answer for himself had better stay away from this career. For in any case, besides grave temptations, it is an avenue that may constantly lead to disappointments' (p. 114). To pursue politics as a vocation, to accept this life of torment, thus demands a particular personality; one who can incorporate personal charisma with an instrumental concern for both political success and ethical life. David Owen (1994) depicts the spirit of this personality as follows:

> The distinctive feature of the charismatic politician is his capacity to ground 'certain ultimate "values" and "meanings" of life' in his person. In contrast to bureaucratic politics in which decision-making is predicated on a utilitarian weighing of material interests, the politician with a calling bases decision-making on a *responsible* commitment to ultimate values (p. 131)

This form of sober heroism, which demands the political leader to constantly risk him or herself by taking a decisive stand and accepting the consequences, is clearly hard to bear. Weber does, however, indicate the primary qualities that the political personality must possess in order to pursue this vocation. He states: 'One can say that three pre-eminent qualities are decisive for the politician: passion (*Leidenschaft*), a feeling of responsibility (*Verantwortungsgefühl*), and a sense of proportion (*Augenmaß*)' (Weber, 1970, 115).

The immediacy of political judgement

This idea of proportion, of a balance between passion (*Leidenschaft*) and responsibility (*Verantwortung*) seems, at first, to bear some comparison to the 'mean' of Aristotle's ethics. Consider, for example, the following:

> The man who shuns and fears everything and stands up to nothing becomes a coward; the man who is afraid of nothing at all, but marches up to every danger becomes foolhardy. Similarly the man who indulges in pleasure and refrains from none becomes licentious (*akolastos*); but if a man behaves like a boor (*agroikos*) and turns his back on every pleasure, he is a case of insensibility. Thus temperance and courage are destroyed by excess and deficiency and preserved by the mean. (Aristotle, 1976, 94)

While Weber's argument for a synthesis of conviction and responsibility would appear to mirror Aristotle's middle course between excess and deficiency, it is worth noting, however, that, for Weber, the mean is a utopian concept that in practice is never attainable. There is then ultimately no 'right way' or 'middle course', for modern existence is defined and vitiated by an irresolvable struggle between competing life-orders and their value-spheres.[12] There are indeed points of compromise and convergence between these spheres, but these are not defined by an absence of excess and deficiency but by the violence of a life-struggle. Weber thus does not pursue eudemonism but a practical ethics that takes account of the violence of this struggle and the violence of political power.[13] The problem is not one of moderation between the extremes of excess and deficiency but of genuine human conduct that can reconcile two different ethics: conviction and responsibility.

The point of difficulty here is the term *Augenmaß*, which is translated as proportion by Gerth and Mills and as judgement by Lassman and Spiers (Weber, 1994; from Weber, 1958a, 545) and J. P. Mayer (1950). This term should not be understood in terms of a mathematical ratio or confused with Kantian judgement (*Urteil*) but read more literally as 'eye measure'. This is not to suggest that *Augenmaß* is a form of aesthetic judgement but a practical judgement based upon the immediate weighing up of historical circumstances. Christopher Adair-Toteff (1996) rightly notes that 'To translate this [*Augenmaß*] as judgement is simply misleading. By judgement we mean taking time to reflect, to consider, and then to render a verdict. Weber does not mean this; instead, he means the immediate sizing up, the quick measuring of the situation. It also implies the appropriate distance' (p. 8). *Augenmaß* is thus not a proportion of conviction and responsibility but a sense of perspective that enables the political leader to remain at a distance from the reality in question, a distance that equips the leader with a degree of political objectivity. This sense of perspective, for Weber, is crucial: 'This is the decisive psychological quality of the politician: his ability to let realities work upon him with inner concentration and calmness. Hence his *distance* to things and men. "Lack of distance" *per se* is one of the deadly sins of every politician' (Weber, 1970, 115).

This sense of perspective, however, while crucial to the pursuit of successful political leadership, offers us little guide as to how the *Gesinnungsethik* and *Verantwortungsethik* and their corresponding rationalities are to be reconciled. Weber, in line with his own ethic of responsibility or value-freedom, claims to offer no such guide, for such value-judgements lie beyond the bounds of social science. One may note, though, that in 'Politics as a Vocation' Weber frequently ranks the value of an ethic of responsibility over that of an ethic of conviction.[14] This leads Mommsen (1989) to conclude: 'In Weber's view the ethics of responsibility represented the ethic specific to the politician, and more particularly to the democratic politician' (p. 19). This is not to suggest that Weber argues that an ethic of conviction is in itself less worthy than that of an ethic of responsibility, but that in view of the violence of political power responsibility must always prevail. The only possible synthesis between conviction and responsibility is thus one in which passion is subordinated to responsibility, so that political responsibility is the primary value to be pursued with passion, thereby engendering what H. H. Bruun terms a 'responsible ethic of conviction' (see Bruun, 1972, 240–88). Weber (1970) states: 'To be sure, mere passion, however genuinely felt, is not enough. It does not make a politician, unless passion as devotion to a "cause" also makes responsibility to this cause the guiding star of action' (p. 115).

This sentence gives some indication of how the rationalities of the *Gesinnungsethik* and the *Verantwortungsethik* are to be reconciled. In *Economy and Society* Weber (1978a) poses the relation of instrumental and value-rational action as follows:

> Value-rational action may ... have various different relations to the instrumentally rational action. From the latter point of view, however, value-rationality is always irrational. Indeed, the more the value to which action is oriented is elevated to the status of an absolute value, the more 'irrational' in this sense the corresponding action is. For, the more unconditionally the actor devotes himself to this value for its own sake, to pure sentiment or beauty, to absolute goodness or devotion to duty, the less is he influenced by the consequences of his action. (p. 26)

Integration of the *Gesinnungsethik*, characterized by value-rationality, and the *Verantwortungsethik*, characterized by instrumental rationality, must introduce an element of irrationality (from the viewpoint of instrumental rationality) into political life, for politics is guided by, and aims to realize, particular values. This irrationality is not to be eliminated, for it is crucial to political ambition, but is to be held in check by responsible action. In this sense, just as the ethic of ultimate ends is to be integrated with and subordinated to an ethic of responsibility, value-rational action is ultimately to be integrated with and subordinated to instrumental rationality. As a result, as Arthur Mitzman (1971) notes, even the passion that accompanies and directs political leadership is, for Weber, to be of a rational type, one imbued at all times with a sense both of *matter-of-factness* and of one's responsibility to humanity (p. 249).

Weber and Kant: from autonomy to heteronomy

Weber's pursuit of a rational politics based upon an ethical correspondence of political means and ends, purpose and consequences here
seems to follow the directive of Kant's practical imperative. This imperative, in one formulation, instructs us to 'Act in such a way that you
always treat humanity, whether in your own person or in the person of
any other, never simply as a means, but always at the same time as an
end' (Kant, 1991, 91). Rogers Brubaker (1984), however, while noting
the influence of Kant on Weber, rightly points out the difficulty of this
reading:

> In Kant's classic formulation, autonomy is the condition of being
> subject to self-created and self-imposed obligations; heteronomy, in
> contrast, is the condition of being subject to obligations which one
> has not created. This morally charged opposition between auton-
> omy and heteronomy persists in the moral thought of Weber and
> the existentialists, but the connection established by Kant between
> autonomy and rationality is severed ... For Weber ... autonomy
> resides not in the formulation of universal laws but in the value-cre-
> ating activity unconstrained by any criteria – except in Weber's case,
> by the criterion of self-consistency. (p. 100–1)

Kant's faith in human autonomy and the triumph of human reason is
reflected in his deontological ethics, which state that the moral rightness of action is determined not by consequences but by the goodness
of the rational will (practical reason). Moral rightness, for Kant, is thus
defined not by action itself but by a formal principal of duty:

> An action done from duty has its moral worth, *not in the purpose* to
> be attained by it, but in the maxim according with which it is
> decided upon; it depends therefore, not on the realization of the
> object of action, but solely on the *principle of volition* in accordance
> with which, irrespective of all objects of the faculty of desire, the
> action has been performed. (Kant, 1991, 65)

The maxim that here determines the moral rightness of all actions is
the categorical imperative, which demands that 'I ought never to act
except in such a way *that I can also will that my maxim should become a
universal law*' (ibid., 67). This maxim serves the rational will as its basic
principle, and confers moral rightness on action according to its confor-
mity to the moral law. Kant's ethics thus constitute a 'rule deontology',

which, as Christian Lenhardt (1994) notes, claims that 'the moral rightness of an act lies not in the act itself (nor of course in its consequences), but in the maxim or rule from which the actor acts or intends to act' (p. 31).

Weber, in contrast to Kant, views the instrumental reason engendered by rationalization as defining a modern existence that is necessarily heteronomous. For Weber, faith in the categorical imperative is thus neither practical nor realistic but simply another form of the *Gesinnungsethik* (Lenhardt, 1994, 30), for autonomy is itself restricted on the one hand by the continuing ethical irrationality of the world, and on the other by the instrumentalism of Enlightenment reason. Weber does not, however, completely give up Kant's struggle for rational autonomy; rather he recognizes the problems of Kant's deontological ethics and argues that the political leader must necessarily commit him or herself to a series of obligations that are not self-imposed. Autonomy, as Brubaker notes, is thus, for Weber, not realized in a universal law, but in the self-imposed commitment to heteronomy. This self-imposed commitment, for the political leader, involves not simply the autonomous pursuit of ultimate values but an obligation to face the restrictions placed on political action by the ethical irrationality of the world. For Weber, it is this obligation to pursue an ethical correspondence of political means, ends and secondary consequences, to recognize the heteronomy of political life, which is of primary importance. He states: 'If one makes any concessions at all to the principle that the end justifies the means, it is not possible to bring an ethic of ultimate ends and an ethic of responsibility under one roof or to decree ethically which end should justify which means' (Weber, 1970, 122).

It is clearly wrong to argue then that, for Weber, 'Moral strength, especially in the political actor, consists in giving up the ethic of conviction' (Lenhardt, 1994, 33). As I have argued throughout this chapter, Weber proposes that the political leader, in order to follow politics as a vocation, must integrate an ethic of conviction with an ethic of responsibility. This integration, as is shown by the above comparison with Kant, demands that the politician must, above all, take personal responsibility for the pursuit of ultimate values. This is the key to the reconciliation of the *Gesinnungsethik* and *Verantwortungsethik*:

> it is immensely moving when a *mature* man – no matter whether old or young in years – is aware of a responsibility for the consequences of his conduct and really feels such responsibility with heart and soul. He then acts by following an ethic of responsibility

and somewhere reaches the point where he says: 'Here I stand; I can
do no other'. That is something genuinely human and moving. And
every one of us who is not spiritually dead must realize the possibility of finding himself at some time in that position. In so far as this
is true, an ethic of ultimate ends and an ethic of responsibility are
not absolute contrasts but rather supplements, which only in
unison constitute a genuine man – a man who *can* have the 'calling
for politics'. (Weber, 1970, 127)

Conclusion

This definition of political maturity, of an individual feeling a passionate responsibility for the consequences of his conduct, is the closest
Weber comes to formulating a concept of human virtue. This concept,
which is not found in postmodern political theory, places an impossible burden on the political leader, but as Karl Jaspers (1965) rightly
states: 'If Max Weber's demands were excessive, the human situation
was to blame, not his lack of realism' (p. 225). It is precisely this
realism that leads Weber to call for the political leader to integrate the
Gesinnungsethik and *Verantwortungsethik*, and to face the disenchantment of the world and not be disenchanted. This (Lutheran) calling,
which consigns us to a fate to which we 'must submit and make the
best of' (Weber, 1992, 160), demands the politician to work against the
fabric of modern life itself and to reconcile principles that are formally
irreconcilable. Weber argues that the political leader must, in view of
the ethical irrationality of the world, subordinate the *Gesinnungsethik*
to the *Verantwortungsethik* and thus value- to instrumentally rational
action, but at the same time guard against the reduction of all ultimate
values to achievable, mundane ends. This double bind perhaps constitutes the basis of a possible form of resistance to the rationalization of
the world, for ultimate values are to be recognized and upheld while at
the same time action is to be guided by an acute sense of responsibility. This position, which in many ways is similar to that espoused in
'Science as a Vocation' (see Chapter 4), involves a constant struggle
against the instrumental nature of modern culture, but Weber insists
that one should not give up or lose faith in the face of this struggle.
Indeed, he calls for us to engage in, rather than withdraw from, the
problems of this world. He reminds us, for example, that while 'successful political action is always the "art of the possible" … the possible

is often reached only by striving to attain the impossible that lies beyond it' (Weber, 1949, 23–4). It is, for Weber, precisely on such active engagement in this-worldly but value-orientated work that genuine resistance to the rationalization and disenchantment of the world may be based.

Part II

Weber and Postmodern Theory: Lyotard, Foucault and Baudrillard

6
Intermediate reflection

Part I analysed Weber's theory and critique of the rationalization and disenchantment of the world (Chapters 2 and 3), and then two possible routes of resistance to this process, namely the pursuit of science (Chapter 4) and of politics (Chapter 5) as a vocation. The second half of this work explores thematic parallels between Weber's theory of the rationalization and disenchantment of modernity and the critiques of contemporary (Western) culture developed by Jean-François Lyotard (Chapter 7), Michel Foucault (Chapter 8) and Jean Baudrillard (Chapter 9). There are two main points of interest here: first, the way in which the these three 'postmodern' theorists develop and extend (even if implicitly rather than explicitly) Weber's analysis of the rise, nature and trajectory of modern culture, and second, the way in which postmodern theory offers a transgressive response to the drive of modern rationalism, and thus an escape route from the ongoing rationalization and disenchantment of the world.[1] These questions, however, in themselves raise three key points of difficulty: first, what is meant by the term 'postmodern'; second, in what sense are Lyotard, Foucault and Baudrillard 'postmodern' theorists; and third, on what grounds may a reading between Weber and postmodern theory proceed?

First, the term 'postmodern', by its very nature, defies simple definition.[2] The term, read literally as the union of 'post-' and 'modern', would seem to signify an order, ethos or movement which is beyond, against or *after* that of modern. Such on approach, though, should be treated with caution, for any idea of the postmodern as subsequent to or later than the modern is itself modern rather than postmodern in nature. It places the postmodern within a modern order of linear time, and thereby ties it to an underlying theme or *meta-narrative* of historical progress or evolution.

The present work rejects this view. It is suggested, instead, that the post-modern neither succeeds nor completely breaks from the modern,[3] but exposes and transgresses the limits of modernity by embracing the experimental moment concealed within this order. The postmodern disrupts modernity and its related narratives from the inside, and posits new forms of historical time which contain their own strategic potential: the future anterior (Lyotard), genealogy or historical difference (Foucault) and symbolic exchange or cyclical time (Baudrillard). With this, the postmodern is tied to a new experimental ethos, one outlined by Lyotard (1984b) as follows:

> A postmodern artist or writer is in the position of a philosopher: the text he writes, the work he produces are not in principle governed by pre-established rules, and they cannot be judged according to a determining judgement, by applying familiar categories to the text or to the work. Those rules and categories are what the work of art itself is looking for. The artist and the writer, then, are working without rules in order to formulate the rules of *what will have been done*. Hence the fact that work and text have the characters of an *event*; hence also, they always come too late for their author, or, what amounts to the same thing, their being put into work, their realization (*mise en oeuvre*) always begin too soon. *Post modern* would have to be understood according to the paradox of the future (*post*) anterior (*modo*). (p. 81)

This definition of the postmodern will be employed in the present work. In these terms, the postmodern evades modern linear time by working concurrently in the future (post) and past (anterior), combining the past and future in the form of the 'what will have been'. The postmodern does not simply mark a break from either tradition or modernity, but proceeds through the historical deconstruction of our modern past in order to open the possibility of new undefined futures.[4] And this, for Lyotard, means waging a war against the totalising instinct of the modern, and seeking the dissolution of all grand narratives, particularly those which claim a universal end (including Hegel's speculative proposition and Marx's scientific socialism), even if this end is 'freedom'.

This call to abandon modern narratives, including those of progress, universality and 'enlightenment' which still tend to define the socio-logical tradition today, asks us to embrace the particular over totality, and demands a reactivation or unbinding of cultural differences or nar-ratives which have been captured, unified or perhaps even effaced by modern culture. This affirmation of multiplicity, is to proceed, for

Lyotard, through the unlearning of modernity itself, a practice that works against the didactic ethos of modern philosophy by searching for the endless possibilities contained within the 'childhood' of thought. To seek this childhood, which has yet to be captured by the modern quest for authority and totality, one must learn to unlearn the modern ideals of clarity, progress and universality. This process calls for the formation of oneself in reverse, and is the antithesis of the teleology of the modern project, for it proceeds through experimentation towards an undefined end. This experimental or 'paralogical' ethos, which, in Lyotard's terms, may be observed in the work of Aristotle (the rule of the undetermined),[5] Kant (reflective judgement),[6] Wittgenstein (the learning of the rules of language),[7] Freud (the idea of 'working through', *Durcharbeitung*),[8] and even in the idea of deferred understanding found in Talmudic law,[9] is the key to the future anterior of the postmodern, and is based on a refusal to restrict the nature of thought itself by the imposition of familiar concepts, categories or definitions. The postmodern is thus always in advance of itself or 'after the event', for it works forwards then backwards to establish the rules of what 'will have been' done. And on this basis, the future anterior defines the postmodern in two interrelated senses. It defines the opening of an unknown future through a return to the elements of what will have been modern through a process of unlearning. It defines also an aporetic mode of experimentation that operates without pre-established rules in order to retain the open possibility of work that 'will have been' done.

In the terms of this dual definition it is possible to define the work of Michel Foucault as postmodern.[10] Foucault, like Lyotard, is highly critical of the totalising ethos of modern thought, which, he argues, expurgates alterity through the historical reduction of difference to the same. He argues: 'modern thought is one that moves no longer towards the never-completed formation of Difference, but towards the ever-to-be-accomplished unveiling of the Same' (Foucault, 1970, 340). This elimination of difference is a product of the anthropological bias of modern culture, which creates and sustains 'Man' both as a subject and object of knowledge while disregarding the limits of thought itself. This bias, Foucault argues, is tied to a humanist narrative of historical progress that understands and evaluates history according to the status of its own anthropological construct: 'Man'. This narrative reconstructs history as an order of linear progress through the retrospective imposition of its own modern (anthropological) norm. And in doing so, this

'Whiggish' history elevates the present over the past by reading the past in terms of a present ideal, a practice which ultimately reduces historical otherness to a comparable but lesser form of the same.

Foucault attempts to unlearn this movement towards the sameness of modern culture (which is also identified by Weber, see Chapters 2 and 3) and belief in historical 'progress' through the genealogical exposition of difference within history (see Chapter 8). This practice reveals the historical limits of power and knowledge through the counter-historical dissipation of modern identity, a practice that disrupts the linear history of modern 'progress' through exposition of the disparity of historical origins and historical descent. This form of history operates at a micro-level, working against all grand narratives to reveal the limits of the modern order. Foucault states: 'Genealogy does not oppose itself to history as the lofty and profound gaze of the philosopher might compare to the molelike perspective of the scholar; on the contrary, it rejects the meta-historical deployment of ideal significations and indefinite teleologies' (Foucault, 1977, 140). The aim of this experimental history is to disturb the ontological security of modern identity and hence to provoke the possibility of otherness through exposition of the cultural difference concealed by, and within, the order of modern rationalism. This practice may be deemed an exercise in the future anterior in so far as it seeks the possibility of a different but undefined future through the experimental unlearning of grand narratives, and through a return to the elements which are concealed within, but excluded from, modern culture.

In these terms, it is also possible to define Jean Baudrillard as a postmodern thinker, for like Lyotard and Foucault he invites us to unlearn history as a narrative of linear progress. He argues, against the accepted Enlightenment view, that Occidental history is a fall (rather than an ascent) from a 'primitive' (in fact highly complex) symbolic order to a modern order of value that is characterized by equivalence and sameness (see Chapter 9). This fall is not, for Baudrillard, a strictly linear descent, but the temporary outcome of an agonistic relation between two orders (the enchanted symbolic order and the rational order of value) which exist on radically different principles (linearity versus cyclical exchange), and which can never fully efface the other. The modern order of value thus always remains vulnerable to the threat of symbolic exchange, and it is on this basis that the undoing of Western rationalism, and with this a reversal of rationalization, remains a possibility. And it is to this end that Baudrillard formulates his own postmodern future anterior. He adopts various strategies of seduction to reactivate the (pre-modern) symbolic order within contemporary life and thereby open an array of future possibilities. Here he plays on the radical power of symbolic exchange, which continues to haunt modernity in the form of its death, and threatens to annul the accumulation of value through its principle of reversibility. Indeed, it is, for Baudrillard, through the strategic deployment of this principle, through the empowerment of the primordial within the modern, that the hegemony of the modern order of value may be destabilized and perhaps even overturned, for, in his own words, 'everything which is symbolically exchanged constitutes a mortal danger for the dominant order' (Baudrillard, 1993a, 188).

It can be argued from the above that Lyotard, Foucault and Baudrillard, despite the clear differences that exist between their work, share a mutual concern for a postmodern unlearning of Western narratives of progress, and for the development of experimental practices to enable this process.[11] The question which remains is of the grounds on which it is possible to read between this strand of postmodern thought and the work of Max Weber. For not only do Lyotard, Foucault and Baudrillard make reference to his work only rarely,[12] but Weber, as a theorist of grand narratives such as intellectualization and rationalization, would appear to be a possible target rather than a source of postmodern critique.[13] In answer to this question, the present work will read 'between' Weber and these three postmodern theorists in terms of what Barry Smart (1993) has called their 'disenchantment *with* modernity' (p. 86). The aim here is not to analyse contemporary forms of rationalization and disenchantment (see Ritzer, 1999), or to consider the nature of what may be termed 'postmodernity', for these tasks lie beyond the scope of this work, but rather to focus on the analyses and criticisms of, and responses to, modern culture which are advanced in the work of Weber and the three postmodern theorists.

There are two main aims of this work, which will become clearer during the course of the following chapters. First, to show not only that Weber's work addresses a number of the same issues as postmodern theory (for example, the nature and trajectory of modern rationalism; the differentiation of modern culture; and the question of cultural rationalization and disenchantment), but that postmodern theory, implicitly rather than explicitly, develops and extends his account of the rise, nature and trajectory of modern culture. Second, to examine the strategies of affirmation and re-enchantment that may be developed from the work of Lyotard, Foucault and Baudrillard in order to resist the drive of modern instrumental reason. These strategies are

Nietzschean in orientation, and respond to the question of cultural nihilism or *disenchantment* by calling for a *revaluation* of all modern values. This response is thus quite different from that found in the work of Weber, who argues that such a revaluation lies outside of the limits of (value-free) social science (see Chapter 4). This difference is fundamental for it gives rise to opposing strategies of resistance to the rationalization and disenchantment of the world: to an *ascetic* response on one hand (Weber), and a creative, artistic, *aesthetic* response on the other – the postmodern (Holton and Turner, 1989, 91). The following chapters will consider this latter trajectory of thought, though, contrary to Holton and Turner (1989), it will be emphasized that, while aesthetic in form, postmodern thought is deeply, perhaps even predominantly, *political* in nature (though the division between these two realms is itself increasingly difficult to uphold). Beyond this, this work, will examine *three* of Weber's value-spheres as possible sites for postmodern resistance to the rationalization and disenchantment of the world: the aesthetic (Lyotard), the political (Foucault) and the erotic (Baudrillard) spheres.[14] It is hoped that examining the work of these three key thinkers in this way will cast new light on Weber's sociology of rationalization and his theory of the crisis of modernity, and, moreover, enable us to specify the strengths and weaknesses of transgressive (postmodern) critiques of modern culture.

7
Weber, Lyotard and the Aesthetic Sphere

> Being prepared to receive what thought is not prepared to think is what deserves the name of thinking.
>
> Lyotard (1991, 73).

The writings of Max Weber and Jean-François Lyotard appear at first glance to lie in radical opposition. The work of Weber, on the one hand, is of a typically modern nature, centring on the power politics of the nation-state, the meaning of social action and the affinity between religious ethics and the rationalization and disenchantment of the world. The work of Lyotard, on the other, became typically postmodern, and attacks modern forms of representation, authority, power and justice. In spite of this, however, there are important points of convergence between these two thinkers over the question of cultural rationalization. These points will be addressed in the present chapter through analysis of Weber's and Lyotard's respective positions on three key issues: first, the nature of modern and postmodern science; second, the form and consequences of cultural differentiation; and, finally, the aesthetic sphere as a possible site of resistance to, or even escape from, Western rationalism. Special reference will be made to the work of Charles Turner (1990) throughout the course this chapter, for it provides a useful starting point for reading between Weber and Lyotard, and for addressing the question of cultural differentiation in particular.

Postmodern science

Lyotard's *The Postmodern Condition* (1984b) raises a basic question that, somewhat surprisingly, is neglected by Weber in 'Science as a Vocation' (see Chapter 4): what constitutes 'science'? Lyotard answers this question initially by drawing a distinction between the pragmatics of 'science' and those of the wider realm of 'knowledge':

> Knowledge [*savoir*] in general cannot be reduced to science, nor even to learning [*connaissance*]. Learning is the set of statements which, to the exclusion of all other statements, denote or describe objects and may be declared true or false. Science is a subset of learning. It is also composed of denotative statements, but imposes two supplementary conditions on their acceptability: the objects to which they refer must be available for repeated access, in other words, they must be accessible in explicit conditions of observation; and it must be possible to decide whether or not a given statement pertains to the language judged relevant by the experts. (Lyotard, 1984b, 18)

In distinction to science, 'knowledge' comprises not only denotative statements but also notions of 'know-how', 'knowing how to live' and 'knowing how to listen'. Lyotard asserts that knowledge, in its broad sense, is thus different from science for it involves 'a question of competence that goes beyond the simple determination and application of the criterion of truth, extending to the determination and application of criteria of efficiency (technical qualification), of justice and/or happiness (ethical wisdom), of the beauty of a sound or colour (auditory and visual sensibility) etc.' (ibid.). The underlying pragmatics of the two genres is thus quite different, for 'knowledge' is based not only on the formation of denotative statements but also on the formation of prescriptive and evaluative utterances,[1] whereas scientific knowledge is based exclusively upon the language game of denotation. This distinction, which mirrors the neo-Kantian (and Weberian) distinction between 'is' (science) and 'ought' (ethics), means that science, at least in principle, is concerned with the 'truth-game' of fact (detonation) rather than value (prescription). Lyotard proposes:

> Scientific knowledge requires that one language game, denotation, be retained and all others excluded. A statement's truth-value is the criterion determining its acceptability. Of course, we find other classes of statements, such as interrogatives ... and prescriptives ... But they are only present as turning points in the dialectical argumentation, which must end in a denotative statement. In this context, then, one is 'learned' if one can produce a true statement about a referent, and one is a scientist if one can produce verifiable

or falsifiable statements about referents accessible to the experts. (ibid., 25)

Scientific knowledge, unlike earlier forms of 'narrative' or mythical knowledge (which remain tied to traditional or 'customary' social practices and have no conception of an external reality; see Chapter 9), is, at least in theory, set apart from the social bond, for it claims the existence of an objective reality (referent) or nature which exists independently of the 'social'.[2] Scientific knowledge, furthermore, is verified through 'rational' procedures of argumentation and proof, which again places it in fundamental opposition to traditional (mythical) narratives which construct their own (diegetic) reality and possess a time-honoured authority in their own right. These differences, Lyotard protests, are well known but nonetheless important, for they point to the impossibility of judging the validity of narrative forms in the terms of modern science, for these two types of knowledge are founded upon radically different principles. Science, however, by its very nature, not only questions the validity of mythical narratives but also dismisses them as a form of knowledge that is neither derived nor proven through 'rational' methods.

Lyotard is particularly scathing of this practice, and of the hierarchical relationship it establishes between Western ('rational') and non-Western ('non-rational') cultures:

This unequal relationship is an intrinsic effect of the rules specific to each game. We all know its symptoms. It is the entire history of cultural imperialism from the dawn of Western civilization. It is important to recognize its special tenor, which sets it apart from all other forms of imperialism: it is governed by the demand for legitimation. (Lyotard, 1984b, 27)

Lyotard analyses this demand for the legitimation of knowledge at some length. He argues that science raises rather than obscures the problem of its own legitimacy (ibid., 18), a position that immediately places him at odds with Weber, for whom science presupposes rather than raises the question of its own value (see Chapter 4). Lyotard suggests that with the transition to the world of modern science, two new features appear in the 'problematic of legitimation'. First, science leaves the metaphysical search for a transcendental authority behind, and instead establishes the conditions of truth through the rules of its own game (an argument which is consistent with Weber's rationalization thesis; see Chapter 2). Second, it becomes clear that science, in spite of appearances, is in fact unable to free itself from narrative, for beyond the realm of argumentation and proof it remains tied or even subordinated to a wider quest for the sociopolitical legitimation of knowledge. In this latter respect, Lyotard outlines two main modern or *grand* narratives of legitimation. The first is political in nature, and rests on the belief that 'all peoples have a right to science'. This narrative, found in the discourse of the French Enlightenment, ties knowledge to an idea of universal emancipation, and posits a connection between the state control of education, the training and freedom of the 'people' and the 'progress' of the 'nation'. The second is the 'speculative narrative', which, for Lyotard, is more philosophical than political in nature, and involves a different relation between science, the nation and the State. This narrative, as found in the work of Fichte and Hegel, suggests that 'knowledge first finds legitimacy within itself, and it is knowledge that is entitled to say what the State and what Society are' (ibid., 34).

Lyotard claims, however, that in the postmodern world legitimation of knowledge proceeds on a different basis, for 'The grand narrative has lost its credibility, regardless of what mode of unification it uses, regardless of whether it is a speculative narrative or a narrative of emancipation' (Lyotard, 1984b, 37).[3] This controversial statement, the implications of which will be discussed below, points to a fundamental change in the way that scientific knowledge is legitimated, and, more deeply, to a transformation of the nature of science itself. Indeed, Lyotard proposes that postmodern science is quite different from its modern counterpart, for it is not governed by a general metalanguage but is the outcome of an open conflict between heteromorphous language games or 'little narratives'. Postmodern science is 'founded' upon a principle of dissensus rather than consensus, but at the same time presupposes some degree of *local* agreement between its players (scientists) over the rules of the game (science). And this local agreement, for Lyotard, forms the basis of postmodern legitimation, or legitimation by what he terms 'paralogy': a form of legitimation which respects the heterogeneity of different language games but which also challenges existing games through the search for new rules, and which thereby seeks 'not the known, but the unknown' (ibid., 60).

This change in the basis of legitimation is accompanied by two radical shifts in the nature of science: first, a 'multiplication in methods of argumentation', and second, 'a rising complexity level in the process of establishing proof' (Lyotard, 1984b, 41). Postmodern science no longer consists of a single metalanguage but a plurality of languages, for science itself is the outcome of a pragmatic game in which the acceptability of the moves or propositions made depends on the 'contract' drawn between scientists. Lyotard here claims, against the position forwarded by Weber (see Chapter 4 and below), that two types of progress arise from the linguistic practice of science: 'normal progress' or (modern) 'innovation', which results from the making of a new move (argument) within the established rules of an existing game, and 'revolutionary progress' or (postmodern) 'paralogy', which results from the invention of new rules and thus a new game.

The second change in the nature of science, which involves the production of scientific proof more than argumentation itself, is that scientific truth is increasingly connected to expenditure and thus power. Lyotard (1984b) writes:

> A new problem appears: devices that optimize the performance of the human body for the purpose of producing proof require additional expenditures. No money, no proof – and that means no verification of statements and no truth. The games of scientific language become the games of the rich, in which whoever is the wealthiest has the best chance of being right. An equation between wealth, efficiency, and truth is thus established. (pp. 44–5)

From the end of the eighteenth century onwards, a reciprocal equation between science and wealth is also established, for just as there can be no science without wealth there equally can be no wealth without technology. Science itself becomes a force of production, for technology optimizes the performance of tasks, and hence optimizes the capacity for the production of surplus value. This marks the irruption of the commodification of knowledge, which Weber overlooks in his outline of the five historical values of science in 'Science as a Vocation' (see Chapter 4), and which, for Lyotard, is a key feature of post-industrial society: 'Knowledge is and will be produced in order to be sold, it is and will be consumed in order to be valorized in a new production: in both cases, the goal is exchange' (ibid., 4). The production of knowledge is here subordinated to a principle of instrumental rationality, for knowledge itself is seen to be of value only in so far as it contributes to the optimization of the capitalist system's performance. Beyond this, however, Lyotard sees an even darker connection between scientific knowledge and power, and in particular between technological investment and state or military domination, arguing first that it is conceivable that nation-states may one day fight for the control of knowledge rather than territory, and second that scientists, technicians and instruments are, in practice, purchased not to find truth, but to augment and secure political power (see ibid., 46).

Postmodern science, however, at least in principle, stands against this identification of science with the system, and against the capitalist quest for 'performativity'. Lyotard claims that this type of science seeks to transcend existing rules or games, and in so doing exposes the fundamental instability of all systems. He illustrates this point through reference to the works of Benoit Mandelbrot (fractal theory) and René Thom (catastrophe theory), which emphasize the fundamental instability and uncertainty of both 'nature' and 'society'. Postmodern science concerns itself with precisely this fact, and, in particular, attacks the idea that a system, be it 'natural', social or political, may exhibit perfect control over itself: 'Postmodern science – by concerning itself with such things as undecidables, the limits of precise control, conflicts characterized by incomplete information, *"fracta"*, catastrophes, and pragmatic paradoxes – is theorising its own evolution as discontinuous, catastrophic, nonrectifiable, and paradoxical' (Lyotard, 1984b, 60). This science hence challenges the idea of a 'noiseless' society based upon a faultless logic of means–ends control, including the bureaucratic society that, for Weber, is characteristic of modernity. Indeed, Lyotard claims, contrary to Weber,[4] not only that bureaucratic societies contain the seeds of their own destruction – for they 'stifle the systems or subsystems they control and asphyxiate themselves in the process (negative feedback)' (ibid., 55–6) – but that postmodern science opens an experimental realm of uncertainty, even of freedom, which eludes any system's control. Lyotard agrees with Weber that this realm of freedom may be restricted by the instrumental control and repression of the ability to formulate new games (paralogy), but in spite of this maintains that science itself remains an 'open system' which is distinct from any one authority. And it is with the aim of preserving such 'openness' that Lyotard concludes *The Postmodern Condition* with an appeal for public free access to data banks, arguing that this would enable groups to make knowledgeable decisions, and, further to this, would preserve knowledge as a force against the instrumental rationalism and 'terror' of the modern order.

Cultural differentiation and the collapse of the grand narrative

In spite of the historical distance between Weber and Lyotard there exist a number of affinities between their respective analyses and criticisms of modern culture. Weber, for example, observes that with the rationalization of the world, modern culture separates out into a number of competing value-spheres, but that these spheres, while possessing a degree of autonomy, tend towards rationalization (see Chapter 3). Lyotard, like Weber, sees the transition to modernity as characterized by a movement towards cultural sameness, for it involves the effacement of local differences by the authority of political and philosophical metanarratives. He proposes, however, unlike Weber, that with the advent of the postmodern condition this process is undone, for with the collapse of all metanarratives, postmodern culture, while still resting upon a social bond, is differentiated into an infinite number of competing local narratives or language games which are not necessarily tied to a quest for performativity (see above). Weber and Lyotard here share a comparable critique of the modern order, though ultimately they depart over the nature, value and possibility of cultural differentiation.[5]

Charles Turner (1990) is the only commentator to have examined this issue in detail. He proposes that Lyotard and Weber diverge over the question of cultural differentiation, for: while they both appear to share a rejection of totalising philosophies of history, Lyotard's work, on the one hand, is limited 'to the analysis of purposive-rational action', whereas Weber's, on the other, 'refuses pluralism, remains sensitive to the enduring power of value-rationality, and acknowledges the constitutive role of tragedy in history' (C. Turner, 1990, 108). Turner draws two further distinctions between Weber and Lyotard: first, they employ different intellectual tools to 'fashion their analyses', the former employing neo-Kantian value-philosophy, the latter Wittgensteinian language games, and second, Lyotard uses these language games to analyse an historical 'epoch', while Weber remains critical of this concept, arguing that it is 'the product of an unscientific need for a "feeling of totality"' (ibid., 109).

On this basis Turner draws an opposition between Weber's 'Intermediate Reflection' (or '*Zwischenbetrachtung*') and Lyotard's *Postmodern Condition*. He argues that whereas Lyotard embraces pluralism in the form of a multiplicity of local narratives, Weber rejects the pluralist or postmodern moment of the rationalization of the world (the differentiation of the value-spheres; see Chapter 3) and instead searches for a universal cultural reality. He writes: 'Weber's concern is directed to the manner in which individual value-spheres can become the sites for the construction of universalist claims, that is, foundations for the unity of culture' (C. Turner, 1990, 110). This difference, for

Turner, is essentially a methodological one, for Lyotard adopts a language games approach which asserts the existence of a plurality of linguistic practices and the absence of an overarching metalanguage, while Weber, by contrast, remains committed to a neo-Kantian value-philosophy, which 'also asserts the absence of such a metalanguage but the presence in *each* sphere of a normative standard' (ibid., 111).

Turner expands on this difference by drawing a distinction between Wittgensteinian and neo-Kantian philosophy, or, more specifically, between the analytic status of 'rules' and 'values': rules, for Wittgenstein (and thus Lyotard), are 'bound up with or immanent to the linguistic practices they constitute', whereas values, for neo-Kantians (including Weber), have 'a validity wholly independent of the existence of the empirical reality they order in constituting an object domain' (C. Turner, 1990, 111). And on the basis of this methodological difference, Turner draws a radical opposition between the substantive positions of Weber and Lyotard. He proposes that Lyotard, on the one hand, not only understands culture as comprising an infinite number of local narratives but rejects the possibility of elevating any one of these narratives to the status of a grand or metanarrative. Weber, on the other, conceptualizes modern culture in terms of a number of competing value-spheres, and, according to Turner, treats individual value-spheres as possible sites for the construction of universalist claims. This means that the potential for the reconstruction of a meaningful social reality remains, and, on this basis, Turner claims that Weber 'refuses to substitute for an ethical "totality" a series of postmodern partial standpoints' (ibd., 115).

At the same time, however, Weber remains sensitive to the tragic nature of modern culture, for he argues that the pursuit of an ultimate value necessarily offends the claims of opposing values from both within and without the same value-sphere. The attempt to construct a universalist claim on the basis of a particular value or value-sphere rests on intense human commitment, for it demands one to hold a particular conviction while at the same time recognising the existence of other values, values which are 'held as firmly by others as ours are by us' and which may block the actualization of our beliefs. Turner believes that it is precisely this matter of human conviction, or value-rationality, and the related idea of tragedy that is lacking in Lyotard's postmodernism. He concludes:

> Without this desire, this 'Here I stand I can do no other', which
> Weber theorized as value-rationality, there can be no tragedy, only

the comforting and bureaucratic purposive-rationality of game-playing. In 1952, Weber's friend and devotee Karl Jaspers wrote a little book called *Tragedy is Not Enough*. It seems that for many pluralist postmodernists, tragedy is too much. (C. Turner, 115)

Turner's account provides a useful starting point for reading between Weber and Lyotard, but overlooks a number of important affinities between their respective positions. First, contrary to Turner, both Weber *and* Lyotard are hostile to the concept of a historical epoch. Weber, as Turner notes elsewhere (C. Turner, 1992, 60–85), is committed to a neo-Kantian form of perspectivism which acknowledges the existence of an infinite number of competing viewpoints or values, and which is thus hostile to the idea of totality which underlies the concept of an epoch.[6] Lyotard, like Weber, also rejects this concept, though initially for a different reason. He stands against treating modernity (and by extension postmodernity) as an epoch, for the modern, he claims, is not in itself a historical entity but rather the expression of a particular philosophical ethos: 'Modernity is not an epoch but a mode (the word's Latin origin) within thought, speech, and sensibility' (Lyotard, 1992, 35). The key point here, which is not to be found in the work of Weber, and which Turner misses, is that modernity and postmodernity are not, for Lyotard, historical periods that follow each other in succession, and which mark out the progression of linear time.[7] Rather the modern and the postmodern are inextricably bound, for the postmodern is the experimental moment of the modern, the moment which the modern must eventually efface in order to become truly itself (see Chapter 6). Lyotard (1984b) hence proclaims: 'A work can only become modern if it is first postmodern' (p. 79).

Lyotard, like Weber, is also hostile to the idea of totality which grounds the concept of an 'epoch'. He commits himself instead to a Nietzschean agonistics that affirms rather than unites the differences between opposing values or parties: 'Let us wage a war on totality ... let us activate the differences and save the honour of the name' (Lyotard, 1984b, 82). Turner fails to note this, and with this overlooks the fact that Weber and Lyotard are united in their attempt to move away from Hegelian and Marxist narratives of historical 'progress'. Weber's (Nietzschean) critique of historical progress and belief in the incommensurability of values (see Chapters 2 and 3), in this regard at least, is close to Lyotard's postmodern agonistics, while Lyotard, like Weber, also embraces a number of the key tenets of Baden neo-Kantianism. Lyotard (1988a) maintains, for example, that there is a hiatus between the subject and the object (p. 7), that there is, as Rickert asserted, an infinite horizon for investigation (ibid., 22), and that prescriptives (the 'ought') can never be derived from descriptives (the 'is') (Lyotard and Thébaud, 1985, 17 and 59). In view of this, Weber and Lyotard, at least methodologically, are not as far removed from each other as they may at first appear, and on this point Turner (1990) eventually concedes that 'Lyotard seems to have rediscovered Weber's version of neo-Kantian value-philosophy and simply expressed it in a postmodern idiom' (p. 112).

Weber and Lyotard also share common ground in their respective criticisms of Western reason. For Weber, the rationalization of the world subordinates value-rationality to instrumental reason, and with this contributes to the nihilism of modern culture (see Chapter 2). His answer to this process is to place limits on the rule of instrumental rationality, thereby protecting the realm of ultimate values while at the same time enabling the possibility of informed and thus responsible value-judgements (see Chapters 4 and 5). Lyotard, while never actually using the term 'instrumental rationality', is equally critical of the instrumental logic of Western culture. He is critical, in particular, of the tendency for plurality and difference to be dissolved by the modern ('rational') drive for order and efficiency, a process which occurs at the level of thought, in terms of the quest for order through systematic representation (see following section), and also at the level of the institution: 'The plural, the collection of singularities, are precisely what power, kapital, the law of value, personal identity, the ID card, responsibility, the family and the hospital are bent on repressing' (Lyotard, 1984a, 10). Lyotard's response to this process of repression, however, is quite different from that forwarded by Weber, for he attempts to reactivate the multiple singularities, differences and aporias that are effaced by the force of instrumental reason.

This practice takes a number of different forms. First, Lyotard embraces the idea of the future anterior, the 'what will have been', which celebrates the aporetic moment of the modern, and thus works directly against the means–ends logic of instrumental rationality (see Chapter 6). Second, he invokes the paralogical search for instabilities against the modern drive for efficiency and performance (see above), and declares that any system, including that of an instrumentally rational bureaucracy, is fundamentally unstable. Third, he employs the notion of the *différend*, and seeks to honour the differences between values, phrases or language games rather than uniting (and thereby effacing) them through the imposition of a single rule: 'As distinguished from a litigation, a differend [*différend*] would be a case of conflict, between (at least) two parties, that cannot be equitably resolved for lack of a rule of judgement applicable to both arguments' (Lyotard, 1988c, xi).[8] Fourth, in line with this, Lyotard celebrates the collapse of the grand narrative and embraces an agonistics consisting of a multiplicity of local narratives or language games. Charles Turner (1990) treats Lyotard as extolling 'the comforting and bureaucratic pur-posive-rationality of game-playing' (p. 115). There is little evidence to suggest, however, that Lyotard's language games are in fact comforting, bureaucratic or instrumentally rational in nature. Rather, quite the opposite would appear to be true. Lyotard stresses that language games, like all games, possess an intrinsic value (value-rationality), and are thus not necessarily played in order to win. He insists: 'A move can be made for the sheer pleasure of its invention: what else is involved in that labour of language harassment undertaken by popular speech and by literature?' (Lyotard, 1984b, 10). Lyotard argues that language games are neither comforting nor bureaucratic, for like Adorno's 'micrologies' they form the basis of a 'strategy of thought that is not merely defensive' but that is creative, and which by its very nature therefore attacks the instrumental logic of performativity (Lyotard, 1983b, 121).

Weber and Lyotard, while both critical of the bearing of instrumen-tal reason on modern culture, take quite different positions, however, on the question of cultural differentiation (the reverse side of the ratio-nalization process). Weber, to recapitulate, views the differentiation of culture as a tragic event. This is so because, first, cultural differentiation forces the individual to choose between values that are fundamentally irreconcilable, and to adhere to a value-position which is necessarily compromised and thus partial (see Chapter 3). This said, Weber acknowledges that there may, in practice, exist grounds upon which conflicts between values may be resolved: 'The theoretically con-structed types of conflicts between "life orders" merely signify that at certain points these internal conflicts are *possible* and "adequate", but *not* that there is no standpoint from which they could be held to be resolved in a higher synthesis' (Weber, 1970, 323; translation corrected by Charles Turner, 1992, 87). This, however, is not an argument for the possibility of extracting the universal, or forms of community, from the particular (Turner, 1990, 1992), but rather a neo-Kantian statement stressing the divide between ideal-typical constructs (the life-orders and their value-spheres) and empirical reality. In *theory* there exists, for Weber, no clear grounds for resolving conflicts between value-spheres (which are rarely found in reality with 'rational consistency'), though in *practice* there may exist grounds for compromize or reconciliation between opposing values (see Chapter 5).

Science, secondly, which has replaced religion as the primary source of societal legitimation in the rationalized world, is, for Weber, unable to resolve conflicts between opposing values, and is thus unable to issue a metanarrative that can restore unity to mutually antagonistic value-spheres (see Chapter 3). This said, Weber believes scientific rationalism lends modern culture a degree of unity, for it offers a model of instrumental rationalism that, with the rationalization of the world, permeates and homogenizes all life-orders. This process has tragic consequences, for while the process of cultural differentiation appears, like modern culture itself, to offer the individual the freedom to confer the legitimacy of values, in fact, as an extension the rationalization process, Weber proposes that it restricts the basis of individual action, reduces the scope of 'legitimate' value-choices and denigrates the pursuit of ultimate values (see Chapters 2 and 3).

Lyotard asserts, by contrast, that the differentiation of modern culture is not a tragic process. This is not, as Turner suggests, because his work *lacks* a theory of tragedy or because he is simply 'resigned' to the disunity of culture, but because he views the collapse of the grand or metanarrative as a distinctly positive event. Geoffrey Bennington (1988) notes:

> It is important, and characteristic of all of Lyotard's thought, that such a break-up of large-scale narratives (the "grand" or "meta-narratives" of *The Postmodern Condition*) is not the object of lamentation but of affirmation – that intellectuals assign the increasing lack of respect for such narratives to a disenchantment or depression ... is simply a 'pure projection of the disappointment they feel in their need to believe in a major narrative'. (p. 113)

For Lyotard, the differentiation of culture into a plurality of competing narratives or language games is to be welcomed for it signals the end of the modern quest to unite opposing singularities under a single authority. This quest is by its very nature violent, for it effaces difference in the name of the 'One', and at the same time silences all forms of otherness, a process which has also been analysed by Foucault (see Chapter 8) and Baudrillard (see Chapter 9). Lyotard (1992) cites a number of examples of this process: 'Auschwitz', 'Berlin 1953', 'Budapest 1956', 'Czechoslovakia 1968', and 'Poland 1980' (p. 40). He argues that each

of these events involved the rule of 'terror' (the use of force to eliminate the opposing player of a game), and hence illustrates the intimate
connection between violence and the quest for totality (see Lyotard,
1984b, 46). In view of this connection, Lyotard celebrates rather than
mourns the collapse of the modern metanarrative, and with this
affirms the newfound heterogeneity of postmodernity.[9] He reflects:
'The nineteenth and twentieth centuries have given us as much terror
as we can take. We have paid a high enough price for the nostalgia of
the whole and the one' (ibid., 81–2).

It would be wrong to accuse Weber of such nostalgia. While seeing
the differentiation of culture as a tragic consequence of the rationalization of the world, he neither seeks a return to the organic unity of pre-
modern culture nor attempts to find a basis for the construction of a
new social totality, but instead takes a pragmatic stand against rationalization itself (see Chapters 4 and 5). This, still places him at odds
with Lyotard, for whom concepts such as rationalization, bureaucratization, intellectualization and modernization are nothing more than
equivalent metanarratives which give a sense of totality by subordinating cultural difference to a single historical movement. While noting
the modern tendency for plural singularities to be repressed by the play
of instrumental rationality, Lyotard suggests that in the postmodern
world there is no overriding metanarrative of instrumental rationalism.
The postmodern differentiation of culture into a plurality of local language games both reinforces the fluidity of the social bond, and
reaffirms the 'complex and mobile' potentiality of the self (see Lyotard,
1984b, 15). Lyotard states, as if in reply to Weber's theory of the
rationalization of the world:

This 'atomization' of the social into flexible networks of language
games may seem far removed from the modern reality, which is
depicted, on the contrary, as afflicted with bureaucratic paralysis.
The objection will be made, at least, that the weight of certain institutions imposes limits on the games, and thus restricts the inven-
tiveness of the players in making their moves. But I think this can
be taken into account without causing any particular difficulty.
(ibid., 17).

Lyotard's answer to the rationalization process is to stress the open nature
of language games, which, he claims, always rest upon a set of rules that
encourage 'the greatest flexibility of utterance'. This flexibility is present
even in institutions, for while, as Foucault notes (see Chapter 8), the

institution privileges certain classes of statements and places certain constraints upon communication, the limits it imposes on language 'moves'
are never established once and for all. 'Rather', Lyotard claims, 'the limits
are themselves the stakes and the provisional results of language strategies,
within the institution and without', and 'Reciprocally, it can be said that
the boundaries only stabilize when they cease to be stakes in the game'
(ibid., 17). With this Lyotard dissolves the constraints of instrumental
reason into a war between different, individually determined, narrative
positions. This move, again places him in marked opposition to Weber,
for whom there could be no such solution to the rationalization of culture
and to the constraints this process places on individual autonomy.
Indeed, for Weber, the very freedom for the individual to engage in creative, value-rational action is itself limited by the force of instrumental
reason, which means, in turn, that the grounds for self-determination
('taking a stand') always remain compromised (see Chapter 5).

The later Lyotard

In his late writings (from the late 1980s onwards), however, Lyotard is
far more circumspect with regard to the emancipatory potential of language agonistics. Here a Weberian narrative of instrumental rationalization haunts his thought as he reflects upon the many ways in which
the potentiality of cultural differentiation is effaced by the forces of
both technological development and global market capitalism. This
narrative takes the form of a number of scattered remarks rather than a
fully developed position, but these remarks are important nonetheless.
In *The Inhuman* (Lyotard, 1993b), for example, Lyotard, like Weber,
reminds us of the distinction between technological development and
'human' progress. He argues, in particular, that the development of
technology, or 'techno-science', is driven by the quest for maximum
efficiency and performance, and as such leads to the emergence of new
'inhuman' (technological) forms of control rather than to the emancipation of 'humanity'. Lyotard reasserts the instrumental nature of the
modern system, arguing that 'All technology ... is an artefact allowing
its users to stock more information, to improve their competence and
optimize their performances' (ibid., 62). In this view, techno-science
may be seen to stand against all instances of the unknown, including
the aporia of the future anterior, and thus to have little respect for
forms which are different or other to itself. This is compounded by the
fact that technological development is intimately connected to the

drive for profit (a point raised initially in *The Postmodern Condition*, see above). Lyotard proposes that this directs the production of knowledge and conditions the nature of knowledge itself, for information, itself a commodity, is increasingly produced in differentiated, digestible forms ('bits') for ease of mass exchange, transmission and consumption, and with the aim of enabling the optimal performance of the global system. Lyotard, like Weber, draws the following observation: 'Thought today appears to be required to take part in the process of rationalization' (ibid., 71). And, as Weber suggests, thought 'takes part' here in a double sense, for it contributes to, or perhaps even drives, the rationalization process, while at the same time being subject to rationalization itself.

Lyotard addresses this double process further in *Postmodern Fables* (Lyotard, 1997). In this work, he sees the instrumentalization of thought extending even into the realm of contemporary social and political theory. He argues, for example, that ideas of difference, alterity and multiculturalism have become nothing more than streams of cultural capital, streams which themselves fashion, and are fashioned by, the demands of the global market. Hence, the following irony: 'What cultural capitalism has found is the marketplace of singularities' (ibid., 7). The result of this discovery, which even reduces the 'postmodern' celebration of difference or otherness to a marketable strategy, is that ideas are stripped of their intrinsic value (value-rationality) and are judged by their value as commodities. This leads to the production of thought that is itself devoid of difference, for streams of cultural capital 'must all go in the right direction' and 'must converge' (ibid., 6). Global capitalism, while appearing to affirm the potentiality of cultural differentiation, in fact subordinates difference and alterity to an instrumental logic of exchange, performance and control. And here, Lyotard turns away from his earlier arguments regarding the flexibility of language games and the subversive nature of postmodern knowledge, and instead focuses on the factors that prevent the realization of cultural heterogeneity. In doing so, he constructs a narrative of the instrumental rationalism of contemporary culture which runs parallel to Weber's rationalization thesis, and which asserts the tendency for cultural differentiation to pass over into cultural sameness.

Art, figure and the aesthetic sphere

In spite of this, the possibility of subverting the instrumental rationalism of modern culture remains, for Lyotard, through engagement in radical artistic practice. In this respect, Lyotard would seem to follow Weber, who suggests that the aesthetic sphere possesses, at least in theory, the capacity to disrupt the rational structures that dominate the modern world. This section will analyse Weber's and Lyotard's respective writings on art, before a final assessment of the possibility of escaping or undoing rationalization through work within the aesthetic sphere.

Weber and Lyotard view the historical transformation of art in terms of a developmental logic of rationalization and disenchantment. Weber (1970) informs us that early forms of art were primarily of religious value: 'Magical religiosity stands in a most intimate relation to the aesthetic sphere. Since its beginnings, religion has been an inexhaustible fountain of opportunities for artistic creation, on the one hand, and of stylising through traditionalization, on the other' (p. 341). This relationship between religion and art, he observes, remains constant as long as art itself continues to be the result of the 'spontaneous play' of either charismatic or magical forces, but changes with the rationalization of the world, for with this art, in similar fashion to other value-spheres, becomes intellectualized, and develops into 'a cosmos of more and more consciously grasped independent values which exist in their own right' (ibid., 342). Lyotard's ideas are in accordance with this account:

> Art no longer plays the role it used to, for once it had a religious function, it created good forms, some sort of myth, of a ritual, of a rhythm, a medium other than language through which the members of a society would communicate by participating in a same music, in a common substratum of meaning ... And this generally went on in churches. Daily life was the realm of discourse, but the sacred was that of form, i.e. that of art. This has now become impossible. Why? Because we are in a system that doesn't give a rap about sacredness. (Lyotard, 1984a, 27)[10]

He proposes, in a similar fashion to Weber, that with the rationalization and disenchantment of Western culture art is stripped of its ritual function, and with this religious or naive art is superseded by a rational discourse of aesthetics and by the needs of capitalist production.[11] For Lyotard, this process involves the repression of 'figure' (the singular, possibly sacred, form that cannot be represented in discourse) by the instrumental drive of modern consumer culture. He writes:

> figural forms have been destroyed by the system which has predominated in the West from the nineteenth century on; these figural forms could not resist the requirements of the reproduction of

capital. In this sense, religion has been destroyed, and its forms of coexistence, its communications through figures, have become impossible. (ibid., 71–2)

Lyotard develops and extends Weber's argument regarding the disenchantment of art to suggest that Western culture increasingly obeys an instrumental logic of performance and control, one that imposes order on the free play of the imagination (see below) and subordinates creative thought to the demands of the capitalist market. And, for Lyotard, the effects of this process are consistent with those outlined in Weber's work, namely the progressive elimination of ritual or religious forms of art, the restriction of creative forms by an instrumental (capitalist) rationality, and with this the denigration of value-rational artistic practice.

This said, Weber and Lyotard both see art or the aesthetic sphere as offering a potential means of escape from the rationalized world. Weber, for example, believes art to have a different fate from that of science in so far as it stands outside of the course of historical 'progress' (see Chapter 4), and thus the course of rationalization. He proclaims:

Scientific work is chained to the course of progress; whereas in the realm of art there is no progress in the same sense. It is not true that a work of art of a period that has worked out new technical means … stands therefore artistically higher than a work of art devoid of all knowledge of those means and laws. (Weber, 1970, 137)

On this basis Weber treats the aesthetic as a 'non-rational' or 'anti-rational' value-sphere that offers, at least in theory, a means of escape from the rationalized world. Indeed, he claims that art offers a 'redemptory function', a form of 'inner-worldly, irrational salvation' that competes directly with claims of salvation religion: 'Art takes over the function of a this-worldly salvation, no matter how this may be interpreted. It provides a *salvation* from the routines of everyday life, and especially from the increasing pressures of theoretical and practical rationalism' (ibid., 342).

Lyotard's position on art and aesthetics, while broadly similar, is more complex. First, Lyotard holds a different view from Weber of the nature of 'progress' in science, and, consequently, of the connection between science and art. He argues, following Kuhn (1996) rather than Weber, that there are in fact two types of progress in science (see above): 'normal progress', or in Lyotard's terms 'innovation', which involves the making of a new move within an existing set of rules, and 'revolutionary progress', or 'paralogy', which is based on the formulation of a different set of rules and with this the founding of a new game. This latter form of paralogical 'progress' defines the basis of postmodern science, in which the rules of an experiment are not laid down a priori but are searched for after the event. And given this, Lyotard proposes that the fates of art and science are *not* necessarily different, for in both there exists an aporetic moment which seeks the potentiality of the unknown. More precisely, postmodern science mimics radical art in its paralogical pursuit for instabilities that challenge the existing set of discursive rules, and in view of this there can be no simple (Weberian) separation between art and (postmodern) science, for they share a similar ethos of experimentation. Indeed, it would appear that, for Lyotard, the experimental basis of such art might in fact inform the nature of postmodern science, which is itself close to assuming an artistic form. And in this respect, Lyotard's position on the connection of science, art and rationalization is quite different from that held by Weber. In spite of this, Lyotard, *like Weber*, asserts the potentiality of radical art to disrupt the order of Western (instrumental) rationalism; indeed, this is a theme that runs throughout the entirety of his work.

Lyotard's basic position on aesthetics, or, to use David Carroll's term, *paraesthetics*,[12] is contained within his doctoral thesis *Discours, Figure* (Lyotard, 1971), in which he presents 'figure' as the unrepresentable other of discursive signification.[13] In this work Lyotard suggests that while discourse operates as a system of representation which defines meanings according to their relation to other concepts in that system, figure is the realm of the singular, of that which refuses to, or simply cannot, be captured and systematized by the concept. This realm of figure does not lie in simple opposition to discourse, but is the dangerous other which disrupts and subverts the logocentric rule of discursive signification (the rule of the concept). Bill Readings rightly observes: 'If the rule of discourse is primarily the rule of representation by conceptual *oppositions*, the figural cannot simply be opposed to the discursive. Rather, the figural opens discourse to a radical heterogeneity, a singularity, a difference which cannot be rationalized or subsumed within the rule of representation' (Readings, 1991, 4). Lyotard emphasizes the radical capacity of figural forms to disrupt discourse from within its own space, and, further to this, establishes a connection between the repressed potential both of desire and of figure. Drawing on the work of Freud, he argues, in short, that figure operates through the free play of unconscious energy, and on this basis offers the possibility of over-turning all forms of rational closure, enabling above all the 'transgression of the object, transgression of form, transgression of space' (Lyotard, 1984a, 65).

Lyotard extends this position in a series of essays published in the early 1970s, a number of which are collected in the volume *Driftworks* (Lyotard, 1984a). This collection, which attempts to disrupt the artificial unity of thought by 'drifting' between the work of Nietzsche, Marx and Freud, is important in three main respects. First, it reaffirms the radical potentiality of figure. More precisely, Lyotard claims to follow Kandinsky, Klee, Itten and Albers in seeking to affirm figures which do not acquire their value through their position within an oppositional system, such as language (discourse), but which have an immediate value in and of themselves. This is so because figure belongs neither to the realm of language nor to that of 'practical transformation' but to an order of sense, and as such stands outside of the systematic order of representational thought. Lyotard attempts to develop a politics on the basis of this radical alterity, a politics based not on critique – which not only rests upon a hierarchical relation between the critic and the criticized but inevitably gets drawn into the oppositional system it seeks to attack[14] – but on the affirmation of disruptive forms which refuse to be captured by any one system.[15] Indeed, this attempt to formulate a politics of affirmation is the basic task of *Libidinal Economy* (1974), in which Lyotard eschews the idea of critique in favour of the affirmation of singular 'intensities'.[16] In this work, Lyotard takes a position of Nietzschean affirmation against what he sees as the nihilism of semiotics (see Lyotard, 1989, 7), and develops a theory of the 'tensor', which unlike the sign does not reduce the event to a series of structural oppositions within a representational system but instead affirms it in its singular intensity. The concluding section of *Libidinal Economy* (1974) summarizes Lyotard's intention: 'No need for declarations, manifestos, organizations, provocations, no need for *exemplary actions*. Set dissimulation to work on behalf of intensities. Invulnerable conspiracy, headless, homeless, with neither programme nor project, deploying a thousand cancerous tensors in the bodies of signs. We invent nothing, that's it, yes, yes, yes, yes' (Lyotard, 1993a, 262).

Second, *Driftworks* reasserts the connection of art and desire. Lyotard proposes that 'desire baffles knowledge and power' and that art, or at least figure, involves the free play of the unconscious. In view of this, the work of the artist is, for Lyotard, immediately radical: 'the artist does not externalize systems of internal figures, he is someone who undertakes to free *from* phantasy, *from* the matrix of figures whose heir and whose locus he is, what really belongs to the primary process' (Lyotard, 1984a, 74). This play between art and the primary processes is important, for art, Lyotard claims, works against prohibition at all levels, and thereby lends itself to a politics that attacks all forms of libidinal and institutional repression. This form of politics, which is based on the *'letting go* of consciousness', is, for Lyotard, both disruptive and effective. He cites May 1968 as an example: 'twenty or ten years of secondary discourse ... had changed nothing, one night of primary processes changed many things' (ibid., 82–3).

Third, Lyotard considers, on the basis of the above, the broader connection of art and politics. The work of art, he claims, has a deconstructive role, for, in the words of Roger McKeon (1984), it acts as 'an instrument allowing us to *see* through the gaps of dominant ideologies, and the source from which new methods could be drawn in the struggle against the system(s)' (p. 1). This role is in itself highly political, and in turn offers a possible model for political activity. Lyotard proposes that the artistic deconstruction of representation and form can be transferred into everyday political practice,[17] for aesthetics is to inform politics and not vice versa. In these terms, art is not be subordinated to the requirements of political discourse, as is the case with 'revolutionary' art, but should be free to deconstruct on its own terms. This necessarily leads to a separation of art and (political) theory, but, for Lyotard, this diremption is healthy, for art subsequently is able to retain its autonomy, while politics in turn is able to draw upon the deconstructive practices of aesthetics. He writes:

> I imagine there will always be a difference between artists and theorists, but that is rather a good thing, for theorists have everything to learn from the artists, even if the latter won't do what the former expect ... so much the better in fact, for theorists need to be practically criticized by works that disturb them. (Lyotard, 1984a, 30)

And in view of this, art, for Lyotard, remains a source, or perhaps even *the* source, of inspiration for the political imagination.

Lyotard's work on art and politics from the late 1970s onwards continues to assert the potentiality of figure (the unrepresentable), and remains critical of political forms of representation, but drifts from a Nietzschean commitment to pure affirmation, which he subsequently termed 'evil' and 'naive' (Lyotard, 1988a, 13), to a more measured analysis of Kant's analytic of the sublime.[18] In this period, Lyotard turns to Kant's 'third Critique', *The Critique of Judgement*, and in particular to the first part of this work, the 'Critique of Aesthetic Judgement' (Kant, 1952, 8–227). Lyotard's interest in this work is manifold but centres on Kant's theory of the sublime, which I will briefly summarize.[19]

In the first part of *The Critique of Judgement* Kant draws a distinction between the beautiful and the sublime. The beautiful, on the one hand, involves an agreement between the faculties of imagination and understanding, and, as a judgement relating to taste, is induced by the form of its object. The sublime, on the other hand, involves a 'cacophonous' relation between the faculties of imagination and reason, and arises from that which is without form. In view of this, while the beautiful and the sublime are both indeterminate forms of judgement and please by their own account, they are fundamentally different, for whereas the beautiful is connected to the form of its object and is thus limited, the sublime, by contrast, arises from the without-form and is thus limitless. Hence, whereas the beautiful involves simply pleasure, as 'the powers of imagination and understanding engage with each other according to a suitable "ratio"' (Lyotard, 1994, 72), the sublime is a moment of excess that involves both pleasure and pain. The pain of this moment arises from the inability of the mind or senses to represent objects that are 'too big according to their magnitude or too violent according to their power' (Lyotard, 1988a, 40). This occurs, for example, when the imagination is called upon to comprehend an exceptionally large or indefinite series, for 'Beyond its absolute of presentation, thinking encounters the unpresentable, the unthinkable in the here and now, and what Burke calls horror takes hold of it' (Lyotard, 1994, 110).

The sublime feeling, however, is also pleasurable.[20] This pleasure comes from the use of reason, for with the failure of the imagination to present form the mind discovers that it has the capacity to conceive of the infinite, and thus has the power to transcend everything that sense can measure and thus present. The sublime feeling in this case arises from the play between the finite nature of the senses and the infinite capacity of reason. Lyotard (1994) states: 'The object that is presented to reason in the phenomenon is never "big" enough with respect to the object of its Idea, and for the imagination the latter is always too "big" to be presentable' (p. 233). The outcome of the resulting *différend* between the faculties of presentation and conception is that the immediate apprehension of forms retreats as ideas of reason begin to dominate the imagination, and this gives rise to a feeling of pleasure. This process, however, does not signify the instrumental suppression of imagination by reason, but means that reason is forced to find new forms of presentation in order to represent that which is without-form or without-limit. And here Lyotard draws an important distinction between modern and postmodern approaches to the sublime. The former, merely attempt to present the fact that the unpresentable exists. Lyotard cites modern art as an example, for it avoids representation by presenting things negatively: 'it will enable us to see only by making it impossible to see; it will please only by causing pain' (Lyotard, 1984b, 78). In contrast, the postmodern approach seeks to present rather than conceal the unpresentable, and thus to put forward 'the unpresentable in presentation itself' (ibid., 81). Best and Kellner (1991) explain 'The sublime ... is precisely that which cannot be put into words, that which resists presentation in conventional forms and words, that which requires new language and forms' (p. 170). It is the pursuit of such new language and forms which, for Lyotard, is postmodern or paralogical, as it involves the experimental search for new forms of presentation, and hence the quest to move beyond the rules (limits) of the existing (language) game.

A number of conclusions may be drawn from the above. The most obvious of these is that Lyotard's work on art and politics is far more detailed and complex than that of Weber, whose theory of the aesthetic sphere remains largely undeveloped. This said, both theorists share a comparable view of the rationalization and disenchantment of art in particular, and culture more generally, and both also see art, at least in principle, as offering a possible means of escape from the drive of modern (instrumental) rationalism. This latter point is of special interest, for while Weber and Lyotard appear to be in agreement, they are in fact divided over the actual possibility of fleeing the 'rational' world through engagement in aesthetic practice.

For Lyotard, as seen above, radical art presents a fundamental challenge to the order of Western rationalism. In his early work he stresses the potential of figure to disrupt rational systems from within their own space, and beyond this emphasizes the connection of art and the unconscious, which, he claims, 'baffles power and knowledge'. This radical potentiality of the aesthetic sphere also surfaces in his later work on the sublime. First, Lyotard (1988b) proposes that the indeterminacy of the sublime is radically other to the instrumental nature of contemporary culture:

> To Wall Street and to NASA, the question of the sublime is not critical, to be sure. Not only is it necessary to represent, but one must also calculate, 'estimate' in advance the represented quanta and the quanta of the representatives. This is the very definition of economic knowledge. The understanding, which figures and counts (even if

only approximately), imposes its rule on to all objects, even aesthetic ones. This requires a time and a space under control. (pp. 40–1).

Second, the sublime forces the mind to search for new forms of presentation, thereby forcing reason away from a means-ends model of control and towards an engagement with the unknown. And in this respect, Lyotard's undetermined (postmodern) approach to the sublime again stands firmly against the basic (means–ends/instrumental) logic of modern cultural forms.

Weber, by contrast, is more circumspect in regard to the capacity of the aesthetic sphere to either resist or disrupt the rationalization of the world. He states that, in theory, the aesthetic sphere is essentially 'non-rational' or 'anti-rational' in nature, and hence offers a form of salvation from the 'increasing pressures of theoretical and practical rationalism'. Like Lyotard then, he recognizes the radical potential of aesthetic practice. But if one searches outside of the 'Intermediate Reflection' ('*Zwischenbetrachtung*') for further confirmation of this fact, a more cautious argument is to be found. In 'Science as a Vocation', for example, Weber (1970), in reply to the 'craving for experience' of the German youth, warns of the outcome such practice:

> the spheres of the irrational, the only spheres that intellectualism has not yet touched, are now raised into consciousness and put under its lens. For in practice this is where the modern form of romantic irrationalism leads. This method of emancipation from intellectualism may well bring about the very opposite of what those who take to it conceive as its goal. (p. 143)

This passage, though stated as an argument against the rejection of the world through religious activity, applies equally to work within the aesthetic sphere, for Weber suggests that the 'spheres of the irrational' (which include the aesthetic sphere) are likely to tend towards rationalization if pursued with any rational intent. This means, by extension, that any measured pursuit of 'romantic irrationalism', in the form of aesthetics or eroticism (see Chapter 9), is intrinsically problematic, for in raising the irrational into consciousness it is more likely to contribute to, rather than escape from, the rationalization process.

This argument against the *practical* potentiality of the aesthetic sphere concurs with Weber's theory of the rationalization of culture more generally,[21] but at the same time places Weber in fundamental opposition to Lyotard. For whereas Weber sees an inevitable movement towards rationalization in all spheres of life, including the aesthetic sphere,

Lyotard, by contrast, sees a space in every system that is other to the rule of instrumental reason, and which is opened up, above all, by the play of figural or aesthetic forms. In this respect Weber and Lyotard ultimately depart, for while Weber does not reject this argument outright (this would presuppose a value-judgement), he proposes instead that radical aesthetic practice is likely to be contaminated by precisely the rationalism it seeks to oppose. And on this basis, Weber, unlike Lyotard, chooses not to commit himself to a strategy of aesthetic work, but instead pursues a pragmatic, ascetic form of (neo-Kantian) critique that works within but against the limits of modern culture (see Chapters 4 and 5).

Conclusion

One may conclude from the above that, on the whole, Lyotard views the possibility of subverting the instrumental rationalism of Western culture with greater optimism than Weber. For Lyotard, both postmodern science and radical artistic practice, which are not far removed from each other, contain an emancipatory moment that stands against the instrumental nature of the modern order. For Weber, this moment is effaced at the very point of its inception: science offers the potential to master life but at the same time gives rise to new technologies of domination, while art offers a means of escape from the rationalized world but is likely to be seduced by the very rationalism it seeks to oppose. Lyotard and Weber hence put forward quite different responses to the rationalization and disenchantment of the world. Lyotard, on the one hand, affirms the postmodern search for instabilities, the irreconcilability of the *différend* and the potentiality of radical forms of artistic practice, whereas Weber, on the other, adheres to a more measured line of resistance, and seeks to place limits on the development and uses of instrumental reason (see Chapters 4 and 5). The key difference here is that Lyotard, unlike Weber, establishes a new narrative of emancipation (paradoxically, a metanarrative of the collapse of metanarratives), one that posits the unconditional freedom to be found in the aesthetic sphere. This said, however, both thinkers remain sensitive to the (instrumental) forces that prevent the experimental or emancipatory moment of modernity from being realized. In so doing, they not only point to the limits of what is modern but also identify the forces that limit the potentiality of that which may be termed 'postmodern'.

8
Weber, Foucault and the Political Sphere

[T]he historian must ... venture forth by lending his or her ear to
what is not presentable under the rule of knowledge.

Lyotard (1988c, 57).

[K]nowledge is not made for understanding; it is made for cutting.

Foucault (1977, 154).

There are a number of strong similarities between the work of Max
Weber and Michel Foucault. These similarities arise primarily from a
shared concern for the impact of cultural rationalization upon 'the
leading of life' (*Lebensführung*), or, more precisely, the bearing of
instrumental rationality (for Foucault power/knowledge) on individual
freedom. This shared concern, as Colin Gordon (1987) has suggested, is
apparent in their respective studies of 'forms of domination and tech-
niques of discipline, their concern with what Weber called "the power
of rationality over men", their writings on methodology and intellectual ethics, their interest in Nietzsche – and the effect of that interest
on the critical reception of their thought' (p. 293).[1] This chapter, while
noting these shared interests, will focus, however, on a key point of
divergence between Weber and Foucault, namely their contrasting
responses to the instrumental rationalism of modern culture. The
analysis, in response to the work of David Owen (1994), will centre on
the distinction between Weber's (ascetic) cultural science and
Foucault's (transgressive) genealogical history, and on the distinct
political practices to which each gives rise. A comparison will be drawn
between the different political ethics advanced by the two theorists,
and finally an analysis of the normative basis of their respective works
will be pursued.

Foucault's genealogical practice

The work of Foucault, like that of Weber, contains an account and critique of the instrumental rationalism of modern Western culture. This
is evident, for example, in *The Order of Things*, which charts the development of intellectual culture from the sixteenth century onwards,
and connects profound changes in the historical foundations of knowledge (the *episteme*) to the emergence of new forms of thought and cultural classification. This account focuses on the shifts in the structure
of knowledge that enabled the transition from Renaissance and classical thought to modern culture, which, through disciplines such as
political science and philology, first created 'Man' as both a subject and
object of knowledge. This narrative of the historical rationalization of
culture, is, in the words of Scott Lash (1987), 'a periodization of *instrumental* rationality' (p. 360), for Foucault defines the modern, in con-
tradistinction to classical and Renaissance culture, as an order in which
scientific knowledge gives rise to new, more complete forms of political
domination. This periodization of instrumental rationality frames the
majority of Foucault's historical writings: *Madness and Civilization*
(Foucault, 1967) depicts the movement from the Stultifera Navis to the
modern asylum; *Discipline and Punish* (Foucault, 1991b) the transition
from physical torture to modern discipline and correction; and *The
History of Sexuality* (Foucault, 1990) the descent from the classical age
of sovereign power to the modern order of bio-power (see below). And
these accounts are parallel in concern and scope to Weber's 'Science as
a Vocation', for they suggest that cultural rationalization, while
promising individual autonomy and human 'progress', in fact leads to
new technologies of domination, for it provides the means for
increased knowledge of, and power over, 'Man'.

   Foucault's *resistance* to this process of rationalization, though, is
unlike that advanced by Weber, for it proceeds through two forms of
historical practice. First, Foucault develops an archaeology of truth
which exhumes and 'defines the conditions under which a true knowledge is possible' (Foucault, 1986a, 15) in order to expose the 'history of
that which renders necessary a certain form of thought' (Foucault,
1971, 60). Second, he outlines a genealogical counter-history of the
present that maps discursive production in a present-relevant field of
power and knowledge in order to expose and transform the limits that
define 'the contemporary field of possible experience' (Foucault, 1986a,
15). This latter practice is informed by, but also extends the scope of,
the former, for it moves beyond an analytic of discursive production to

a critical analysis of the interpenetration of history, truth, power and the present. It is this exercise, which challenges the instrumental rationalism of modern institutions and the progressive 'sameness' of modern culture, which is of specific interest in this chapter.

Foucault outlines the basis of this genealogical practice in his 1971 essay 'Nietzsche, Genealogy, History'. Genealogy, he argues, is an untimely meditation that disturbs the singularity of human memory through dispersion of the historical origin and exposition of the alterity concealed within history. This practice seeks to rid the present of its internalized enslavement to the past through dissipation of the historical identity of modern 'Man', and the restoration of political philosophy to a critical philosophy of the limit.[2] In doing so, it removes the anthropological subject ('Man') from the centre of political practice, and instead demarcates and decentres the limits of cultural identity through exposition of historical difference. Foucault (1977) argues:

> The purpose of history, guided by genealogy, is not to discover the roots of our identity but to commit itself to its dissipation. It does not seek to define our unique threshold of emergence, the homeland to which metaphysicians promise a return; it seeks to make visible all of those discontinuities that cross us. (p. 162)

This historical practice shatters the appearance of unilinear human progress by revealing the unstable multiplicity of historical descent. It does so by operating at a micro-level, eschewing grand narratives in favour of local events (see Foucault, 1991a, 150), and addressing 'a layer of material which had hitherto had no pertinence for history and which had not been recognized as having any moral, aesthetic, political or historical value' (Foucault, 1980, 50–1). Genealogy proceeds by recalling, reassembling and magnifying these forgotten, obscured or subjugated fragments of history, mapping them within historical relations of power and knowledge, not to resurrect the past in terms of the present, but to write instead 'the history of the present' (Foucault, 1991b, 31).

This idea of a history of the present is developed from Nietzsche's essay 'On the Uses and Disadvantages of History for Life' (Nietzsche, 1983, 57–123; see Dean, 1994), in which genealogy is employed to oppose three Platonic modalities of history: the *monumental* veneration of historical events, the *antiquarian* continuity of identity through the preservation and reverence of the past, and the *critical* judgement of the past on the basis of present truths.[3] In opposition to these modalities, Nietzsche proposes three new means for the use of history. It is worth quoting Foucault's depiction of these at length, for they encapsulate the aims of his historical practice, and form the methodological basis of his 'history of the present',[4]

> The first is parodic, directed against reality, and opposes the theme of history as reminiscence or recognition; the second is dissociative, directed against identity, and opposes history given as continuity or representative of a tradition; the third is sacrificial, directed against truth, and opposes history as knowledge. They imply a use of history that severs its connection to memory, its metaphysical and anthropological model, and constructs a counter-memory – a transformation of history into a totally different form of time. (Foucault, 1977, 160)

Foucault proposes that this form of transfigurative history is itself an experimental mode of political resistance and transgression, for it exposes the conditions under which knowledge is formed and functions, and may be used to exploit the instability of history wherever discourses are in competition or in the process of transformation.

Foucault's use of genealogy hence centres on the fragility of discursive redistribution, on the conflict, for example, between the spectacle of the scaffold and 'carceral' society, and between the discourse of the *ars erotica* and *scientia sexualis* (see below). Foucault employs genealogy to rework these points of discursive conflict to reveal and transform the limits of what we are and what we may possibly become. This practice, like archaeology, is a form of counter-history, because it is 'nothing more than a rewriting: that is, in the preserved form of exteriority, a regulated transformation of what has already been written' (Foucault, 1989a, 140). It is also, a form of critical description which, beyond archaeology, works against the grain of 'official' knowledge to level the hierarchical ranking of ideas, and to reveal the discursive and institutional modalities of subjection and rationalization which produce 'true', functional forms of knowledge. It is a practice which pits discourse against discourse through a retrieval of marginal or subjugated knowledges which have been disqualified or obscured by 'official' histories.[5] This resuscitation of subjugated knowledge – that of the madman, the patient, the delinquent – destabilizes our rationalized present by reminding us of the proximity and potentiality of historical difference. In doing so it opens new possibilities of political transfiguration, for it reveals the historical closure of difference in an ontological critique of the powers that define the possibility of being and becoming other. This ontology constitutes a form of political practice that disturbs the singularity of memory (and identity) by revealing the historical limit as a site of practical and theoretical transgression (see Simons, 1995, 81–104; Gane, 1996). Foucault (1991c) argues:

> The critical ontology of ourselves has to be considered not, certainly, as a theory, a doctrine, nor even as a permanent body of knowledge that is accumulating; it has to be conceived as an attitude, an ethos, a philosophical life in which the critique of what we are is at one and the same time the historical analysis of the limits that are imposed on us and an experiment with the possibility of going beyond them. (p. 50)

The possibility of transgressing the limits of modern subjectivity, which are both restricting and empowering, lies in the empowerment of a cultural alterity concealed within the history of the present. Foucault's genealogical counter-histories do not recall the past to recommend a nostalgic return to previous times, but use history to open possibilities of cultural and political transfiguration. *The Use of Pleasure* (Foucault, 1986b) and *The Care of the Self* (Foucault, 1988), for example, do not explore the different sexual ethics of ancient Greece and Rome simply to reminisce or even to prescribe a particular way of life, but to disturb the limits of the rationalized world through historical exposition of cultural difference, and to thereby reveal the possibilities of becoming other.[6]

It is thus a mistake to understand Foucault's genealogical practice as a conservative form of anti-modernism, one which, as suggested by Habermas (1981, 13), removes 'into the sphere of the far away and the archaic the spontaneous powers of imagination, of self-experience and of emotionality'. Rather, this practice is a radical form of political provocation that seeks to invigorate the present by using the past to reveal and contest the limits of existence today. The aim of this practice is to destabilize the power-knowledge relations that order both memory and identity, and to thereby open the possibility of a 'heterotopian' future (Rajchman, 1985, 49) that (at least in theory; see below) is left undefined. Indeed, Foucault claims to employ genealogy not to prescribe a particular route to a particular future, but rather to open the limits of political possibility itself to demarcation and, beyond this, transgression.[7]

Foucault's use of genealogy

Foucault first applies this historical practice in *Discipline and Punish*, which he terms 'a genealogy of the present scientifico-legal complex from which the power to punish derives its bases, justifications and rules, from which it extends its effects and by which it masks its exorbitant singularity' (Foucault, 1991b, 23). This genealogy erects a historical counter-memory against the Enlightenment narrative of 'progress' through a dissemination of the powers underlying the transition of punishment from physical torture to the present culture of correction and discipline. The aim of this exercise is to locate the historical specificity of law within a political landscape of power and knowledge, and to rework the shift from feudal to modern punishment in order to reveal changes in the underlying fabric of societal power relations.[8]

This work opens with a horrific account of the public torture and execution of a regicide in Paris in 1757, an event Foucault (1991b) explains in terms of its ritual reaffirmation of sovereign power. He says:

> The public execution ... belongs to a whole series of great rituals in which power is eclipsed and restored (coronation, entry of the king into a conquered city, the submission of rebellious subjects); over and above the crime that has placed the sovereign in contempt, it deploys before all eyes an invincible force. Its aim is not so much to re-establish a balance as to bring into play, as its extreme point, the dissymmetry between the subject who has dared to violate the law and the all-powerful sovereign who displays his strength. (pp. 48–9).

By the end of the eighteenth century, Foucault argues, this volatile regime of princely centred power had been replaced by a new contractual order, and punishment as a spectacle largely disappeared. The sovereign power to punish here gave way to that of the reforming jurists, who sought to requalify individuals as juridical subjects, and punished by sign and analogy rather than by physical force. This semiotic modality of punishment, however, was short-lived, for it soon gave way to a scientific, instrumentally rational knowledge of 'man' and to an economy of power centred on the production of 'docile' individuals, reflected in the birth of corrective institutions and the technology of panoptic surveillance.[9]

For Foucault, this historical separation of pain and punishment is not to be read as a sign of human progress, for the criminal was freed from the horrors of the scaffold only through the incarceration of life more generally within a new network of normalising power. This process, which is a manifestation of the rise of instrumental rationalism in the West, and is marked by the birth of the prison and the discourse of criminal science, rests on the punishment of the soul rather than body, and connects punishment to the production and transformation of individuals. On this basis, Foucault treats 'punishment as a political tactic' (see Foucault, 1991b, 23), and sees modernity as an age of 'rational' domination. He observes: 'Humanity does not gradually progress from combat to combat until it arrives at universal reciprocity, where the rule of law finally replaces warfare; humanity installs each of its violences in a system of rules and thus proceeds from domination to domination' (Foucault, 1977, 151). His genealogy traces and magnifies the devices that have enabled this continuity, exposing, for example, the prison timetable as a means for cataloguing, routinising and rationalising life, and the examination as a means for measuring, classifying and standardising individual performance. These instances disturb the chimera of modern progress, and suggest that liberation from torture proceeded through the subjugation of life to a new technology of domination. Foucault (1991b) claims:

> although the universal juridicism of modern society seems to fix limits on the exercise of power, its universally widespread panopticism enables it to operate, on the underside of the law, a machinery that is both immense and minute, which supports, reinforces, multiplies the asymmetry of power and undermines the limits that are traced around the law. (p. 223)

Power itself is at once both beneath and beyond the law.

Foucault develops this exposition of formative micro-powers in the first volume of the *History of Sexuality*. Extending the thesis of *Discipline and Punish*, he argues that power no longer exists as the sovereign right of life or death, but as a normalising strategy that invests itself within the individual, permeating life to its core. He calls this *bio-power*, a technology of normalization that disciplines humanity at the level of life through material subjugation of the body. One crucial manifestation of this bio-power is sexuality, which, for Foucault, captures and penetrates life irrespective of subjective consciousness or representation, producing and reproducing both body and life through power and discourse. Foucault pursues a *dissociative* history of this process, and reveals a hidden regime of life production within the seemingly 'repressive' identity of Victorian sexuality. This regime, he argues, is based on the investment and reinvestment of normalising bio-power in the individual through the *scientia sexualis*: a vast array of technical discourse that includes medicine, psychiatry and pedagogy. He draws the conclusion that

Sex was a means of access both to the life of the body and the life of the species. It was employed as a standard for the disciplines and as a basis for regulations. This is why in the nineteenth century sexuality was sought out in the smallest details of individual existences; it was tracked down in behaviour, pursued in dreams; it was suspected of underlying the least follies, it was traced back to the earliest years of childhood; it became the stamp of individuality – at the same time what enabled one to analyse the latter and what made it possible to master it. (Foucault, 1990, 146)

Genealogy is employed to reveal the mechanisms through which bio-power permeates the individual, propagates the discourse of sexuality, and is exercised through this knowledge. Foucault argues that the constitution of subjectivity is inextricably bound to relations of power and knowledge, and, furthermore, that the accumulation of 'rational' knowledge (including the discourse of sexuality) gives rise to new forms of domination and discipline which permeate all aspects of modern life. And in this respect, Foucault's genealogical histories complement Weber's analysis and critique of the rationalization and disenchantment of the world, for they offer an account of the rise and operation of instrumental rationalism in different institutional settings (the prison, the clinic, the asylum), and indicate the ways in which this rationalism extends to normalize, and perhaps even govern, life itself (the concept of bio-power).

Cultural science and genealogical history

These points of convergence between Weber and Foucault, which arise mainly from their respective accounts of the rise of 'bureaucratic' or disciplinary societies, have been discussed at length by theorists such as Colin Gordon (1987), Scott Lash (1987) and John O'Neill (1995). Little attention has been paid, though, to the fact that the work of Weber and Foucault, although equally critical of instrumental rationalism, differs markedly in form and intent, for while Foucault employs genealogy to open the possibility of transgressing the limits of the modern order (see above), Weber's work is neither genealogical in nature nor affirms this anarchic spirit of transgression, but seeks rather to work concurrently within and against the limits of modernity (see Chapters 4 and 5). The forms of resistance to instrumental rationalism advanced in the work of Weber and Foucault are very different, as are the political and ethical positions forwarded in their respective writings, as can be illustrated through analysis of the distinction between Weber's (modern) cultural science and Foucault's (postmodern) genealogy.

One of the few commentators to have analysed the connection of these two types of intellectual practice is David Owen (1994; see Gane, 1998b). Owen (1994) argues that Weber's work shares a similar evaluative interest to that of Nietzsche and Foucault, namely whether the 'autonomous individual' can become 'the dominant human type in modern culture' (p. 123), and that his cultural science, in pursuing this interest, constructs a 'history of the present' which, like the work of Foucault, is genealogical in nature. This argument is important for it challenges the conventional view that Weber's methodology rests upon an application of the principles of Baden neo-Kantianism. Owen claims that Weber's cultural science is rather an extension of Nietzsche's genealogical perspectivism, arguing that Weber sides with Nietzsche and against Rickert in rejecting the possibility of an objective value of truth, that Weber's doctrine of value-freedom embodies Nietzsche's commitment to reflexivity and probity, and that his ideal-type methodology embraces Nietzsche's value perspectivism (see ibid., 87–93). Owen suggests that the actual purpose of Weber's work is the same as Nietzsche's: 'to provide a "context of meaning" within which the development of *Menschentum* may be understood and evaluated in terms of the fate of man in modernity' (ibid., 101). On this basis, Owen reads Weber's work, in particular his sociology of religion, as a genealogy of modernity, one that is broadly similar in form to those forwarded by Nietzsche and Foucault in so far as it is concerned 'with how we have become what we are, that is to say, with articulating a history of the present' (ibid.).

There are, however, a number of important difficulties in this reading of Weber. First, Owen's presentation of Weber's work is in many respects one-sided, for it accentuates the 'Nietzschean commitments' of Weber's methodology, while playing down its debt to neo-Kantian philosophy, and the points at which it departs from Nietzsche's work. Owen makes no reference, for example, to Weber's neo-Kantian theory of concept formation and reality, and accentuates Nietzschean themes that are found in Weber's early (1895) 'Inaugural Freiburg Lecture' (Weber, 1989), in particular those regarding the 'greatness and nobility of our human nature', while overlooking the critique of historical progress and evolution which may be found in neo-Kantian value-philosophy. Habermas (1984) rightly reminds us of the importance of neo-Kantian thought here: 'Neo-Kantianism gained special significance for the critique of evolutionist approaches in the social sciences because of its theory of value ... This is the background to Weber's position in the controversy over value judgements in social science' (p. 154).

Second, it is clearly difficult to identify a single evaluative interest which runs through the entirety of Weber's work, for while, as Owen argues, Weber is concerned with the development of *Menschentum* and with the 'fate of man in modernity', these questions, as Wilhelm Hennis (1988) and Lawrence Scaff (1991) have argued, do not represent Weber's sole evaluative interests (see Chapter 1).

This leads to a third difficulty: because Weber is interested in the development of *Menschentum* and in the fate of 'man', his work constitutes a 'history of the present' and is thus genealogical. Owen is right to note that a number of Weber's studies – particularly those which address the rise of capitalism and the fate of the Western order, for example *The Protestant Ethic*, 'Science as a Vocation' and 'Politics as a Vocation' – do facilitate an understanding of the present. This said, the present-relevance of Weber's historical sociology is not always clear; indeed, often it has to be reconstructed according to a particular evaluative interest, for works such as *The Religion of India* (Weber, 1967b) or *The Agrarian Sociology of Ancient Civilizations* (Weber, 1976) contain very few references to the present. The problem here is that all historical studies, if read with an active evaluative interest, can be understood in terms of their relevance to the present, and on this basis, if one follows Owen, can be seen to be genealogical. In view of this, the distinction between historical writing and genealogical practice must be drawn with greater precision.

There are a number of important distinctions between Weber's historical sociology and the genealogical practice of Nietzsche and Foucault that Owen neglects. First, Weber's historical account of the rise of capitalism, or, more broadly, modernity, is comparative but also *developmental* in nature. This account, against the arguments of Lyotard and Foucault (see Chapter 7 and above), traces the origins of Western culture and establishes a metanarrative of the stages and trajectory of its subsequent development (see Chapter 2). Second, genealogy, as Foucault, following Nietzsche, argues, is not simply history that is relevant to the present but a critical *and* transgressive practice. While Owen rightly notes that Weber's work is critical in nature (a position which is put forward in the first part of the present work), there is little evidence to suggest that it seeks either to be transgressive or to open the possibility of transgression. Clearly, Weber's sociology of religion and Foucault's genealogies of discipline and sexuality are different in form and intent. On the one hand, Weber's historical analyses seek clarity and objectivity in order to enable a factual understanding of social action at the levels of causality and meaning. On the other, the work of Foucault is itself a transgressive practice which seeks to open the possibility of becoming other, and which, following Nietzsche, calls for a 'revaluation' of the values of modernity. Foucault, contrary to Weber, here does not employ history to establish clear, objective facts – indeed he argues that it would not matter if his genealogies were fictions – but to overturn and overcome modern values through affirmation of the otherness concealed within our past.

The historical practices of Weber and Foucault are hence quite different from each other, and are, moreover, connected to two opposing forms of political practice. Weber's work, while retaining a heuristic quality, seeks to transcend opinion (*doxa*) in a bid to establish, clarify and understand the nature of social action. In view of this, Zygmunt Bauman characterizes Weber as a modern legislator, for not only does he attempt to bring some degree of order to the chaos of modern values, but, in doing so, 'argues the case for the truth of the sociologist through denigrating the cognitive value of lay knowledge' (Bauman, 1992, 123). Weber, while committed to a neo-Kantian ethic of value-freedom (*Wertfreiheit*) in academic work, in particular makes a case for the value of specialized vocational activity that goes beyond the work of the mere dilettante. Indeed, it is precisely this vocational activity that, through the responsible work of the scientist (Chapter 4) and political leader (Chapter 5), opens the possibility of resistance to the rationalization of the world. And in this respect, Weber questions but also conveys the authority of the specialist to engage in 'legislative activity'.

Foucault, like Weber, is critical of intellectual work which attempts to confer the legitimacy of an 'ought', and which thereby prescribes a direction for political practice. He argues: 'I hold that the role of the intellectual today is not that of establishing laws or proposing solutions or prophesying, since by doing that one can only contribute to the functioning of a determinate situation of power that to my mind must be criticized' (Foucault, 1991a, 157). Unlike Weber, however, he extends this critique of authority to all acts of legislation, from the practice of establishing objective historical facts through to political activity itself. He argues that the purpose of intellectual work is neither to educate nor to legislate, but to open history to the free play of lay interpretation. This practice, which centres on the local rather than the 'world-historical', and which proclaims the 'death of the author' rather than the authority of a universal subject, calls for a new type of 'specific' intellectual, and not a universal 'master of truth and justice'. Foucault (1980) proclaims:

> A new mode of the 'connection between theory and practice' has been established. Intellectuals have got used to working, not in the 'universal', the 'exemplary', the 'just-and-true-for-all', but within specific sectors, at the precise points where their own conditions of life or work situate them ... This is what I would call the 'specific' intellectual as opposed to the 'universal' intellectual. (p. 126)

The specific intellectual, for Foucault, escapes from the dogma of political leadership through the non-evaluative exposition of the historical limits of power and knowledge. This strategy leaves the ends of intellectual and political work (between which, for Foucault, there is no clear separation) undefined, and with this transfers the responsibility for the nature and direction of political practice from the author (the legislator) to the reader (the interpreter).

The political ethics of legislative and interpretive practice

Weber's modern legislative activity and Foucault's postmodern practice of interpretation are also tied to opposing political ethics. On the one hand, Weber's work is grounded upon a practical ethic of conduct, an ethic that claims, for example, that it is the duty of the vocational politician to pursue and protect ultimate values while at the same time bearing responsibility for the consequences of their actions. This type of political activity is to proceed through the rational evaluation of the purpose, means and ends of actions, and rests upon a sense of responsibility in intellectual and political work (see Chapters 4 and 5). On the other, Foucault's genealogical practice rests upon a postmodern ethics of difference, an anti-humanist ethics committed to the exposition of otherness within history rather than the affirmation of legislative responsibility. The legislative definition of individual duty is, for Foucault, simply another form of dogmatism, another exercise of authority or power that constrains transgressive activity. In view of this, the question for Foucault is not of an 'ought', an imperative prescribing the value of responsible individual commitment, but of work which refuses to represent others and which leaves the future open to possibility (see Foucault, 1991a, 29).

The marked difference between these two ethics, these two forms of resistance to the instrumental drive of modern rationalism, becomes clear if one contrasts their respective positions before what Weber terms the 'ethical irrationality' of the world.[10] It is important to note, first, that Foucault and Weber both emphasize the historical relation of politics and violence. Weber (1970), for example, defines the state as 'the *monopoly of the legitimate use of physical force* within a given territory' (p. 78), arguing that 'The decisive means for politics is violence' (p. 121),[11] while Foucault (1980) inverts Clausewitz's assertion that war is politics continued by other means, to suggest instead that 'power is war, a war continued by other means' (p. 90). For Weber, this connection of politics and violence effectively defines the role of the vocational politician: he or she is to take a definite stand while at the same time weighing up the relation of political means and ends, and bearing personal responsibility for the consequences.

However, the intimate relation of politics and violence, while a point of concern, does not, for Foucault, shape the content of his writings, for he formally declares no control over, and interest in, the destination of his work, and thus the political effects produced by his genealogical histories.[12] Indeed, Foucault claims to employ genealogy not to prescribe a specific end but to *reconstitute* subjugated knowledge, knowledge which, under the force of its own intrinsic dynamism, may expose and destabilize the limits of the present. This disengaged practice, which refrains from commentary and analysis, effectively leaves subjugated knowledge, that of the parricide Pierre Rivière or the regicide Damiens, to its own devices. This is a practice that Jacques Derrida (1977) notes with respect to *Madness and Civilization*:

> In writing a history of madness, Foucault has attempted ... to write a history of madness *itself. Itself.* Of madness *itself.* That is, by letting madness speak for itself. Foucault wanted madness to be the subject of his book in every sense of the word: its theme and its first person narrator, its author, madness speaking about itself. (pp. 33–4).

This separation of the author from the authority of the work he or she produces disjoins political authorship from the pursuit of particular ends, and rejects political responsibility in favour of the contingency of discursive play.[13] This practice, which attempts to free knowledge from dogma by opening history to difference and alterity, unmasks the historical conditions and authority of knowledge regardless of the consequences which may follow. Genealogy is thus a radical but dangerous practice, for it leaves open the possibility of political transfiguration by eschewing political rationality and responsibility in favour of the free play of discursive forces.

Weber's practical ethics and Foucault's ethics of difference hence appear to reside in stark contrast. For Weber, it is the duty of both the political leader and the intellectual to take account of the bearing of their work on the future. This idea is prominent in the 1895 inaugural lecture, in which Weber (1989) argues:

> It is certain that there can be no work in political economy on any other than an altruistic basis. The overwhelming majority of the fruits of the economic, social, and political endeavours of the present are garnered not by the generation now alive but by the generations of the future. If our work is to retain any meaning it can only be informed by this: concern for the *future*, for *those who will come after us*. (p. 197)

Weber is acutely aware of the relation of politics and violence, and because of this argues that the intellectual must take responsibility for the future, even if, or perhaps precisely because, the consequences of our actions are not always as intended. He voices this same concern over twenty years later in 'Politics as a Vocation', in which he stresses the need for the political leader to weigh up the relations between the means and ends, intentions and possible consequences, of action (see Chapter 5). Weber, unlike Foucault, refuses to leave political ends open to interpretation, rather, following Fichte, he 'takes account of precisely the average deficiencies of people' and refuses to 'presuppose their goodness and perfection' (Weber, 1970, 121). He places no faith in the eudemonistic outcome of political practice, and indeed argues that, given the ethical irrationality of the world, the political leader must take personal responsibility for political consequences rather than leaving 'the results with the Lord' (ibid., 120). Foucault, by contrast, while not an advocate of an ethic of ultimate ends, places his faith in the potentiality of interpretation and the possibility of self-transfiguration, and on this basis disengages himself from the consequences of political practice. In this respect, he shares a similar position to Weber's 'mystic', for he claims to 'resist no evil' and 'withdraws from the pragma of violence which no political action can escape' (ibid., 336).

In spite of these differences, both Weber and Foucault advance an ethical claim for value-freedom in intellectual work. Weber, employing a neo-Kantian distinction between fact and value, argues that subjective value-judgements have no place within the lecture room or academic text, for personal bias should not preclude the scientific ascertainment of objective historical facts. He states, for example, that 'I am ready to prove from the works of our historians that whenever the man of science introduces his personal value judgement, a full understanding of the fact ceases' (Weber, 1970, 146). Foucault, by contrast, employs value-freedom as a political strategy. He claims that his genealogical history is neither normative nor prescriptive, but instead attempts 'to produce some effects of truth which might be used for a possible battle, to be waged by those who wished to wage it, in forms yet to be found and in organizations yet to be defined' (Foucault, 1989b, 191). This dismisses the dogmatism of modern political theory, arguing that his 'open' genealogical histories do not prescribe a theory of contemporary life, but use the past to provoke us to question the identity of our present.[14] He states of *Discipline and Punish*, for example, that 'The inquiry is limited to an investigation covering the period up to about 1830. But even in this case readers, whether critics or not, took it as a description of modern society. You won't find an analysis of the present in the book' (Foucault, 1991a, 37).

This said, Weber and Foucault, both violate their respective claims to value-freedom. Weber, for example, values an ethic of political and intellectual responsibility in its own right (see Chapters 4 and 5), and this value is itself embodied in his doctrine of ethical neutrality or value-freedom (*Wertfreiheit*). This doctrine proclaims that questions of 'ought' are to be kept separate from questions of what actually 'is', for it is the task of social science to convey the validity of objective facts not subjective ideals. Weber (1949) argues that this process can only proceed through the suspension of questions of 'ought' from scientific investigation: 'it can never be the task of an empirical science to provide binding norms and ideals from which directives for immediate practical activity can be derived' (p. 52). But even this statement, itself posits a practical ideal, an ideal that affirms the commitment of the scientist to the clear distinction of facts and values, thus indicating that Weber's empirical science operates on the basis of a 'normative' statement, a judgement of what should be. This judgement, however, while raising doubt as to the presuppositions of 'value-free' methodology, defines rather than compromises Weber's commitment to value-freedom, for it places the value of responsibility at the heart of intellectual and political activity. This commitment to value-freedom defines the very nature of Weber's historical work, which, as argued above, seeks to establish objective facts rather than to motivate political forms of transgression.

The charge against Foucault is perhaps more serious. His genealogical practice, while claiming not to prescribe an 'is' or an 'ought', is tendentious, for it not only presupposes its own value but conceals the position and purpose of its historical attack. Foucault claims, for example, not to offer a theory of contemporary life. A close reading of his genealogical history, which mysteriously manages to remain outside of the modern powers of normalization, reveals however that this is not in fact the case, for his historical analysis of 'carceral' society is accompanied by a largely ahistorical description of the present:

> *Our* society is not one of spectacle, but of surveillance: under the surface of images, one invests bodies in depth; behind the great abstraction of exchange, there continues the meticulous, concrete training of useful forces; the circuits of communication are the supports of an accumulation and a centralization of knowledge; the play of signs defines the anchorages of power; it is not that the beautiful totality of the individual is amputated, repressed, altered by *our* social order, it is rather that the individual is carefully fabricated within it, according to a whole technique of forces and bodies. (Foucault, 1991b, 217; emphasis mine)

Likewise, in *The History of Sexuality* Foucault (1990) tells us that *'We* ... are in a society of "sex", or rather a society "with a sexuality"': the mechanisms of power are addressed to the body, to life, to what causes it to proliferate, to what reinforces the species, its stamina, its ability to dominate, or its capacity for being used' (p. 147; emphasis mine). In this respect Foucault clearly violates his claim to a *sacrificial* history which neither asserts a dogmatic description of the present nor judges the past on the basis of present truths, for in practice his genealogical histories read both back from, and forward to, an assertion of the disciplinary power of the present. And in view of this, Jürgen Habermas (1987) is right to accuse Foucault of presentism, for

> the attempt ... to explain discourse and power formations only on their own terms, turns into its opposite. The unmasking of objectivist illusions of *any* will to knowledge leads to an agreement with a historiography that is narcissistically oriented toward the standpoint of the historian and instrumentalizes the contemplation of the past for the needs of the present. (p. 278)

Foucault's work, in sum, replaces an antiquarian continuity of historical identity with a new metanarrative of Western development, one that gives a linear account of the rise and periodization of different technologies of instrumental reason. This is the case in spite of his own ridicule of the 'fear which makes you seek, beyond all boundaries, ruptures, shifts, and divisions, the great historico-transcendental destiny of the Occident' (Foucault, 1989a, 210). Foucault attempts to avoid this problem by focusing on local knowledges which expose, and thus potentially destabilize, the instrumental means by which historical difference is repressed and effaced by the Western order. This practice, however, still rests upon and contributes to a metanarrative of Western development, for Foucault, in similar fashion to Lyotard – whose account of the collapse of the metanarrative is itself metanarratival in form – reactivates local narratives precisely because of the broader historical and political contexts in which they are embedded. This, in turn, lends weight to, rather than destroys, an overarching metanarrative of the instrumental nature of modern culture.

Foucault's genealogical practice is thus not as disinterested as it claims, for it proceeds through the selection, evaluation and prioritization of historical evidence with the aim of destabilising the 'carceral' domination which it portrays as intrinsic to modernity. His claim simply to offer '"propositions", "game openings" where those who may be interested are invited to join in' rather than 'dogmatic assertions that have to be taken or left en bloc' (Foucault, 1992, 74) must thus be treated with a degree of scepticism. His genealogical counter-histories, while claiming to be free from prescriptives, are in fact not free from directives and are, to use Habermas's term, 'cryptonormative', for they are not only critical of the nature of the modern order but are based upon a call for transgressive activity.[15] They are thus 'instrumental' as well as 'visionary or dream-like' (Foucault, 1991a, 29), and not only contain statements regarding the nature of contemporary society, but are tendentious in so far as they seek to energize an undefined movement against the order they depict. In view of this, Foucault's work is not as free from its own values or *authority* as it declares itself, and in this respect fails to free itself fully from the (modern) legislation of an 'ought'.

Conclusion

The work of Foucault is at once close to and far removed from that of Weber. Foucault, like Weber, offers an account of the rise of the

9
Weber, Baudrillard and the Erotic Sphere

> In seduction ... it is the manifest discourse ... that turns back on the deeper order ... in order to invalidate it, substituting the charm and illusion of appearances.
>
> Baudrillard (1990a, 53).

> Achieving depth through erotic adventures is something quite problematical.
>
> Max Weber (quoted in Marianne Weber, 1975, 381).

The previous two chapters addressed the possibility of resistance to the rationalization of the world, first, through analysis of Lyotard's theory of postmodern science and aesthetics (Chapter 7), and second, through assessment of Foucault's project of genealogical transfiguration (Chapter 8). The present chapter addresses a further strategy through which such resistance may be possible, namely that of re-enchantment. It is argued that this strategy is pursued by Jean Baudrillard, whose work emphasizes the threat symbolic forms continue to pose to the order of Western rationalism. This chapter focuses on Baudrillard's account of the subversive nature of the 'symbolic order', and examines the possibility of developing a strategy of re-enchantment from the play of symbolic forms. This analysis centres on Baudrillard's theory of the radical opposition of the symbolic order to the capitalist order of value, and examines the possible challenge of the former to the latter through a comparative analysis of Weber's position on the erotic sphere and Baudrillard's theory of seduction.

Symbolic exchange and the law of value

Baudrillard's analysis of modernity is founded upon a radical critique of capitalist production and economic exchange. This critique, which frames his theory of enchantment and re-enchantment, proceeds initially through an attack on the concept of use-value: value tied to the fulfilment of scarcity and need, utility and function, but free from the accumulation of surplus value.[1] Baudrillard argues that Marx's critique of political economy attacks the principle of capitalist exchange but at the same time retains an idea of 'pure' use-value, and in this respect stops short of a radical critique of the concept of value itself. And with this, Marx's critique of economic exchange does not go beyond but reproduces the ideological basis of the capitalist system, for it fails to treat use-value as the creation of a system of needs which itself is tied to the production and accumulation of economic value (see Baudrillard, 1981, 63–87).[2] Baudrillard claims:

> needs ... can no longer be defined adequately in terms of the naturalist-idealist thesis – as innate, instinctive power, spontaneous craving, anthropological potentiality. Rather they are better defined as a *function* induced (in the individual) by the internal logic of the system: more precisely, *not as a consummative force liberated* by the affluent society, but *as a productive force* required by the functioning of the system itself, by its process of reproduction and survival. In other words, there are only needs because the system needs them. (ibid., 82)[3]

In accepting this system of needs and thus the necessity of production (and labour), Marx fails to break free of the logic of capitalist production,[4] for rather than attack the principle of production itself (the order of value), his critique of political economy legitimates use-value through the concept of need, thereby reproducing the functional ideology of capitalist exchange. This move effectively leaves production itself unquestioned: 'A spectre haunts the revolutionary imagination: the phantom of production. Everywhere it sustains an unbridled romanticism of productivity. The critical theory of the mode of production does not touch the *principle* of production' (Baudrillard, 1975, 17).

Baudrillard extends this argument – which suggests that going beyond capital cannot entail a celebration of 'more' – through a critical analysis of the 'political economy of the sign'. He argues that the sign too is a reified object that is tied, like the commodity, to the production and circulation of economic value. The sign and commodity have the same basic logic and structure. First, the logic of the commodity is to be found within the structure of the sign:

> It is because *the logic of the commodity and of political economy is at the very heart of the sign*, in the abstract equation of signifier and signified, in the differential combinatory of signs, that signs can function as exchange value (the discourse of communication) and as use value (rational decoding and distinctive social use). (Baudrillard, 1981, 146)

Second, the structure of the sign is homologous to the structure of the commodity:

> It is because *the structure of the sign is at the very heart of the commodity form* that the commodity can take on, immediately the effect of signification ... because its very form establishes it as a total *medium*, as a *system of communication* administering all social exchange. Like the sign form, the commodity is a code managing the exchange of values. (ibid.)

Baudrillard develops this idea of the homology of the sign and the commodity through an extension of Ferdinand de Saussure's theory of linguistic value, which claims that the structure of language, itself a system of values, is comparable to the structure of economic value in that it is composed

1 of a *dissimilar* thing that can be *exchanged* for the thing of which the value is to be determined, and
2 of *similar* things that can be *compared* with the thing of which the value is to be determined (Saussure, 1974, 115).

Baudrillard, following Saussure, breaks the sign and the commodity into their constituent parts to show the connection of these dissimilar (economic exchange-value, the signifier) and similar (use-value, the signified) elements. He formulates this connection of use-value and the signified, economic exchange-value and the signifier as follows:

$$\text{(Commodity)} \quad \frac{\textit{EcEV} \text{ (Economic Exchange-Value)}}{\textit{UV} \text{ (Use Value)}} = \frac{\textit{Sr} \text{ (Signifier)}}{\textit{Sd} \text{ (Signified)}} \quad \text{(Sign)}$$

In view of this, the radical other to exchange-value is, for Baudrillard, neither use-value, which, contra Marx, is nothing more than an abstraction of a system of needs which itself is defined by economic exchange, nor sign value, which is homologous to economic value. Rather, it is the enchanted form of *symbolic exchange*, which exists outside of and contrary to the order of value (production) itself. This form of exchange, which Baudrillard develops from Marcel Mauss's analysis of gift exchange (potlatch in particular) and Georges Bataille's theory of general economy, is based upon the cyclical reciprocity of the ritual rather than the linear production and accumulation of value.[5] Baudrillard (1981) proposes:

> In symbolic exchange, of which the gift is our most proximate illus-
> tration, the object is not an object: it is inseparable from the con-
> crete relation in which it is exchanged, the transferential pact that it
> seals between two persons: it is thus not independent as such. It
> has, properly speaking, neither use value nor (economic) exchange
> value. The object given has symbolic exchange value. (p. 64).

This form of symbolic exchange value exists in fundamental opposition to both economic exchange-value and the economy of the sign,
for it rests upon an order of culture which is radically other to the ideologies of scarcity, need, wealth and function which legitimate capitalist exchange. Baudrillard argues that these Western ideologies only
exist as effects of a productivist economy, and have no place within
the reciprocal relations of symbolic exchange, which are defined by
sacrifice, return and annulment, and not by linear accumulation. He
argues, moreover, that in the symbolic order objects are not defined
and consumed according to their function, for they never exist outside
of the narrative of gift exchange. Objects thus possess no autonomy
within the symbolic order, and consequently are not reified as signs.
And in view of this, (enchanted) symbolic exchange lies in radical
opposition to the (disenchanted, rational) order of the commodity and
sign. This opposition may be represented as follows (see ibid., 128):[6]

$$\frac{EcEV \text{ (Economic Exchange-Value)}}{UV \text{ (Use-Value)}} = \frac{Sr \text{ (Signifier)}}{Sd \text{ (Signified)}} \quad \text{(General Political Economy)}$$

SbE (Symbolic Exchange)

This formulation conveys the fundamental opposition of political
economy (the homology of commodity and sign) to the symbolic
order, an opposition, or, more precisely, a struggle for primacy, which,
for Baudrillard, defines the basis of societal order and social change.

The historical processes of modernization and rationalization are manifestations of this struggle in so far as they involve a transition from a social order dominated by the principle of symbolic exchange to an order in which symbolic exchange is blocked and restricted by the law of value. This inversion of the hegemony of the symbolic order and the order of value occurs, Baudrillard argues, the moment gift exchange is broken by the production of value outside of the narrative of the ritual. From this point onwards, annulment through symbolic exchange is displaced by the play of autonomous objects (signs) and by the linear accumulation of value. He claims:

> It is from the (theoretically isolatable) moment when the exchange is no longer purely transitive, when the object (the material of the exchange) is immediately presented as such, that it is reified into a sign. Instead of abolishing itself in the relation that it establishes and thus assuming symbolic value (as in the example of the gift), the object becomes autonomous, intransitive, opaque, and so begins to signify the abolition of the relationship. Having become a sign object, it is no longer the mobile signifier of a lack between two beings, it is "of" and "from" the reified relation (as is the commodity at another level, in relation to reified labour power). Whereas the symbol refers to lack (to absence) as a virtual relation of desire, the sign object only refers to the absence of relation itself, and to isolated individual subjects. (Baudrillard, 1981, 65)[7]

This transition from the predominance of the symbol to that of the sign, from an enchanted world characterized by symbolic exchange to the 'rational' world of commodity production, exchange and consumption, marks the birth of modernity. This passage is accompanied by the emergence of new social forms that break from the symbolic narratives of past history and obey a logic of accumulation rather than one of reversibility and self-effacement. And here, for the first time, objects (including individuals) are freed from the cyclical narratives of gift-exchange and are fired, as signs or commodities, into self-referential orbits within a capitalist system.

Baudrillard's genealogy of value: the transition to modernity

Baudrillard (1993a) argues, in *Symbolic Exchange and Death*, that this transition to modernity accelerates through three orders of simulacra. These orders of appearance, which are accompanied by mutations of the law of value, together form a historical series, one that parallels Weber's rationalization thesis in so far as it traces the modern disenchantment of symbolic or mythical forms. This series is as follows.

1   *First-order simulacra: the counterfeit or natural stage (use-value)*
This stage has its origins in the Renaissance, and involves the transition from feudal or archaic society, in which signs are limited in number and restricted in circulation, to democratic society, in which signs are openly produced and compete against each other. This transition from society based on rank and the reign of the *obligatory* sign to that based on the participation of all classes and the reign of the *emancipated* sign coincides with the birth of the counterfeit. Baudrillard (1981) argues:

> Competitive democracy succeeds the endogamy of signs proper to status-based orders. With the transit of values or signs of prestige from one class to another, we simultaneously and necessarily enter into the age of the *counterfeit*. For from a limited order of signs, the 'free' production of which is prevented by a prohibition, we pass into a proliferation of signs according to demand. (p. 51)

The counterfeit works through the invention and imitation of 'nature'. It constructs an *analagon* of man through the production of signs that give a theatrical representation of Renaissance (bourgeois) life. This process of imitation operates through the construction of a natural referent, and proceeds through the transubstantiation of nature into a single substance: stucco. This substance is used to embrace all forms and to imitate all materials, and with this becomes an equivalent for all other substances. Baudrillard argues that a distinction is erected here between the referent (the real) and the sign, but that this distinction is nothing more than a projection of the sign itself. He terms this the 'mirage of the referent', arguing that 'The referent in question here is no more external to the sign than is the signified: indeed, it is governed by the sign. It is carved out and projected as its function: its reality is of that which is *ornamentally inscribed on the sign itself*' (ibid., 151).

2   *Second-order simulacra: the production or commodity stage (exchange-value)*
This stage, which coincides with the Industrial Revolution, is defined by the destruction of reproduction by analogy and effect, and by the rise of technical production and reproduction. Baudrillard illustrates this transition by contrasting the automaton (first-order simulacra),

which operates through analogy and maintains a difference between appearance and reality, and the robot (second-order), which operates through mass equivalence and liquidates the distinction between the simulacrum (appearance) and the original (the real). Baudrillard (1993a) explains: 'The automaton is the *analogon* of man and remains responsive to him ... The machine is the *equivalent* of man, appropriating him to itself as an equal in the unity of a functional process. This is the difference between first- and second-order simulacra' (p. 53). In this latter order of technical reproduction the counterfeit, which refers to an original, is superseded by the mass production of signs and objects and is replaced by the series, in which, as Walter Benjamin foresaw (1973), an infinite number of identical objects are produced without reference to an original. At this point there is no longer a division between the order of the sign and its projection of external reality. Baudrillard argues that here the signifier subsumes the referent and circulates in its own self-referential orbit. This negation of the real, and thus any reference to an original or natural object is, for Baudrillard, the defining characteristic of this order. He argues: 'The extinction of the original reference alone facilitates the general law of equivalences, that is to say, *the very possibility of production*' (ibid., 55). And this order of simulacra, once established, subjects everything to the rule of mechanical efficiency and mass equivalence, and operates according to the market law of value: 'No more semblance or dissemblance, no more God or Man, only an immanent logic of the principle of operativity' (ibid., 54).

3   *Third-order simulacra: simulation or structural stage (sign-value)*
The second-order simulacrum of serial reproduction is transitional, for as the machine establishes its hegemony over reproduction, production itself gives way to coded signification and operational simulation. Baudrillard (1993a) argues:

> As soon as dead labour gains the upper hand over living labour (that is to say, since the end of primitive accumulation), serial production gives way to generation through models. In this case it is a matter of a reversal of origin and end, since all forms change from the moment that they are no longer mechanically reproduced, but *conceived according to their very reproducibility*, their diffraction from a generative core called a 'model'. We are dealing with third-order simulacra here. There is no more counterfeiting of an original, as there was in the first order, and no more pure series as there were in

the second; there are models from which all forms proceed according to modulated differences. (p. 56)

This order of modulation is dominated by the indeterminacy of the code. Here, simulacra proceed through exercises of simulation that are designed to test and control. And this, Baudrillard argues, is the age of digitality in which cybernetic models replace living labour through manipulation of the genetic code, and simulacra operate through reduction of reproduction to a test modelled on the binary form of DNA (question – answer, 0 – 1).

4   *Fourth-order simulacra: the fractal or viral stage*

In *The Transparency of Evil* Baudrillard (1993b) extends this three-stage classification of simulacra through the addition of a fourth order: the *fractal*. This is an order of vitiation in which all individual categories and distinct fields become corrupted and confused. Baudrillard argues:

> At the fourth, the fractal (or viral, or radiant) stage of value, there is no point of reference at all, and value radiates in all directions, occupying all interstices, without any reference to anything whatsoever, by virtue of pure contiguity. At the fractal stage there is no longer any equivalence, whether natural or general. Properly speaking there is now no law of value, merely a sort of *epidemic of value*, a sort of general metastasis of value, a haphazard proliferation and dispersal of value. Indeed, we should really no longer speak of 'value' at all, for this kind of propagation or chain reaction makes all valuation impossible. (ibid., 5)

The fractal disperses all limits and decentres all systems, giving rise to a culture in which categories proliferate beyond traditional boundaries and circulate in a network devoid of referential value. Indeterminacy rules, for all types and terms are commutable, and substitution is possible between all spheres, including Weber's value-spheres. This, for Baudrillard, is demonstrated by the birth of the transpolitical (Baudrillard, 1990b, 25–70), the transaesthetic (Baudrillard, 1993b, 14–19), the transsexual (ibid., 20–5) and the transeconomic (ibid., 26–35): spheres which are no longer restricted to politics, aesthetics, sex and economics for they expand and infect all other spheres, forming a vast undifferentiated field. This expunction of difference leads, paradoxically, to the combined success and effacement of all spheres:

> Each category is generalized to the greatest possible extent, so that it eventually loses all specificity and is reabsorbed by all the other

categories. When everything is political, nothing is political any more, the word itself is meaningless. When everything is sexual, nothing is sexual any more, and sex loses its determinants. When everything is aesthetic, nothing is beautiful or ugly any more, and art itself disappears. (ibid., 9).

This effacement of all forms of differentiation constitutes *the* most violent assault on the symbolic order, for here all differences and alterities are attacked by the 'transversalism' of Western culture. And in this respect, the fractal is the most 'advanced' stage of Western development, for it destroys the enchanted forms of reciprocity that enable symbolic exchange, and with this all forms of otherness which pose a threat to itself. The result of this process, Baudrillard argues, is that Western culture systematically removes everything other to itself from the world, and in the process consigns us to the 'hell of the same'.

This classification of the four orders of simulacra is not, however, to be read strictly as a theory of the linear destruction of symbolic exchange but as a genealogy of the law of value, and as an account of the fundamental opposition of this law to the symbolic order. Western history is thus not to be understood as a movement towards the complete disenchantment and elimination of all symbolic forms, for since the symbolic order exists outside of the order of value, as its radical other, it can never be fully removed from the world by this order. In addition, despite the descent of signification to fourth-order simulacra within the order of value itself, different orders of simulacra (for example, mass production and simulation) may themselves coexist in contemporary cultural forms. This means that modernity is not, for Baudrillard, strictly a unilinear process of regression from an enchanted world (characterized by symbolic exchange) to a disenchanted fourth-order of value, but a process whereby symbolic forms, though reduced to a subordinate position within contemporary culture, continue to haunt this world in the form of its other (an example is seduction, see below). This fact is crucial as it effectively means that forms of enchantment and re-enchantment are, for Baudrillard, never completely excluded from Western culture, and may even be reactivated to destabilize capitalist modernity. This is because the strength of the symbolic order lies, paradoxically, in its essential weakness, for it exists outside of, and operates on a different principle from, the modern economies of power and value. Indeed, Baudrillard proposes, that 'The excluded form [the symbolic] prevails, secretly, over the dominant form [the order of value]' (1990a, 17), and beyond this, that 'Symbolic rituals can absorb anything, including the organless body of capitalism' (Baudrillard, 1993b, 144). These ambitious statements imply that Western rationalism always remains vulnerable to its enchanted, symbolic other, and with this point to the active possibility of reversibility and re-enchantment (see below).

The symbolic order and the order of value reside then in an uneasy coexistence, and while the nature of this coexistence has changed over time, with the latter order attacking and blocking the basis of symbolic exchange, Western rationalism nonetheless remains exposed to the weakness of its enchanted other. And in many ways this account of the repression of symbolic exchange by the order of value, and of the potential threat of the former order to the latter, runs parallel to Weber's rationalization thesis. Baudrillard's analysis accentuates the different principles that govern the modern and pre-modern world – the production of value and the annulment of gift-exchange respectively – and broadens the scope of Weber's thesis through analysis of contemporary science (computer simulation, fractal mathematics, cybernetics, etc.), economic exchange-value and semiotics. In doing so, he departs from Weber's rationalization thesis in a number of important respects, most notably in emphasising the radical basis of the pre-modern order and in arguing that the boundaries between value-spheres are levelled in contemporary culture. In spite of this, however, the key historical problem for both thinkers is essentially the same: the progressive disenchantment of magical religiosity (the symbolic form) by 'rational' science.[8]

The radical opposition between what Baudrillard terms the symbolic order and the order of value is in fact to be found in Weber's work, if only in nascent form. The clearest example is to be found in the 'Intermediate Reflection' (the *'Zwischenbetrachtung'*), in which Weber contrasts the cyclical fate of pre-modern life to the linear fate that characterizes modern existence:

> The peasant, like Abraham, could die 'satiated with life'. The feudal landlord and the warrior hero could do likewise. For both fulfilled a cycle of their existence beyond which they did not reach. Each in his way could attain an inner-worldly perfection as a result of the naive unambiguity of the substance of his life. But the 'cultivated man' who strives for self-perfection, in the sense of acquiring or creating 'cultural values', cannot do this. He can become 'weary of life' but he cannot become 'satiated with life' in the sense of completing a cycle. For the perfectability of the man of culture in principle

progresses indefinitely, as do the cultural values. (Weber, 1970, 356; see also ibid., 140)

This passage offers an illustration of the different trajectories of the symbolic order and the law of value. The fate of the 'pre-modern' individual is contained within the bounds of a symbolic narrative, beyond which there is no knowledge, no desire to know, and thus no external reality or referent. This 'naive' cycle of life offers the possibility of individual satiation, for mastery of the world proceeds not through the production and accumulation of knowledge but through magical or mythical means. The life of the modern individual, by contrast, is distinguished by the endless pursuit of knowledge (see Chapter 4), a life that can never be complete because of the inevitability of death. Weber proclaims:

> the individual life of civilized man placed into an 'infinite progress', according to its own imminent meaning should never come to an end; for there is always a further step ahead of one who stands in the march of progress. And no man who comes to die stands upon the peak which lies in infinity. (ibid., 139–40)

Here, the cyclical fate of the symbolic order is broken by the linearity of progress, by the infinite perfectability of knowledge. The modern individual can, in short, never live a definitive life for this life is itself defined by a will to know which can never be fulfilled.

Weber and Baudrillard concur that science is unable ultimately to eradicate the presence of the 'arationalism' or irrationalism of the symbolic or magical world. For Weber, science is necessarily an incomplete enterprise that breaks the organic cycle of life but is unable to engage in the irrational world of values, thereby leaving the modern order open to the claims of mythical doctrines that attribute meanings to the world. Alongside this, modern forms of 'legal-rational' domination repress but also remain susceptible to more 'primitive' forms of charismatic authority. For Baudrillard, meanwhile, the order of value is unable to eradicate the symbolic order because this order has a fate that is radically other to, and independent of, that of the former. The rational 'progress' of the West, for both theorists, thus remains vulnerable to the symbolic order, to forms of symbolic 'arationalism' that exist outside of, and in opposition to, scientific rationality. The radical otherness of this 'arationalism', which has been considered in different terms in Chapter 7 through analysis of the aesthetic sphere, hence appears to present a profound challenge to Western rationalism, and, by extension, to the process of rationalization. This possibility will be examined further in the remainder of this chapter through analysis of Weber's remarks on the erotic sphere and Baudrillard's writing on the principle of seduction.

The erotic sphere and seduction

The erotic sphere, like the aesthetic sphere, is, for Weber, fundamentally 'arational' or irrational in nature. Weber's analysis of this sphere opens with an account of the historical rationalization of what he terms 'the greatest irrational force of life': sexual love (Weber, 1970, 343; see also Weber, 1978a, 602–4). This account centres initially on the relation of sexual love and religion. Weber observes that originally the relation of sex and religion was particularly intimate for sexual activity was often part of 'magic orgiasticism' or the unintended result of 'orgiastic excitement'. He argues, however, that over time a fundamental tension developed within this relation as a result of 'evolutionary factors', factors that mark the rationalization both of religion and sex. On the side of religion, for example, tension arose with the cultic chastity of priests, which was determined by the view that sexuality was 'dominated by demons'. On the side of sexuality, this identification of sex as an evil 'residue of the Fall' was accompanied by the sublimation of sex into eroticism. Here, Weber argues, the 'naive naturalism' of sex was transcended as sex itself was raised to a sphere of conscious activity. And this process is a part of the general rationalization and intellectualization of culture more generally, a process that in turn identified the irrational nature of eroticism. Weber (1970) argues:

> The total being of man has now been alienated from the organic cycle of peasant life; life has been increasingly enriched in cultural content, whether this content is evaluated as intellectually or otherwise supra-individual. All this has worked, through the estrangement of life-value from that which is merely naturally given, toward a further enhancement of the special position of eroticism. Eroticism was raised into the sphere of conscious enjoyment (in the most sublime sense of the term). Nevertheless, indeed because of this elevation, eroticism appeared to be like a gate into the most irrational and thereby real kernel of life, as compared with the mechanisms of rationalization. (pp. 344–5)

The intellectualization of culture enhances the tension between religion and sex, as may be seen in the conflict between eroticism and religious ethics of brotherliness. On one side of this relation, innerworldly, rational asceticism stands firmly against the erotic relation as a brutal form of passion, and rejects 'every sophistication of the sexual into eroticism as idolatry of the worst kind' (ibid., 349). On the other, passion itself is seen to constitute beauty, the rejection of which is seen to amount to blasphemy. And this, as Weber indicates above, is part of a deeper conflict: between the rationalism of the everyday world and the irrational or arational freedom of the erotic experience. Indeed, the erotic sphere would seem to offer a means of escape both from the asceticism of a religious ethic of brotherliness and from the modern order of instrumental rationalism. Weber's passionate reflection on this point in the 'Intermediate Reflection' ('*Zwischenbetrachtung*') affirms this latter possibility:

> The lover realizes himself to be rooted in the kernel of the truly living, which is eternally inaccessible to any rational endeavour. He knows himself to be freed from the cold skeleton hands of rational orders, just as completely as from the banality of everyday routine. This consciousness of the lover rests upon the ineffaceability and inexhaustibleness of his own experience. The experience is by no means communicable and in this respect it is equivalent to the 'having' of the mystic. This is not only due to the intensity of the lover's experience, but to the immediacy of the possessed reality. (ibid., 347)

The erotic sphere, for Weber, is thus a sphere that returns us from the rationalism of the modern world to the 'immediacy' of experience. This sphere offers the possibility of an undefined freedom which escapes the grasp of instrumental rationality through the resurrection of a reciprocal relation based upon 'truly living' reality rather than cold rational judgement. This is a freedom from the morality of ascetic brotherliness and the rationality of the intellectual sphere. It is an order of symbolic exchange, an order of fate defined by the reciprocity of a symbolic relation. The direction of this fate, however, remains unknown, for it lies outside of the order of rationality, in the aleatoric realm of destiny rather than the security of reasoned reflection. And it is precisely here, for Weber, that the attraction of the erotic relation lies: 'No consummated erotic communion will know itself to be founded in any way other than through a mysterious *destination* for one another: *fate*, in this highest sense of this word' (ibid., 348).

Baudrillard's theory of seduction can be read as a radical development of Weber's analysis of the erotic sphere. For Baudrillard, seduction is an agonistic relation between two parties that proceeds, like
Weber's erotic relation, through the mastery of immediate appearances
rather than through considered rational judgement. It is a form of
symbolic exchange which infects objects and signs from the outside,
subordinating them within a reciprocal relation between individual
subjects and objects, a relation which always remains cyclical and
reversible. On this basis, seduction, for Baudrillard, eludes and threatens the Western order of value:

> Seduction ... never belongs to the order of nature, but that of
> artifice – never to the order of energy, but that of signs and rituals.
> This is why all the great systems of production and interpretation
> have not ceased to exclude seduction – to its good fortune – from
> their conceptual field. For seduction continues to haunt them from
> without, and from deep within its forsaken state, threatening them
> with collapse. (Baudrillard, 1990a, 2)

Seduction is not to be confused with sex, which, for Baudrillard, is
merely its disenchanted other, in so far as it is defined by function and
nature rather than by the mythical play of appearances. In contrast to
sex, seduction is not centred on reproduction or the accumulation of
pleasure, rather it is a surface relation that effaces anatomy, and is
driven towards an unknown fate by the cyclical challenge of its own reciprocity. Baudrillard proclaims: 'The law of seduction takes the form of
an uninterrupted ritual exchange where seducer and seduced constantly
raise the stakes in a game that never ends ... Sex, on the other hand, has
a quick, banal end: the orgasm, the immediate form of desire's realization' (ibid., 22).[9] By extension, seduction also is not to be confused with
desire, which, like sex, is chained to a functional definition of 'nature'
and to a linear economy of bodily pleasure. Indeed, it is precisely this
definition of nature and this form of economy, centring on the production and accumulation of (libidinal) value, which the symbolic relation
of seduction opposes. Baudrillard argues:

> In order to understand the intensity of ritual forms, one must rid
> oneself of the idea that all happiness derives from nature, and all
> pleasure from the satisfaction of a desire. On the contrary, games, the
> sphere of play, reveal a passion for rules, a giddiness born of rules,
> and a force that comes from ceremony, and not desire. (ibid., 132)

Seduction then is a relation born not from 'natural' attraction but from ritual and artifice. In this respect, it is comparable to Weber's eroticism, which involves the 'boundless giving of oneself' and radical 'opposition to all functionality, rationality, and generality' (Weber, 1970, 347). Baudrillard argues that seduction is a relation that, like Weber's erotic relation, operates at the level of pure appearances, absorbing autonomous objects and signs within the reciprocal relation in which they are exchanged, and at the same time annulling their meaning. It too thus presents a means of escape from a depth model of reason and rationality, offering the possibility of a return to an order of fate within which objects and signs are abolished through symbolic exchange. And it is on this basis that the principle of seduction presents itself as a principle of possibility, a principle which haunts the modern order and which threatens to reverse and efface the effects of Western rationalism. Indeed, as Baudrillard (1990a) argues: 'Seduction continues to appear to all orthodoxies as malefice and artifice, a black magic for the deviation of all truths, an exaltation of the malicious use of signs. Every discourse is threatened with this sudden reversibility, absorbed into its own signs without a trace of meaning' (p. 2).

The possibility of symbolic exchange, at least in the form of seduction, is thus, for Baudrillard, always present, even within cultures characterized by the presence of third- and fourth-order simulacra. This possibility lies in the celebration of appearance rather than the pursuit of meaning, in the preservation rather than disenchantment of that which remains secret. The strength of seduction lies not in the unmasking of the truth of the world, an exercise that would seek to distinguish appearance from reality, but in a return to a world of pure appearance. And it is through this strategy of comparative 'weakness' that seduction remains outside of the forces of rationalization. Baudrillard (1990a) proposes:

> Any movement that believes it can subvert a system by its infrastructure is naive. Seduction is more intelligent, and seemingly spontaneously so. Immediately obvious seduction need not be demonstrated, nor justified – it is there all at once, in an alleged reversal of all the alleged depth of the real, of all psychology, anatomy, truth, of power. It knows (this is its secret) that *there is no anatomy*, nor psychology, that all signs are reversible. Nothing belongs to it, except appearances – all powers elude it, but it 'reversibilizes' all their signs ... The only thing truly at stake is the mastery of the strategy of appearances, against the force of being

and reality. There is no need to play being against being, or truth against truth; why become stuck undermining foundations, when a light manipulation of appearances will do. (p. 10)

Possibilities for re-enchantment

Baudrillard develops this principle of seduction into a radical theoretical strategy. The purpose of theory, he argues, is not to disenchant myth in order to uncover the meaning of the world but precisely the opposite: to annul the production of meaning itself and to thereby resurrect the enchantment of appearances. This form of theory celebrates ambiguity rather than clarity, and proceeds through a sacrificial form of writing that resists and dispels the accumulation of knowledge. Baudrillard (1990c) proclaims: 'The real joy of writing lies in the opportunity of being able to sacrifice a whole chapter for a single sentence, a complete sentence for a single word, to sacrifice everything for an artificial effect or an acceleration into the void' (p. 29). Baudrillard's own anagrammatic and aphoristic style is an exercise in this form of sacrificial writing, a poetic form which seeks to reverse and disperse rather than elucidate meaning, and which aims not to interpret but to mystify and enchant the world.

This strategic application of the principle of seduction stands in radical opposition to the modern (sociological) culture of conceptual production and interpretation. Baudrillard (1990a) argues:

> To produce is to materialize by force what belongs to another order, that of the secret and of seduction. Seduction is, at all times and in all places, opposed to production. Seduction removes something from the order of the visible, while production constructs everything in full view, be it an object, a number or concept. (p. 34)

This strategy thus also stands in radical opposition to Weber's interpretative sociology, and to any approach more generally which seeks to unveil the meanings that underlie the realm of immediate appearances. Baudrillard here argues that interpretation itself contributes directly to disenchantment, for its very aim is to strip life of its hidden meanings, thereby destroying the enchantment of all that is secret. In this respect, interpretative sociology is nothing more than a form of theoretical pornography,[10] for it is a practice which denudes all appearances through the projection of an underlying reality: '*All meaningful discourse seeks to end appearances*: this is its attraction and its imposture' (ibid., 54).

In view of this, Baudrillard works against the practice of interpretation in a bid to enchant or perhaps even re-echant, the world. He stipulates the following principles upon which such work may proceed:

> Cipher, do not decipher. Work over the illusion. Create illusion to create an event. Make enigmatic what is clear, render unintelligible what is only too intelligible, make the event itself totally unreadable. Accentuate the false transparency of the world to spread a terroristic confusion about it, or the germs or viruses of a radical illusion – in other words a radical disillusioning of the real. Viral, pernicious thought, corrosive of meaning, generative of an erotic perception of reality's turmoil. (Baudrillard, 1996c, 104)

This strategy of (re-)enchantment seeks to restore the possibility of symbolic exchange through a theoretical project of re-mystification. It, like seduction, embraces immediate appearances rather than reason, with the aim of restoring the world to an infinitely complex but intelligent puzzle. This radical strategy runs against all forms of Enlightenment thought, for it seeks to re-enchant the secret of the symbolic form through the diversion rather than production of knowledge. This practice brings to light the reversible fate of the symbolic order *within* the apparent linearity of modern culture, and proceeds through a theoretical application of the principle of gift-exchange: 'The absolute rule is to give back more than you were given. Never less, always more. The absolute rule of thought is to give back the world as it was given to us – unintelligible. And, if possible, to render it a little more unintelligible' (ibid., 105).[11] And this principle, for Baudrillard, defines the very purpose of postmodern science: to complicate, disorder and ultimately re-enchant the seemingly 'rational' world in which we live (see also Chapter 7).[12]

Weber, in spite of his personal adventures in the erotic sphere,[13] is fundamentally opposed to this strategy of resistance to the rationalization of the world. His commitment to clarity and precision in intellectual work and to the interpretation of the causes and meanings of social action stands in marked opposition to the pursuit of (re-)mystification. Weber, unlike Baudrillard, makes no attempt to extend the principle of eroticism or seduction into an attack on Western rationalism either from *within* (the pursuit of seductive intellectual strategies) or *without* (the resurrection of naive symbolic forms).

Rather, he turns away from both these possibilities and instead commits himself to an ascetic vocation that seeks to demystify rather than mystify the world (as argued in Chapters 4 and 5). There are a number of important reasons for this that together lend themselves to a forceful critique of Baudrillard's position.

First, Weber argues that even the 'arational' or irrational life-orders tend towards rationalization (this argument is also elucidated in Chapter 7 with regard to the aesthetic sphere). As previously noted, he proposes:

> the spheres of the irrational, the only spheres that intellectualism has not yet touched, are ... raised into consciousness and put under its lens. For in practice this is where the modern intellectualist form of romantic irrationalism leads. This method of emancipation from intellectualism may well bring about the very opposite of what those who take to it conceive as its goal. (Weber, 1970, 143)

On the basis of this statement, Weber would appear to reject erotic or seductive activity as anything more than a *temporary* means of escape from modern rationalism, arguing that *conscious* engagement in irrational or arational activity is likely to result not in the re-enchantment of the world but in its opposite: rationalization. And this argument applies equally to Baudrillard's postmodern science, which is highly rational in structure, content and purpose.

Second, Weber argues that there is no possibility of returning to the naive state of the pre-modern world, for the intellect once realized is irrevocable. This argument, which parallels Kleist's argument for the impossibility of redemption from self-consciousness in 'On the Marionette Theatre' (Kleist, 1981), states that there can be no genuine attempt to unlearn modern rationalism. Moreover, it suggests that there can be no invention of genuinely 'arational' or irrational forms by rational activity. Weber (1970) illustrates this point through reference to art and religious prophecy:

> If we attempt to force and 'invent' a monumental style in art, such miserable monstrosities are produced as the many monuments of the last twenty years. If one tries intellectually to construe new religions without a new and genuine prophecy, then, in an inner sense, something similar will result, but with still worse effects. (p. 155)

There can, by extension, be no rational reinvention of mythical or symbolic forms and no return to the naiveté or immediacy of pre-modern culture, and with this no rational attempt to disturb Western rationalism from the outside. Jean-François Lyotard (1984a) makes this same point, arguing that any attempt to reconstruct and redeploy symbolic forms is necessarily futile, for 'Primitive culture cannot be invented: it is given by definition' (p. 72).

Third, whereas Baudrillard's work assumes a nostalgic tone, and rests upon what Lyotard (1984a) has termed the 'paradisaic representation of a lost "organic" society' (p. 15), Weber's work by contrast is pragmatic and forward-looking. Weber, at the conclusion of 'Science as a Vocation', for example, refuses to yearn and tarry for new prophets who will disrupt the order of modernity, but instead pledges to act differently by attempting to meet the 'demands of the day'. He places little faith either in pre-modern symbolic forms, such as seduction, or modern 'arational' or irrational forms, such as eroticism or mysticism, arguing instead that we must face disenchantment through responsible, rational work both within and against this world. This vocational work involves questioning the meaning and value of rationalization, placing limits on the rule of science (Chapter 4), and reconciling responsible action with the preservation of ultimate values or ends (Chapter 5). It thus stands in diametrical opposition to Baudrillard's call to cipher rather than decipher the world.

Conclusion

On the above grounds Weber rejects, first, the possibility of resisting the rationalization of the world through either seduction or erotic activity, and, second, the more general possibility of re-enchantment. The notion of redemption from modern rationalism through the manipulation of 'arational' or irrational forms is, for Weber, ultimately nothing more than a form of idealism based upon a nostalgic lust for a pre-modern world. This criticism applies to Baudrillard's vision of a reactivation of symbolic exchange, and, by extension, to his idea of a subversive, seductive science. Baudrillard's idealized notion of symbolic exchange would appear to overestimate the power of pre-modern forms to disrupt the rationalization and disenchantment of the world, and with this underestimate the strength of the rational world to resist re-enchantment. Weber, while sharing an interest in the fate of the symbolic order and in the potentiality of the erotic sphere, is by contrast, less optimistic than Baudrillard. He remains deeply pessimistic as to both the outcome of rationalization and the possibility of re-enchantment, and, as argued in Chapters 4 and 5, emphasizes that resistance to rationalization can only proceed through further clarification and understanding of the world. And it is here that Baudrillard and Weber ultimately depart, for whereas the former commits himself to seductive, 'arational' and enchanting intellectual practice, the latter rejects this position and places his faith in ascetic, rational, *this-worldly* work.

10
Conclusion

> Were I to wish for anything I could not wish for wealth and power, but for the passion of the possible, that eye which everywhere, ever young, ever burning, sees possibility.
>
> Kierkegaard (1992, 56)

The writings of Weber, Lyotard, Foucault and Baudrillard, can be seen to contain a comparable account and critique of the rise, trajectory and nature of modern culture. Weber, to recapitulate, explains the transition to modernity in terms of an ongoing process of rationalization. This process involves the disenchantment of religious forms of legitimation by the claims of 'rational' science, and with this the emergence of new forms of domination that are bureaucratic rather than charismatic or traditional in nature, and which are tied to the needs of market capitalism rather than to ethical or spiritual beliefs. Weber views this transition as tragic in nature for it promises but in fact restricts individual freedom: while the rationalization process makes social life more predictable (at least in theory), it does so by placing limits on the scope for value-rational action (see Chapter 2), and while it differentiates culture into a number of competing value-spheres, these spheres themselves tend be seduced in time by the force of instrumental reason (see Chapter 3).

The postmodern theorists discussed in the previous three chapters develop and throw light on different aspects of this rationalization thesis. The work of Lyotard, like that of Weber, emphasizes the radical differences between mythical and scientific knowledge, and proceeds to identify the instrumental nature of modern culture, drawing attention, in particular, to the reciprocal relation which exists between the pursuit of scientific knowledge or 'truth' and the accumulation of wealth, and the connection between technological development and state or military power (see Chapter 7). Lyotard, in response, analyses and attacks the metanarratives that legitimate this instrumental pursuit of knowledge, and which, he claims, inaugurate a movement towards cultural sameness through the levelling of differences under the rule of a single rule or authority.

Foucault, like Lyotard, also addresses the rise of instrumental reason that accompanies the transition to modernity. His work analyses the rationalization of culture in terms of the emergence of new forms of knowledge that give increased power of and over 'Man', and addresses the institutional technologies which develop through application of this new (instrumental) rationalism. Foucault (1970), in short, outlines a movement towards sameness in the modern age both at the level of culture, which works towards 'the ever-to-be-accomplished unveiling of the Same' (p. 340), and at the level of life itself, as institutional practices of normalization emerge which standardize, catalogue and routinize individual behaviour (see Chapter 8). And in both these respects, Foucault's analysis of the rise and nature of the modern world develops and extends Weber's rationalization thesis, for it offers a comparable account of the development of instrumental rationalism, and beyond this examines the modern forms and practices of 'legitimate' domination to which this rationalism gives rise.

Baudrillard also offers an account of the transition to modernity which complements Weber's rationalization thesis. His work emphasizes the fundamental differences that exist between the pre-modern world, characterized by the rule of the symbolic order, and the modern world, characterized by the overriding dominance of the homologous orders of the sign and economic value. Baudrillard claims that this latter world is driven by a desire to efface all symbolic or mythical forms that are other to itself, and that this pursuit leads in turn to the 'Hell of the Same'. He follows Weber in arguing that Western rationalism disenchants the mythical basis of the pre-modern world and contributes to the increasing sameness of modern culture, but beyond this also extends Weber's work, first, through accentuation of the radical nature of the symbolic form, and, second, through analysis of contemporary science (computer simulation, fractal and chaos theory, cybernetics, etc.) and of the 'rational' orders of economic exchange value and semiotics (see Chapter 9).

In view of this, it is possible to argue that in spite of the clear differences in style and tenor which separate the writings of Weber, Lyotard, Foucault and Baudrillard, each theorist advances a comparable account of the transition to, and nature of, modernity, and beyond this an argument to suggest that this transition is not a mark of historical or 'human' progress. Furthermore, each of these thinkers puts forward a response to the instrumental nature of modern culture. Weber's response, as argued in Chapters 4 and 5, rests on the belief that there can be no redemption from modern rationalism, for the intellect, once realized, is irrevocable. There can be, he argues, no other-worldly or mystical route of escape from the rationalization of the world, and in view of this, reason should be employed to meet the demands of the day. In taking this position, Weber refuses to tarry for prophets that may disrupt the modern order and instead seeks an active mediation of fate through the pursuit of 'rational', this-worldly vocational work. The value of this work lies not in its capacity to free us from the constraints of the modern order but in its ability to clarify the nature of this order, and to delineate the grounds of possible value-choices and future courses of action. And with this, Weber seeks to establish not only the uses but also the *limits* of modern rationalism, a project which does not call for the transcendence of modernity, but which does constitute a form of resistance to the rationalization of the world in so far as it seeks to protect the realm of ultimate values from the further encroachment of instrumental reason (see Chapters 4 and 5).

In contrast, the work of the postmodern theorists examined in the previous chapters contains not only an analysis and critique of the modern order, but also a call for the transgression of the limits of this order, and an outline of how this transgression may proceed. In each case this transgressive practice rests on a philosophical challenge to the limits of modern rationalism. Lyotard, for example, seeks to undo the cultural sameness which is characteristic of the modern order: first, by embracing the irreconcilable difference (the *différend*) which exists between narratives or values; second, by recalling the experimental or aporetic moment which is concealed within, but effaced by, modern culture (the future anterior); and third, by searching for new forms of presentation which transcend the rules of the existing order (paralogy). Foucault, by contrast, attempts to disturb the sameness of modern culture through the genealogical exposition of forms of historical otherness that are repressed by, and present a challenge to, the order of modern rationalism. These forms, he claims, may be used to reveal *and* transform the limits of what we are and of what we may possibly become, and in this respect genealogy proceeds as both a critical *and* transgressive practice. Finally, Baudrillard seeks to disturb the drive of modern rationalism through the recognition of primordial symbolic forms, forms that remain other to the modern order and which, he claims, threaten this order with the possibility of reversal and collapse.

Weber's ascetic response to the rationalization and disenchantment of the world is clearly different from that offered by Lyotard, Foucault or Baudrillard. Weber's work is distinctly modern in orientation, seeking not only to establish objective historical facts that may be used to inform responsible value-judgements, but to place limits on the development and uses of instrumental reason. Weber remains critical of the nature and trajectory of modernity, while at the same time working within and against the limits of this order. This position stands in marked contrast to that taken by the three postmodern theorists. The postmodern response to the rationalization and disenchantment of the world seeks, by contrast, not to work within the limits of modern reason but to transgress precisely these limits through exposition of forms of difference or otherness (for example, Lyotard's *différend*, Foucault's subjugated knowledge, Baudrillard's symbolic order) that are repressed or effaced by the modern order. This response rests on the belief that such forms, which tend to be a- or irrational in nature, lie concealed within Western history but remain other to the forces of instrumental rationalism, and thus may be employed to expose, destabilize and overcome the limits of the modern order. On this basis, Lyotard, Foucault and Baudrillard, contrary to Weber, affirm the possibility of *transcending* the confines of modern culture, and hence of undoing or even escaping the rationalization process.

This key difference between the work of Weber, on one hand, and that of Lyotard, Foucault and Baudrillard, on the other, may be developed into a point of critique against either modern or postmodern theory. Weber's work may be used, for example, to assess critically the postmodern attack on the modern order, and in particular the postmodern appeal to arational or irrational forms. The second half of the present work, in part, engaged in such an assessment. Chapter 7 drew on Weber's work to argue that Lyotard affirms the possibility of escaping modern rationalism through radical artistic practice, but at the same time overlooks the susceptibility of such practice to the forces of (instrumentally) rational thought. Chapter 8 used Weber to question the ethics of Foucault's genealogical practice, and, in particular, to expose the presuppositions or values which are implicit in his work. Finally, Chapter 9 attacked Baudrillard from a Weberian position, arguing that his appeal to the symbolic order is not only nostalgic in nature but misjudges the capacity of Western reason to resist the challenge from its pre-modern other, and that, in view of this, his theory of seduction (the erotic sphere) offers no lasting solution to the rational constraints of the everyday world.

On this basis it is possible to put forward a Weberian critique of post-modern theory, one which reads the work of Lyotard, Foucault and Baudrillard as Utopian or *other-worldly* in its commitment to the poten-tiality of arational or irrational forms. This said, it is equally possible to reflect critically on Weber's work through the use of postmodern theory. The main point in question here is Weber's rationalist response to the rationalization and disenchantment of the world, which, while admirable in so far as it seeks to engage in the problems of this world, is not without difficulty, for it risks contributing to, rather than resist-ing, precisely the processes it seeks to oppose. This problem is not restricted to Weber's work but haunts sociology more generally, for sociology by its very nature is a rational discipline, or, in the words of Helmuth Plessner, 'an instrument of self-knowledge and disenchant-ment' (quoted in Lepenies, 1988, 49), one that remains tied to the order of modern rationalism, even if it is critical of this order. This problem, which is raised by Baudrillard (see Chapter 9), is particularly pressing in Weber's work, for this work, as an exercise in interpretive sociology, seeks to clarify and explain the causes and meanings of social action, and in doing so lends itself to the further disenchant-ment of the world through exposition of the meaning or reality which lies behind the realm of immediate or mythical appearances. This prac-tice, which effectively seeks to denude the world of its mysteries, leaves Weber's work in an uncomfortable position, for while it is critical of the rationalization and disenchantment of the world, its commitment to understanding social action and to rational (vocational) work is itself subject to this very critique.

The work of Weber may, in view of the above, be used to problema-tize postmodern theory and vice versa. This exercise offers an indication of the weaknesses but also of the *strengths* of the work of Weber, Lyotard, Foucault and Baudrillard. The strengths of Weber's sociology may be seen to lie in its commitment to *this-worldly* work, to work that is both realistic and responsible in nature. The strengths of postmodern theory, by contrast, lie in its exposition of the limits of rational critique, and in its experimental search for forms that challenge the order of modern rationalism. The question which remains for social theory, however, and which is beyond the scope of the present work, is whether these strengths may be developed together to form an approach which is this-worldly *and* experimental, realistic and respons-ible yet at the same time sensitive to the effects of its own rationalism and to the problem of contributing to the further rationalization and disenchantment of the world. The possibility of such an approach, which has been raised by Ulrich Beck and by Scott Lash,[1] lies in crossing the distinction between the modern and the postmodern, and hence in reconciling two seemingly irreconcilable value-positions. Work *within* such a *différend* or aporia, as Lyotard reminds us, need not seek a final resolution, which at best may be said to be unlikely anyway, but can be celebrated in the terms of its own value – rationality as an experimental and potentially productive undertaking in itself. The basic irreconcilability of opposing (modern and postmodern) values should thus not be a cause for dismay or disillusionment, for in the struggle between opposing value-positions new values and alternatives are likely to be born. From this perspective, a realm of possibility may be seen to lie in the seemingly impossible terrain between modern and postmodern thought. And this terrain demands further study, for as Weber (1949) himself observed: 'the possible is often reached only by striving to attain the impossible that lies beyond it' (p. 24).

Notes

Chapter 1

1. This renewed interest may be traced to the mid-1980s, and coincides with the collapse both of state socialism and Marxist theory. Since the 1980s, Weber scholarship has centred on the following: first, methodology, in particular the nature of Weber's neo-Kantianism (see Burger, 1976; Oakes, 1988; and, more recently, Drysdale, 1996, Hennis, 1994 and Ringer, 1998); second, biography and the position of Weber's thought within the history of ideas (see Mommsen and Osterhammel, 1987; Käsler, 1988; Lassman and Velody, 1989; Turner and Factor, 1994; Diggins, 1996; and Whimster, 1999); and third, Weber as a theorist and/or critic of modernity (see Schluchter, 1981; Whimster and Lash, 1987; Hennis, 1988; Scaff, 1989; Owen, 1994; and Horowitz and Maley, 1994). It is this latter line of Weber scholarship that is specifically of interest in the present work.
2. This view has, of course, been contested. Alex Callinicos, in particular, has argued that the collapse of state socialism is in fact the precondition for true Marxist theory and practice. He proclaims: 'Now classical Marxism can finally shake itself of the Stalinist incubus and seize the opportunities offered by a world experiencing greater "uncertainty and agitation" than for many decades. It is time to resume unfinished business' (Callinicos, 1991, 136, see also Callinicos, 1989). This call for a return to the 'true' Marx (undistorted by either Lenin or Stalin) and to 'resume unfinished business', however, has yet to materialize, and has been swept aside by new forms of thought that cast doubt on the nature of ideology, class, progress and revolution. The key figure behind these new forms is not Marx but Nietzsche, whose work heavily influenced Weber and first-wave critical theorists such as Horkheimer and Adorno, and today continues to inform contemporary continental philosophy, post-structuralist and postmodern theory. For a more engaging Marxist reading of the 'postmodern', one that treats postmodernism as a stage in the development of capitalism, see Frederic Jameson (1991).
3. For the key differences between Marx and Weber see Mommsen (1974), chapter 3. There are, of course, also important points of convergence between Marx and Weber. These are discussed in detail by Karl Löwith (1993), and have been developed by Frankfurt school critical theorists such as Adorno and Horkheimer (see, for example, Adorno and Horkheimer, 1992). For an accessible overview of Marx and Weber on modernity see Sayer (1991), in particular Chapter 4, and Antonio and Glassman (1985). For a Marxist critique of Weber see Marcuse (1968), Lewis (1975) and Weiss (1986).
4. I have followed the translators of *Economy and Society* in using 'instrumental rationality' rather than 'purposive rationality' or 'ends-orientated rationality' as the English translation of *Zweckrationalität*. This translation, while not literal, captures the means–ends basis of this type of rationality and

brings out the important contrast between value-rationality (*Wertrationalität*) and the more calculating, dispassionate, and thus 'rational', *Zweckrationalität*.

5. On the curious relation of Durkheim and Weber see Tiryakian (1966). For an argument for the theoretical convergence of the work of Durkheim and Weber see Parsons (1968), and for a recent account that also elucidates the divergence of their work see Münch (1988, 5–56). For a neo-Parsonian reading of Weber, Marx and Durkheim see Alexander (1983).

6. The present work will not address the position of Bataille as an intermediary figure between Nietzsche and postmodern theory. Rather, it will focus directly on the connections between the work of Weber, and that of Lyotard, Foucault and Baudrillard.

7. The present work is concerned chiefly with the theoretical grounds for resistance to rationalization. For a study with more of an empirical outlook see Barry Smart's edited collection *Resisting McDonaldization* (Smart, 1999a).

8. Parsons argues, for example, that 'Weber's central methodological concern was to vindicate the necessity for general theoretical concepts in the sociohistorical sciences. But the only kind of general concepts for which he provided an explicit methodological clarification was his general ideal types. This ... is a hypothetically concrete type which could serve as a unit of a system of action or social relationships' (Parsons, 1968, 640). Contrary to Parsons's argument, the ideal type is not a 'hypothetically' concrete type. Weber (1949) argues: 'The ideal-typical concept will help to develop our skills in imputation in research: it is no "hypothesis" but offers guidance to the construction of hypotheses. It is not a description of reality but it aims to give unambiguous means of expression to such a description' (p. 90). For further discussion of this point see Weber (1978a, 21).

9. A connected line of interpretation, although one found more within mainstream (or what Holton and Turner, 1989, 68, call 'conventional') sociology of the 1960s and 1970s than in specialist Weber scholarship, is that Weber's work as a whole can be interpreted as an account of the rise of capitalism in the West. This argument is rarely encountered today, for as Turner and Holton rightly argue: 'It is now clear that this characterization of Weber's primary sociological concerns is too narrow to provide an adequate and theoretically sophisticated perspective upon Weber's sociological corpus' (ibid.).

10. Tenbruck (1989) argues that Weber's 'undoubted and marked interest in occidental rationalization was ... only the condensation and starting point of a theme that preoccupied him throughout his life. In fact only a small part of his oeuvre was directed to specifically occidental development, while the entirety of his work, including the methodology, owes its existence to the question: what is rationality?' (p. 75). Beyond this, Tenbruck (1989) rejects the possibility of reconstructing Weber's work through the posthumously assembled *Economy and Society*.

11. In similar vein, I would argue that Szakolczai (1998) is mistaken in proposing that Weber's 1920 'Author's Introduction' (the '*Vorbemerkung*') to the 'Collected Essays on the Sociology of World Religions' (*Gesammelte Aufsätze zur Religionssoziologie*) provides the master key to his work. The '*Vorbemerkung*' is clearly of great importance but there is little evidence to

suggest that this essay serves as the key to Weber's early studies of labour relations, or work on the methodology of the social sciences.

Chapter 2

1. This reads in the original: 'was bedeutet Nihilism? – daß die obersten Werthe sich entwerten' (Nietzsche, 1970, 14). Kaufman and Hollingdale translate this passage as: 'What does nihilism mean? *That the highest values devaluate themselves*' (1968, 9). I prefer, however, to translate *enwerten* as to *devalue* (rather than to 'devaluate').

2. As Sam Whimster proposes in his translation of F. H. Tenbruck's 'The Problem of Thematic Unity in the Works of Max Weber': 'the term disenchantment [*Entzauberung*] should not be read so much as the final state of a world purged of illusion, but as an actual process, literally, or dis-enchantment' (Tenbruck, 1989, 48). Ralph Schroeder (1992) offers a slightly different, although consistent, translation of this term: 'the literal translation of the German term *Entzauberung* is "demagification"' (p. 72).

3. This work, admittedly, will be one-sided in two respects. First, it emphasizes the cultural rather than the material conditions that enabled the rise of Western capitalism, and therefore focuses on Weber's sociology of religion rather than his *General Economic History* (1981). For a clear and detailed account of the latter, see Swedberg's *Max Weber and the Idea of Economic Sociology* (1998), chapter 1. Second, it focuses predominantly on the development of Western rationalism and does not address the arguments of *The Religion of China* (Weber, 1968) and *The Religion of India* (Weber, 1967b), or Weber's work on Islam. Here, see Wolfgang Schluchter's *Paradoxes of Modernity* (1996), chapter 3, and Ralph Schroeder's *Max Weber and the Sociology of Culture* (1992), chapter 2.

4. These 'early' or 'elementary' forms of behaviour are, for Weber, 'relatively' rational as 'Only we, judging from the standard of our modern views of nature, can distinguish objectively in such behaviour those attributions of causality which are "correct" from those which are "fallacious", and then designate the fallacious attributions of causality as irrational, and the corresponding acts as "magic"'(Weber, 1978a, 400). This statement is consistent with Weber's perspectival definition of rationality in *The Protestant Ethic*, in which he argues that 'what is rational from one point of view may well be irrational from another' (Weber, 1992, 26), and in 'The Social Psychology of the World Religions' (the '*Einleitung*'), where he states: 'We have to remind ourselves in advance that "rationalism" may mean very different things' (Weber, 1970, 293).

5. The magician is also important as the 'historical precursor' of the prophet and 'saviour'. Weber (1970) argues: 'As a rule the prophet and the saviour have legitimized themselves through the possession of a magical charisma. With them, however, this has been merely a means of securing recognition and followers for the exemplary significance, the mission, or the saviour quality of their personalities. For the substance of the prophecy or of the saviour's commandment is to direct a way of life to the pursuit of a sacred

value. Thus understood, the prophecy or commandment means, at least relatively, to systematize and rationalize the way of life, either in particular points or totally' (p. 327).

6. For a clear and detailed account of the historical development of ancient Judaism see Schroeder (1992, 72–84). Schroeder argues that ancient Judaism promoted a 'world-view based on a single, completely transcendent, and omnipotent god'. He adds: 'This world-view remained the underlying premise of religiosity throughout the development of Judaism and provided the framework for a divine order on which the validity of all claims and commands rested. Within this world-view, there are two shifts. At the time of the Confederacy, Yahweh was the protector of an association of warriors and a god of natural catastrophe. He was partly a functional god who served political aims. During the pre-exilic period, he became both the universalist and wrathful god of the prophets and the understandable and predictable overlord of the priesthood. Still later, in exilic and post-exilic times, the notions of an immanent redeemer who provides individual salvation and of a wise governor of world affairs emerged. Summarising the whole course of this development, we can say that there was a shift from the ritual worship of an anthropolatric god, to an increasing emphasis on universalism and ethical obedience, and finally a move towards ritualism and legalism' (ibid., 82).

7. In the *Anti-Christ*, Nietzsche advances two propositions regarding the origin of Christianity: first, that 'Christianity can be understood only by referring to the soil out of which it grew – it is *not* a counter-movement against the Jewish instinct, it is actually its logical consequence, one further conclusion of its fear-inspiring logic', and second, that 'the psychological type of the Galilean is still recognisable – but only in a completely degenerate form (which is at once a mutilation and an overloading with foreign traits) could it serve the end to which it was put, that of being the type of a *redeemer* of mankind' (Nietzsche, 1990, 146).

8. It is possible to argue that Weber's account is one-sided for it offers a privileged position to (Calvinistic) Protestantism within the study of the world religions (Holton and Turner, 1989, 81). This position may in part be explained by Weber's evaluative interest, which centres on what Schluchter (1981) terms the 'rise of Western rationalism'. This said, Weber's account of this process emphasizes the role of the Protestant 'calling' but overlooks the bearing of the counter-Reformation, in particular the Jesuit movement, on the development of Western rationalism, neglecting, above all, the emergence of Cartesian rationalism in France. On Descartes's influence on the emergence of the 'rationalist state of mind', see, for example, Durkheim (1973, 21–2).

9. This said, there is a clear a difference of emphasis here in the work of Weber and Nietzsche. For Nietzsche, Christian values do not constitute the 'highest values' but rather underlie the cultural decadence and decline of the modern era. For Weber, by contrast, the values of Protestantism are among the highest values, but devaluate themselves through a process of self-rationalization and disenchantment.

10. Weber argues that forms of bureaucratic administration have existed outside of the modern Western world (see, for example, Weber, 1978a, 964

and 969–71, and his remarks on patrimonial bureaucracy in *The Religion of China*, 1968). His argument, is that bureaucracy only develops *fully* in the modern state and in the 'most advanced institutions of capitalism', as it is tied to the existence of a 'rational' money economy (Weber, 1978a, 956).

11. Weber (1978a) says: 'On the one hand, capitalism in its modern stages of development requires the bureaucracy, though both have arisen from different historical sources. Conversely, capitalism is the most rational economic basis for bureaucratic administration and enables it to develop in the most rational form, especially because, from a fiscal point of view, it supplies the necessary money resources' (p. 224).

12. Traditional authority is a double sphere that, because of its demand for unlimited personal obedience, comprises action bound to specific traditions *and* action free of specific rules. The contrast of traditional and charismatic authority is thus complex, but the key point is that the principles of traditional rule 'are not formal principles, as in the case of legal authority' (Weber, 1978a, 227). This distinction is crucial as it distinguishes the *personal* rule of traditional and charismatic authority from the rational, and thus *impersonal*, law characteristic of modern bureaucracies.

13. In this account I have presented the movement towards disenchantment or nihilism, in particular the movement from personal to impersonal legitimation (charismatic and traditional to bureaucratic domination), in the form of a developmental history. Weber, however, rightly offers a cautionary note to this practice: 'charismatic domination is by no means limited to primitive stages of development, and the three basic types of domination cannot be placed into a simple evolutionary line: they in fact appear together in the most diverse combinations' (Weber, 1978a, 1133). In spite of this, Weber himself points to an important, perhaps *ideal-typical*, developmental tendency: 'It is the fate of charisma ... to recede with the development of permanent institutional structures' (ibid.). This remark points to the existence of a developmental logic within history, and reaffirms the *tragic* fate of Western culture. On the problematic relation of developmental sequences and ideal-types, see Weber (1949, 101).

Chapter 3

1. This demarcation of the different life-orders and their value-spheres (into the religious, economic, political, aesthetic, erotic and intellectual) has been the subject of much debate. Habermas, for example, rightly questions the absence of the sphere of law from the '*Zwischenbetrachtung*' (1984, 242). Scaff, by contrast, argues that the 'ethical', unlike the political and economic, does not, for Weber, constitute an autonomous life-order. He argues: 'Although the ambiguous category "ethics" cannot in itself be a sphere of value with its own "lawful autonomy", Weber's entire treatment of the religious sphere of action and valuation must be interpreted as suggesting there are distinctly "absolutist ethical" paths, sharing an affinity with the ascetic religious life, that some choose to follow as a way of counteracting the dilemmas of living in this world' (Scaff, 1991, 94). Meanwhile, Weber's conflation of the religious with the ethical is challenged by Wolfgang

Schluchter (1981), who argues that ethics and religion should be split into separate spheres. On this point, see Charles Turner (1992, 90–1). In addition, Schluchter (1981, 27) and Bellah (1999, 282–4) claim that the 'familial' constitutes a separate value-sphere. There is little evidence in Weber's short analysis of the conflict between prophecies of salvation and the natural sib (Weber, 1970, 328–30), however, to suggest that this is the case.

2. Lawrence Scaff rightly reminds us that value-conflicts take place not only between opposing life-orders but also *within* their individual value-spheres: 'Not only are different value-spheres, such as the political and the ethical, or the ethical and the aesthetic, *not* identical, it is also the case that *within* a sphere of value (e.g. the ethics of personal conduct) a system of uniform rules, say, of a Kantian type, *cannot* be found that will "solve" once and for all the problems of action or choice' (Scaff, 1991, 91–2).

3. Weber (1970) relates this to the conflict between the value-spheres: 'According to our ultimate standpoint, the one is the devil and the other the God, and the individual has to decide which is God for him and which is the devil. And so it goes throughout all the orders of life' (p. 148). Leo Strauss reads these allusions to God and the Devil literally rather than metaphorically. He argues that 'Weber's "idealism", i.e. his recognition of all "ideal goals of all "causes", seems to permit of a nonarbitrary distinction between excellence and baseness or depravity. At the same time, it culminates in the imperative "Follow God or the Devil", which means, in nontheological language, "Strive resolutely for excellence or baseness". For if Weber meant to say that choosing value system A in preference to value system B is compatible with genuine respect for value system B as base, he could not have known what he was talking about in speaking of a choice between God and Devil; he must have meant a mere difference of tastes while talking of a deadly conflict. It thus appears that for Weber, in his capacity as a social philosopher, excellence and baseness completely lost their primary meaning' (Strauss, 1953, 45–6). Contrary to this position, Weber, does not overlook the meaning of baseness and excellence but argues that such a hierarchical evaluation of values cannot and thus should not proceed through scientific means. Science, he argues, can clarify actions and values, but questions of baseness or excellence remain questions of faith. For further discussion of Strauss's natural right critique of Weber, see next third section of the Chapter 3.

4. Gerth and Mills (Weber, 1970) use the subtitle ('Religious Rejections of the World and Their Directions') rather than the title ('Intermediate Reflection') of this essay. A more accurate translation of this subtitle (*'Theorie der Stufen und Richtungen religiöser Weltablehnung'*) is 'A Theory of the Stages and Directions of Religious Rejections of the World' (see Bellah, 1999, 278).

5. I do not wish to suggest that it is only in modernity that the conflict between religion and 'this-world' is inaugurated, for, as Weber argues, salvation religions have always existed in a state of conflict with 'things-worldly'. The difference in modernity, however, is that the relation between salvation religion and the world is effectively reversed, so that worldly or *mundane* values now rule ideal interests or beliefs. In this respect, the conflict between religion and the world is sharpened by rationalization, and beyond this religion itself is reduced to one value-system among many.

6. For a more detailed account of the rationalization of law see Swedberg (1998, 82–107). Swedberg argues that, for Weber, legal history is divided into four main stages: 'Early in history ... there was "legal revelation through "law prophets" (stage 1). This was followed by "empirical creation and finding of law by legal honoratiores" (stage 2); and later by the "imposition of law by secular and theocratic powers" (stage 3). The modern legal situation is characterized by "the systematic elaboration of law and professionalized administration of justice by people who have received legal training in a learned and formally logical manner" (stage 4)' (ibid., 89). The main trend here is, in short, that 'The formal qualities of law ... have grown stronger throughout history, and one can speak of a general tendency for law to become ever more systematized, specialized, and logical' (ibid., 89–90).

7. It would be interesting, if space permitted, to examine the Protestant nature of Weber's work in greater detail. One may note in passing the Protestant tenor both of Weber's methodology and politics. On the former, see Sheldon Wolin (1994). Wolin argues: 'The exacting, even obsessive, demands which Weber imposed on the social scientist form a counterpart to the Calvinist's adherence to the letter of the Scripture and to the rules of piety prescribed by Puritan divines' (Wolin, 1994, 297–8). Weber himself states, for example, that 'We deprive the word "vocation" of the only meaning which still retains ethical significance if we fail to carry out that specific kind of self-restraint which it requires' (Weber, 1949, 5–6). On the Protestant nature of Weber's politics, see Waltzer (1976).

Chapter 4

1. The influence of Tolstoy and Dostoyevsky on Weber is of enormous importance. Paul Honigsheim, recalling the meetings of Weber's Heidelberg circle, notes: 'I don't remember a single Sunday conversation in which the name of Dostoyevsky did not occur. Perhaps even more pressing, even inflaming, was the necessity of coming to grips with Tolstoy' (Honigsheim, 1968, 81). On Weber and Tolstoy see Hanke (1999).

2. For a critique of Weber's reading of Plato see Heinrich Rickert (1989, 81–4). Rickert argues that this reading is plagued by a 'striking negative dogmatism' as it oversimplifies Plato's metaphor of the cave in order to justify the opposition between past and present values of science. Rickert argues that Weber, as a consequence, 'creates too much of an opposition, in a number of respects, between Plato's thoughts on the nature of science and the view we must hold today' (ibid., 81).

3. This said, science is still often called upon to legitimate religious doctrines through, verification of the historical facts of a prophecy. Conversely, the inability of science to prove God's word to be false may be used to lend religious doctrines credibility. See, for example, A.T. Pierson, *Many Infallible Proofs*, chapters 5 and 6.

4. Weber refers to Nietzsche's 'last men' in the following passage of The *Protestant Ethic*: 'Dann allerdings könnte für die "letzten Menschen" dieser Kulturentwicklung das Wort zur Warheit werden: "Fachmenschen ohne Geist, Genußmenschen ohne Herz, dies Nichts bildet sich ein, eine nie

vorher erreichte Stufe des Menschentums erstiegen zu haben' (Weber, 1993, 154). This reference to Nietzsche is obscured in the English translation of this work, as Talcott Parsons translates 'letzten Menschen' as 'last stage' rather than as 'last men' (Weber, 1992, 182). On this point of mistranslation see Kent (1983).

5. I have changed R. J. Hollingdale's translation of 'letzten Menschen' from 'ultimate men' to 'last men'. This passage reads as follows: 'Wehe! Es kommt die Zeit, wo der Mensch keinen Stern mehr gebären wird. Wehe! Es kommt die Zeit des verächtlichsten Menschen, der sich selber nicht mehr verachten kann. Seht! Ich zeige euch *den letzten Menschen* ... Die Erde ist dann klein geworden, und auf ihr hüpft der letzte Mensch, der Alles klein macht ... "Wir haben das Glück erfunden" – sagen die letzten Menschen und blinzeln' (Nietzsche, 1994a, 15).

6. Weber is referring to Lukács's early writings on aesthetics; see, for example, 'Heidelberger Philosophie der Kunst (1912–1914)' (Lukács, 1974, 9). The relation of Weber and Lukács is complex and cannot be addressed in the present work in any detail. For further discussion of this relation see Mitzman (1971), *The Iron Cage* chapter 9, Arato and Breines (1979), Scaff (1991, 215–20) and Karádi (1987).

7. Heinrich Rickert states, quite rightly, that 'Weber was convinced that there was no way theoretical research could deal with the question of the validity of values' (Rickert, 1989, 79). On this complex question of the validity of values see Gillian Rose (1981), *Hegel Contra Sociology*, Chapter 1, and Guy Oakes, (1988) *Weber and Rickert*, Chapters 1 and 3.

8. Durkheim, following Comte, develops a quite different idea of the supervision of science (see Durkheim, 1984, 292–301). He argues that the division of labour, if pushed too far, can be a disintegrative rather than integrative social force, and that, in view of this, the unity of the sciences should be pursued and overseen by a political state or government. This unity may be achieved, for Comte, through means of a positive philosophy, but Durkheim is sceptical of this possibility, arguing that 'philosophy becomes more and more incapable of ensuring the unity of science' (ibid., 298), and that the unity of scientific methods, with the specialization of the division of labour, becomes increasingly difficult to achieve. These positivistic arguments regarding the supervision of science, are very different from those found in the work of Weber. For Weber, the supervision of science means confining this enterprise within its true limits (i.e. it is to address questions of fact rather than value). For Durkheim, such limits do not exist, for science can and *should* be prescriptive in nature. These differences are discussed at length in Chapter 3 of the present work.

9. I have corrected Talcott Parsons's translation of 'letzten Menschen' from 'last stage' to 'last men'; see above, footnote 4.

Chapter 5

1. This chapter addresses Weber's theory of the vocation of politics rather than the political views he held in practice. For a detailed analysis of the latter see Beetham (1974), Mommsen (1984) and Schroeder (1998).

2. Wolfgang Schluchter draws attention to the difficulty of translating *Gesinnungsethik*. He states: '"Ethic of responsibility" is a literal rendering of *Verantwortungsethik*, but there is no equally easy translation for *Gesinnungsethik*, for which I have chosen "ethic of single-minded conviction" instead of the more familiar "ethic of ultimate ends"' (Roth and Schluchter, 1979, 66). I, while noting this difficulty, will refer to *Gesinnungsethik* as 'ethic of conviction' for ease of use.

3. This task subsequently forms the basis of *The Rise of Western Rationalism*, in which Schluchter outlines these three ethics in relation to the substantive content of Weber's sociology (see Schluchter, 1981, 39–59).

4. On this point see also C. Turner (1992, 146–70). Turner dismisses the complexity of the relationship between the *Gesinnungsethik* and the *Verantwortungsethik*: 'The precise relationship between these two distinctions has given rise to a good deal of unnecessary head-scratching and tortuous scholasticism in the literature, but it is in fact fairly straightforward' (ibid., 159). Despite this claim for the simplicity of Weber's position, Turner draws no concrete conclusions as to the relation of these two ethics and their relation to value and instrumental rationality.

5. Gerth and Mills, following the guidance of Marianne Weber, state that the speeches 'Science as a Vocation' and 'Politics as a Vocation' date from 1918 (Weber, 1970, 77 and 129). In fact, according to the research of Wolfgang Schluchter, Max Weber gave the speech 'Science as a Vocation' at Munich University on 7 November 1917 and 'Politics as a Vocation' on 16 January 1919. Both speeches were published, with revisions, in 1919 (see Roth and Schluchter, 1979, 113–16, and Schluchter, 1996, 46–7).

6. Weber argues, following Burckhardt, that power is of a diabolical nature (see Weber, 1994, 75). The affinities between Weber's and Burckhardt's work are discussed at some length by R. Bendix and G. Roth in *Scholarship and Partisanship* (1971), Chapter 14.

7. For Weber, this is a very real problem: 'On the whole, people are strongly inclined to adapt themselves to what promises success, not only – as is self evident – with respect to the means or to the extent that they seek to realize their ideals, but even to the extent of giving up these very ideals. In Germany this mode of behaviour is glorified by the name *Realpolitik*' (Weber, 1949, 23). Here, one may note in passing a possible connection between Weber's two political ethics and the ideals of politics (nationalist conviction) and culture (humanist/liberal moralism) that divided the German middle class immediately after 1871. On the history of this split, and on the subsequent shift of the middle class from a humanist to a nationalist elite, see Norbert Elias (1996, 121–70). For a summary of this work, see my review (Gane, 1997a, 318–21). On the conflict between nationalist and liberal ideals in the work of Weber, see also Wolfgang Mommsen (1989, 24–43).

8. The Lutheran overtone of Weber's emphasis on faith in politics is clearly at odds with Nietzsche, who ridicules Luther: 'Faith is a *pons asinorum* [bridge of asses]' (Nietzsche, 1968, 114). This question of the relation of 'Faith' or 'Works' is particularly interesting, as Weber appears to argue that they must coexist in order for political leadership to be successful. In this respect, it may be argued that Weber's theory of politics is deeply Protestant in nature; see Waltzer (1976).

9. Turner and Factor are not alone in presenting these two political ethics in terms of an either/or. Paul Honigsheim, for example, argues that 'the radical ethic [*Gesinnungsethik*] is oriented toward the image of the saint; the ethic of responsibility toward that of the hero. The individual must choose between the two, and, by deciding for the one, the individual inevitably sins against the other precept' (Honigsheim, 1950, 232). Wolfgang Schluchter, by contrast, recognizes the demand for a practical reconciliation of these ethics but refuses, wrongly I believe, to move beyond a consideration of their formal opposition. He argues: 'the ethical life-style adequate to the disenchanted world seems to lie, as it were, *between* the two ethics. Both are in tune with the times, but only if they are combined. Weber has given some hints that would seem to justify such an interpretation. But I believe that this would be logically unsatisfactory, and would besides be at odds with his own premises' (Roth and Schluchter, 1979, 55).

10. This metaphor of the struggle between God and the Devil appears to come from Luther, who states: 'For what is not of God must of necessity be of the devil' (Luther, 1961, 9). The account given by Turner and Factor is particularly confusing as they argue that this statement 'does *not* imply that one must choose between the alternatives, for there is no contradiction in claiming, for example, that an act is good by virtue of its conscience *and* by virtue of its good consequences' (Turner and Factor, 1984, 33), but still they reject a position between the two political ethics: 'Weber's view seems closer to Otto Baumgarten's, in which the separation of the two types of demands is the dominant theme' (ibid., 49).

11. As Charles Turner (1992) rightly notes, the main difficulty that the politician here must face, and guard against, is the 'degeneration of [political] means into ends' (p. 150).

12. Robert Eden (1983) rightly reminds us that 'Neither Weber nor Nietzsche is concerned with "ethics" in the Aristotelian sense of the rational apprehension of and habituation to justice, moderation, *enkratia*, or prudence' (p. 195).

13. Weber's critique of eudemonism is clearly stated in his inaugural (Freiburg) address: 'there can ... be no real work in political economy on the basis of optimistic dreams of happiness. Abandon hope all ye who enter here: these words are inscribed above the portals of the unknown future history of mankind. So much for the dream of peace and happiness' (Weber, 1989, 197).

14. In particular, Weber is disdainful of the *unconditional* conviction demanded by revolutionary politics. This is borne out by his meeting in 1918 with Austrian economist Josef Schumpeter in Vienna, a meeting described by Karl Jaspers as follows: 'Schumpeter remarked how pleased he was with the Russian Revolution. Socialism was now no longer a discussion on paper, but had to prove its viability. Max Weber responded in great agitation: Communism, at this stage in Russian development, was virtually a crime, the road would lead over unparalleled human misery and end in a terrible catastrophe. "Quite likely", Schumpeter answered, "but what a fine laboratory".

"A laboratory filled with mounds of corpses", Weber answered heatedly' (Jaspers, 1965, 222).

Chapter 6

1. I use the term 'theorist' with some caution as each of these writers is highly critical of both the form and purpose of modern theory. Lyotard, for example, is particularly sceptical of the dogmatic and teleological nature of theoretical work, and argues that 'theorists' should draw from the deconstructive and experimental practices of art (see Lyotard, 1984a, 19–33, and 1981, 71–77). This leads Bill Readings to conclude that 'Lyotard is not a theorist. Lyotard's decisive entry into the French academic scene is an insistence that, after 1968, theory ought to be recognized as part of the problem, not as a potential solution' (Lyotard, 1991, xxix). The key point, however, is that Lyotard attempts to develop a form of (postmodern) theory that is based on experimentation and difference, and free from teleology and binary oppositions. In view of this, I concur with David Carroll's argument that Lyotard's and Foucault's 'awareness of the limitations of theory has led them not to reject theory but rather to work at and on the borders of theory in order to stretch, bend, or exceed its limitations' (Carroll, 1987, xi).
2. There is even controversy over the writing of the term postmodern. Pauline Rosenau (1992) notes, for example, that 'how one writes the word – "postmodern" or "post-modern" – signals a position, a bias. The absence of the hyphen has come to imply a certain sympathy with post-modernism and a recognition of its legitimacy, whereas the hyphen indicates a critical posture' (p. 18). The resistance of the postmodern to simple definition has been the focus of much criticism. Ernest Gellner, for example, argues that 'Postmodernism is a contemporary movement. It is strong and fashionable. Over and above this, it is not altogether clear what the devil it is. In fact, clarity is not conspicuous amongst its marked attributes' (Kellner, 1992, 22). This type of critique largely overlooks the fact that postmodern theory seeks to be both heterogeneous and aporetic in form. For a clear account of the emergence and usage of the term 'postmodern', see Best and Kellner (1991, 5–16).
3. Lyotard argues that the idea of a break from modernity is itself tied to an order of linear time that is quintessentially modern in nature. He states: 'the idea of a linear chronology is itself perfectly "modern". It is at once part of Christianity, Cartesianism and Jacobinism: since we are inaugurating something completely new, the hands of the clock should be put back to zero. The very idea of modernity is closely correlated with the principle that it is both possible and necessary to break with tradition and institute absolutely new ways of living and thinking' (Lyotard, 1992, 90). Zygmunt Bauman also supports the argument that there is no clear break between modernity and postmodernity, but on different grounds. He argues: 'The most conspicuous features of the postmodern condition: institutionalized pluralism, variety, contingency and ambivalence – have been all turned out by modern society in ever increasing volumes; yet they were seen as signs

of failure rather than success, as evidence of the insufficiency of efforts so far, at a time when the institutions of modernity, faithfully replicated by the modern mentality, struggled for *universality, homogeneity, monotony*, and *clarity*. The postmodern condition can be therefore described, on the one hand, as modernity emancipated from false consciousness; on the other, as a new type of social condition marked by the overt institutionalization of the characteristics which modernity – in its designs and managerial practices – set about to eliminate and, failing that, tried to conceal' (Bauman, 1992, 187–8).

4. Charles Jencks argues that Lyotard, along with Jacques Derrida and Ihab Hassan, is in fact a late modernist as he elides deconstruction with postmodernism and thereby simply takes modernist principles to an extreme. Jencks argues that the postmodern differs from deconstruction in that it operates through a double coding of the modern and the traditional, giving rise to pairings such as elite/popular, accommodating/subversive and new/old, and, further to this, that 'the post-modern is the continuation of modernity and its transcendence' (Jencks, 1996, 15). This argument, however, is rather misleading for it overlooks, first, Lyotard's critique of the 'textualism' of deconstruction, and, second, his attempt to return to and reactivate the experimental moment that lies buried within the modern order. This latter practice, which is found in different forms in the work of the three postmodern theorists analysed in the present work, seeks not the 'continuation of modernity' but the overcoming of the modern order through the use of elements, in particular forms of historical difference or otherness, which are concealed within and effaced by modernity. For an excellent account of Lyotard's position on the question of deconstruction, see Bill Readings (1991), *Introducing Lyotard*, Chapter 1.

5. See the Aristotelian epitaph to Lyotard and Thébaud's (1985), *Just Gaming*: 'The rule of the undetermined is itself undetermined'.

6. Lyotard refers to Kant's idea of reflective judgement as: 'the ability of the mind to synthesize data, be it sensuous or socio-historical, without recourse to a predetermined rule' (Lyotard, 1988a, 20).

7. Lyotard (1988a) argues: 'Wittgenstein explains that the rules regulating games are unknown to the players and that no one learns to use language by acquiring a knowledge of its grammatical or lexical aspects as such. Rather everyone learns by groping around in a stream of phrases like children do' (p. 6).

8. Lyotard refers to Freud's notion of 'working through', which is close to the notion of 'free association', and is based on the following dictum: 'do not prejudge, suspend judgement, give the same attention to everything that happens as it happens ... let speech run, give free rein to all the "ideas", figures, scenes, names, sentences, as they come onto the tongue and the body, in their "disorder", without selection or repression' (Lyotard, 1991, 30). He also plays upon the connected idea of 'equally floating attention', which is based on 'the power to be able to endure occurrences as "directly" as possible without the mediation or protection of a "pre-text"' (Lyotard, 1988a, 8).

9. Lyotard, following Lévinas, makes reference to the following passage of the Talmud: 'Do before you understand, and the Jews did, and then they understood' (Lyotard and Thébaud, 1985, 41).

10. There is, to my knowledge, only one reference to the postmodern in Foucault's work (excluding interviews). This is in the essay 'What is Enlightenment?', in which he states: 'Rather than seeking to distinguish the "modern era" from the "premodern" or "postmodern", I think it would be more useful to try to find out how the attitude of modernity, ever since its formation, has found itself struggling with attitudes of "countermodernity"' (Foucault, 1991c, 39). It is precisely this strategy of revealing narratives which run counter to modernity, however, which leads me to term Foucault's work postmodern.

11. I do not wish to overemphasize the homogeneity of postmodernism. There are, as I have argued, similarities between Lyotard, Foucault and Baudrillard that lead me to define them as postmodern theorists. There are also fundamental differences between them, differences that will become clear in the following Chapters, and which illustrate the heterogeneous nature of postmodernism itself. For an illustration of these differences see Baudrillard's attack on Foucault (Baudrillard, 1987) and Lyotard's critique of Baudrillard (Lyotard, 1984b, 15 and 1993a) and Foucault (Lyotard, 1992, 86).

12. There is, to my knowledge, only one minor reference to Weber in Lyotard's work (Lyotard and Thébaud, 1985, 27). Foucault and Baudrillard appear to have read Weber in some detail but, like Lyotard, make little reference to his work (see Foucault, 1991c, 1 and 1992, 78–80) and (Baudrillard, 1993a, 145 and 163).

13. Peter Lassman and Irving Velody, drawing on the work of Sheldon Wolin, argue that the postmodern attack on metanarratives may in fact be found in the work of Weber. They state: 'The strange and paradoxical quality of Weber's thought seems to reside in the fact that what we are presented with is the construction of an "epical" denial of the possibility of an "epical" theory for the modern age. Meanwhile, Weber's insight, unacknowledged, has been rediscovered in the current debates concerning the "post-modern" condition. Weber's account of the modern world is not dissimilar to that of Lyotard in his diagnosis of the loss of credibility of the "grand narratives" that formerly claimed to legitimate knowledge' (Lassman and Velody, 1989b, 172). One may note, however, first, that 'epical' theory – a 'style of theorising which is "inspired mainly by the hope of achieving a great and memorable deed through the medium of thought"' – is quite different to what Lyotard terms a grand narrative, which, to the exclusion of all other narratives, makes an all-encompassing claim to a universal truth. Second, while Weber is critical of a number of the modern grand narratives which legitimate knowledge, those, for example, found in the work of Hegel and Marx, he offers an alternative metanarrative of Western development, one which centres on the world-historical meta-process of rationalization. For further analysis of the respective positions of Lyotard and Weber, see Chapter 7 of the present work.

14. The work of these three postmodern theorists is clearly not confined to three separate spheres. The work of Baudrillard, for example, addresses questions of aesthetics, just as the work of Lyotard is highly political in orientation, and that of Foucault addresses questions relating to the erotic sphere. For the purposes of the present work, however, the work of each of

these thinkers will be analysed in connection to one particular value-sphere: Lyotard, the aesthetic sphere, Foucault, the political sphere and Baudrillard, the erotic sphere.

Chapter 7

1. This is rather an oversimplification of Lyotard's position as he later adds: 'even discussions of denotative statements need to have rules. Rules are not denotative but prescriptive utterances, which we are better off calling metaprescriptive utterances to avoid confusion (they prescribe what the moves of language games must be in order to be admissible)' (Lyotard, 1984b, 65). Lyotard argues that it is the task of postmodern science (paralogy) to unmask and transcend these prescriptives.
2. Lyotard admits, however, that scientific knowledge is indirectly a component of the social bond in so far as it 'develops into a profession and gives rise to institutions, and in modern societies language games consolidate themselves in the form of institutions run by qualified partners (the professional class)' (Lyotard, 1984b, 25).
3. I do not have the space to discuss the validity of this claim. For a critique of Lyotard on this point see Conroy (1985, 376).
4. This said, an idea of the radical instability of all rational systems (the 'irrationality of rationality' thesis) is implicit in Weber's work, particularly in its emphasis upon the unforeseen outcomes of history. This idea, as Smart notes, has been developed by Ritzer (1996) in his theory of McDonaldization: 'The basic thesis is that, however rational the system, there is a strong possibility, virtually a certainty, that there will be unanticipated irrational consequences. The outcomes Ritzer identifies include "adverse effects on the environment" associated with the fast-food industry in particular. For example, the 'need to grow uniform potatoes to create those predictable french fries' is associated with huge farms making extensive use of chemicals, which subsequently contaminate underground water supplies. Other "irrationalities" identified in this context include the destruction of forests to produce paper, "the damage caused by polystyrene" and the disproportionate quantity of "food needed to produce feed cattle"' (Smart, 1999, 15).
5. I use the term 'cultural differentiation' rather than 'cultural fragmentation' as both Weber and Lyotard see a degree of order underlying modern (and postmodern) culture. For Weber, while the life-orders and their value-spheres separate out from each other with the transition to modernity, they remain tied together to some extent by the rationalization of the world, and, in particular, by a general movement towards the rule of instrumental reason (see Chapter 3). For Lyotard, underlying the general agonistics of postmodern society there remains a conception of a (linguistic) social bond (see Lyotard, 1984b, 15). He argues: 'Language is the whole social bond (money is only an aspect of language, the accountable aspect, payment and credit, at any rate a play on differences of place or time)' (Lyotard, 1993a,27).
6. Weber, in his essays on Roscher and Knies (Weber, 1975), is particularly critical of the idea of the 'epoch' and of the idea of Hegelian synthesis. For a

comprehensive account of the opposition between neo-Kantianism and Hegelianism, see Gillian Rose's *Hegel Contra Sociology* (1981), Chapter 1.

7. Wlad Godzich (the translator of *Just Gaming*), anticipating precisely this misunderstanding, warns: 'Postmodern is not to be taken in a periodising sense' (Lyotard and Thébaud, 1985, 16).

8. I am here unable to discuss Lyotard's idea of the differend at any length. For an overview of the complex argument of *The Differend*, see Carroll (1987, 158–84), Bennington (1988, 106–75), Best and Kellner (1991, 167–71) and Readings (1991, 105–27).

9. Lyotard (1984b) argues that 'in the diverse invitations to suspend artistic experimentation, there is an identical call for order, a desire for unity, for identity, for security, or popularity' (p. 73). Bauman's analysis of the violence of the modern quest for order is a direct development of this position. See *Postmodernity and Its Discontents* (Bauman, 1997), chapters 1 and 2.

10. Lyotard (1984a) adds: 'In a society reputed to be archaic, there is a certain function of art that is, in fact, a religious function in the strict sense of the term: art, in this case, belongs to the society's system of self-integration: it is an integral part of the system. One could say, moreover, that the culture of this society is also simply an art. It functions as a religion, as something that joins people by permitting them to communicate ... This type of art has become impossible' (1984a, 71).

11. Lyotard (1997) argues, for example: 'Aesthetics is the mode taken by a civilization that has been deserted by its ideals. It cultivates the pleasure of representing. And so calls itself culture' (p. 235). Weber is similarly sceptical of the disenchantment of modern culture (see Weber 1970, 356–7).

12. David Carroll rightly argues that Lyotard's work attacks 'the rational' discourse of aesthetics. In view of this Carroll employs instead the term 'paraesthetics', which 'indicates something like an aesthetics turned against itself or pushed beyond or beside itself, a faulty, improper aesthetics – one not content to remain within the area defined by the aesthetic. Paraesthetics describes a critical approach to aesthetics for which art is a question not a given, an aesthetics in which art does not have a determined place of a fixed definition' (carroll, 1987, xiv).

13. This work is not yet available in English translation in its entirety. The following sections, however, have been translated: 'The Dream-Work Does Not Think' (Lyotard, 1989, 19–55; 1971, 239–70), 'The Connivances of Desire with the Figural', (Lyotard, 1984a, 57–68; 1971, 271–9) and 'Fiscourse, Digure' (Lyotard, 1983a; 1971, 333–57). I, for reasons of space, only give the barest outline of this complex work. For a detailed overview of the argument of *Discours, Figure* see Carroll (1987, 30–43), Dews (1987, 112–28) Bennington (1988) and Best and Kellner (1991, 148–52).

14. Lyotard (1984a) argues: 'Where do you criticize from? Don't you see that criticising is still knowing, knowing better? That the critical relation still falls within the sphere of knowledge, of "realization" and thus of the assumption of power? Critique must be drifted out of' (p. 13). On the tendency of critique to remain caught within the position of its object, see also Chapter 9 of the present work.

15. See, for example, Lyotard's analysis of music. He argues that the rules of classical composition impose a number of 'grids which filter the flows of energy, in this case sound'. 'These grids', he continues, 'are not things

(there are no things): they are libidinal investments that block the entrance and exit of certain sound-noises, and that maintain and transmit themselves' (Lyotard 1984a, 94–5). Lyotard argues, in response, for 'deafness to the rules of composition', and for the potential of silence and unresolved dissonance to disrupt the rational basis that underlies and orders classical forms of Western music.

16. For a more extensive analysis of *Libidinal Economy* (Lyotard, 1993a), see Carroll (1987, 43–52), Dews (1987, 128–43), Best and Kellner (1991, 152–60): and Williams (2000).

17. Lyotard is clearly alluding to a form of political situationism; see I. H. Grant (1993, xvii) and David Macey (1998, 53).

18. This is not to suggest, that Lyotard simply abandons the work of Nietzsche for that of Kant, for in a number of respects he drifts between the two. He argues in *The Postmodern Condition*, for example, that 'I see a much earlier modulation of Nietzschean perspectivism in the Kantian theme of the sublime' (Lyotard, 1984b, 77). Lyotard also retains his interest in Freud. Indeed, he argues that Kant's distinction between the beautiful and the sublime is in many respects analogous to Freud's theory of the conscious and unconscious. Lyotard (1988b) states: 'secondary repression is to primary repression as the beautiful is to the sublime – and this with respect to the matter or quality of what for Kant is the given, for Freud the notion of excitation, with respect to the capacity to synthesize in Kant and to associate in Freud, with respect to the spatiotemporal form in the former or to the formation unconscious–preconscious in the latter and, finally, with respect to the way in which neither the Kantian sublime nor the Freudian *Nachträglichkeit* lets itself be inscribed in "memory", even as an unconscious one' (p. 5).

19. I do not address Lyotard's argument for the heteronomy of the faculties, and, following this, his argument that Kant failed to restore unity to philosophy through the third Critique. For a brief overview of these important points, see Sim (1996, 99–103).

20. Lyotard (1984b) states: 'The sublime sentiment ... carries with it both pleasure and pain. Better still, in it pleasure derives from pain' (p. 77). Stuart Sim (1996) is thus mistaken in presenting the sublime as a case 'where pain is the experience rather than pleasure' (p. 99).

21. See, for example, the 1920 'Author's Introduction' (the '*Vorbemerkung*') to the *Collected Essays on the Sociology of World Religions* (*Gesammelte Aufsätze zur Religionssoziologie;* see Weber, 1992:13–31) and *The Rational and Social Foundations of Music* (Weber, 1958b).

Chapter 8

1. There are also a number of striking similarities between the 'life-works' of Weber and Foucault; see Szakolczai (1998).

2. This critique of humanism stems from Foucault's reading of Kant, who, he argues, closed the possibility of limit-philosophy when he 'relegated all critical investigations to an anthropological question' (Foucault, 1977, 38). For a detailed discussion of the important relation of Foucault's limit-philosophy

to Kant's *Anthropology from a Pragmatic Point of View*, which Foucault himself translated into French, see James Miller's *The Passion of Michel Foucault* (1993, 137–151).

3. Mitchell Dean (1994, 18–19) provides an excellent outline of the nature of monumental, antiquarian and critical history. I disagree with his claim, however, that 'while Foucault is certainly attracted to Nietzsche's genealogy as a source of inspiration and of "historical sense", it is a mistake to read this as a methodological statement' (ibid., 19). I suggest that Foucault (following Bataille and Blanchot) uses Nietzsche's critique of method to radicalize method itself, adopting, in particular, 'the task of "tearing" the subject from itself in such a way that it is no longer the subject as such, or that it is completely "other" than itself so that it may arrive at its annihilation, its dissociation' (Foucault, 1991a, 31).

4. The correspondence of Foucauldian and Nietzschean genealogy is not explored in detail in this chapter. Foucault, in short, openly acknowledges his distortion of Nietzschean genealogy. He states: 'The only valid tribute to thought such as Nietzsche's is precisely to use it, to deform it, to make it groan and protest. And if commentators then say I am being faithful or unfaithful to Nietzsche, that is of absolutely no interest' (Foucault, 1980, 53–4). For a comprehensive account of this complex relation see Mahon (1992, 119–34).

5. Foucault (1980) defines 'subjugated knowledge' as follows: 'on the one hand, I am referring to the historical contents that have been buried and disguised in a functionalist coherence or formal systematization ... On the other hand, I believe that by subjugated knowledges one should understand something else, something which in a sense is altogether different, namely, a whole set of knowledges that have been disqualified as inadequate to their task or insufficiently elaborated: naive knowledges, located low down on the hierarchy, beneath the required level of cognition or scientificity ... it is through the reappearance of this knowledge, of these local popular knowledges, that criticism performs its work' (pp. 81–2).

6. In view of this I would argue that there is a high degree of continuity between the three volumes of *The History of Sexuality*. Foucault states that the aim of *The Use of Pleasure*, for example, is to 'examine both the difference that keeps us at a remove from a way of thinking in which we recognize the origin of our own, and the proximity that remains in spite of that distance which we never cease to explore' (Foucault, 1986b, 7).

7. Edward Said is one of the few commentators to have understood this aspect of Foucault's work, arguing that it is part of an 'everlasting effort to formulate otherness and heterodoxy without domesticating them or turning them into doctrine' (said, 1988, 6).

8. Foucault's genealogy of punishment is thus deeply political in nature: 'What's effectively needed is a ramified, penetrative perception of the present, one that makes it possible to locate lines of weakness, strong points, positions where the instances of power have secured and implanted themselves by a system of organization dating back over 150 years' (Foucault, 1980, 62).

9. Foucault, is careful though to, note the overlap of these regimes. He argues: 'The reduction in the use of torture was a tendency that was rooted in the

great transformation of the years 1760–1840, but it did not end there; it can be said that the practice of the public execution haunted our penal system for a long time and still haunts it today' (foucault, 1980, 15). For a detailed discussion of the periodization of *Discipline and Punish* see Watson (1994, 132–51).

10. See Chapter 5 of the present work. To recapitulate, the ethical irrationality of the world, for Weber, results from the following: first, that 'The decisive means for politics is violence' (Weber, 1970, 121); second, that political purposes and actual ends often do not correspond: 'The final result of political action often, no regularly, stands in completely inadequate and often even paradoxical relation to its original meaning' (ibid., 116); and third, that good does not always come from good and evil from evil.

11. Weber gives a concrete example of this point in his 1906 essay 'Pseudo-Constitutionalism', in which he reflects on the use of force by the police following the failed 1905 Russian Revolution (see Weber, 1995, 190–1).

12. This position is similar to that of Lyotard, who argues: 'I don't think it is true that one writes for someone ... I believe that it is important that there is no addressee. When you cast bottles to the waves, you don't know to whom they are going and that is all to the good' (Lyotard and Thébaud, 1985, 8–9).

13. Both Foucault and Lyotard toyed with the idea of publishing anonymous, 'unsigned' works (see Szakolczai, 1998, 259, and Macey, 1998, 53).

14. Foucault (1980) proclaims: 'A topological and geological survey of the battlefield – that is the intellectual's role. But as for saying, "Here is what you must do!", certainly not' (p. 62). He states of *I, Pierre Rivière*: 'the reason we decided to publish these documents was to draw a map, so to speak, of those combats, to reconstruct these confrontations and battles, to rediscover the interaction of those discourses as weapons of attack and defence in the relations of power and knowledge' (Foucault, 1978, xi). This idea of political cartography has been developed by Gilles Deleuze (1988) in *Foucault* (pp. 23–46).

15. Habermas (1987) here quotes the work of Nancy Fraser: 'Why is struggle preferable to submission? Why ought domination be resisted? Only with the introduction of normative notions of some kind could Foucault answer this question. Only with the introduction of normative notions could he begin to tell us what is wrong with the modern power/knowledge regime and why we ought to resist it' (p. 284).

Chapter 9

1. Marx (1976) states, for example, that a 'thing can be a use-value without being a value. This is the case whenever its utility to man is not mediated through labour' (p. 131).

2. Baudrillard (1975) also cites Marx's concept of free labour as an example of his inability to break from the ideology of political economy: 'In a work, man is not only quantitatively exploited as a productive force by the *system* of capitalist political economy, but is also metaphysically overdetermined as a producer by the *code* of political economy. In the last instance, the system rationalizes its power here. *And in this Marxism assists the cunning of*

capital. It convinces men that they are alienated by the sale of their labour power, thus censoring the much more radical hypothesis that they might by alienated as labour power, as the "inalienable" power of creating value by their labour' (p. 31).
3. Marx (1992) generally portrays 'needs' as facts of human nature: 'Let us suppose that we had produced as human beings ... In your use or enjoyment of my product I would have the *immediate* satisfaction and knowledge that in my labour I had gratified a *human* need, i.e. that I had objectified *human nature* and hence had procured an object corresponding to the needs of another *human being'* (p. 277)
4. This argument is similar in nature to Lyotard's attack on Marx's theory of alienation for positing the possibility of 'a *true* universality' (Lyotard, 1984a, 20) and to Foucault's critique of ideology for presupposing a 'true' form of representation (Foucault, 1970, 240). The key point for Lyotard, Foucault and Baudrillard is that the critic (in this case Marx) remains, because of the nature of critique itself, 'in the sphere of the criticized' (Lyotard, 1984a, 13). This point is developed by Foucault (1980) in his analysis of Maoist forms of popular justice (see *Power/Knowledge*, chapter 1), and by Lyotard (1984a) in his attack on the politics of 'ultra-leftist organizations' (p. 29).
5. For a concise statement of Mauss's theory of gift exchange see *The Gift* (Mauss, 1966, 6–16). For Bataille's theory of general economy see the first volume of *The Accursed Share* (Batallie, 1991, 19–77). For a detailed account of the relation of Baudrillard to Mauss and Bataille see Julian Pefanis (1991), *Heterology and the Postmodern.*
6. I have modified this formulation slightly by replacing a slanted bar (/) between the orders of value and symbolic exchange with a horizontal bar (—) in order to accentuate this line as one of radical exclusion. Baudrillard proposes: 'The fundamental reduction no longer takes place between UV and EV, or between signifier and signified. It takes place between the system as a whole and symbolic exchange' (baudrillard, 1981, 128). The bar between use- and exchange-value and the signifier and signified is thus different from to that dividing the value-system from symbolic exchange. The former is a bar of logical implication that establishes a structural relation between two terms within the framework of political economy, the latter a bar that marks the fundamental opposition of two radically different orders: the symbolic order and the order of value (political economy). For a detailed analysis of Baudrillard's 'bar games' see Genosko (1994, 1–27). J.-C. Giradin (1974, 127–37), in one of the few commentaries on *For a Critique of the Political Economy of the Sign*, argues that this formulation may be completed through the addition of the following equations,

$$\frac{Wage}{Labour} = \frac{Sd}{Sr} \quad \text{and} \quad \frac{Exchange\text{-}Value}{Use\text{-}Value} \quad \frac{Sd}{Sr}$$

Symbolic Exchange

These formulae, however, contradict the basic structure of Baudrillard's critique, for they invert the order of primacy within the structure of the sign

(Baudrillard, following Saussure and Lacan, argues that the signifier dominates the repressed signified, and in third- and fourth-order simulacra breaks free of both the referent and signified), and thereby break the link made by Saussure between value and the sign. With this move, the homology of the sign and value is destroyed as there is no longer a structual correlation between economic exchange-value and the signified or between use-value and the signifier.

7. This transition to the 'functional' order of the sign is also addressed by Baudrillard in his first book, *The System of Objects*. He here argues: 'The materiality of objects no longer directly confronts the materiality of needs, these two inconsistent primary and antagonistic systems have been suppressed by the insertion between them of the new, abstract system of manipulable signs – by the insertion, in a word, of *functionality*' (Baudrillard, 1996b, 64).

8. It could be said that both Weber and Baudrillard here neglect the scientific basis of pre-modern culture. For a critique of such a tendency see Lévi-Strauss (1966).

9. Baudrillard (1990a) adds: 'in our culture the sexual has triumphed over seduction, and annexed it as a subaltern form. Our instrumental vision has inverted everything. For in the symbolic order seduction is primary, and sex only appears as an addendum' (p. 41).

10. Baudrillard (1990a) argues, for example, that 'What is obscene about this world is that nothing is left to appearances, or to chance' (p. 34).

11. This combined resurrection and application of symbolic exchange defines, for Baudrillard, the very basis of radical thought. He states: 'it is necessary to restore the possibility of returning, that is, to change the form of social relations. If no counter-gift or reciprocal exchange is possible, we remain imprisoned in the structure of power and abstraction' (Baudrillard, 1981, 211).

12. This question of re-enchantment through scientific means has been addressed by George Ritzer in relation to the question of consumption. See Ritzer (1999), *Enchanting a Disenchanted World*, particularly chapters 5 and 6.

13. In a key passage of the 'Intermediate Reflection' ('*Zwischenbetrachtung*') Weber (1970) analyses the fundamental opposition of the erotic and intellectual life-orders: 'The last accentuation of the erotical sphere occurred in terms of intellectualist cultures. It occurred where this sphere collided with the unavoidably ascetic trait of the vocational specialist type of man. Under this tension between the erotic sphere and rational everyday life, *specifically extramarital sexual life*, which had been removed from everyday affairs, could appear as the only tie which still linked man with the natural fountain of life' (p. 346; emphasis mine). Weber (the vocational specialist) here appears to reflect on and affirm the possibility of escape from rationalism that he himself found through engagement in the erotic sphere, or to be more precise through his extramarital relations with Mina Tobler (a concert pianist who was introduced to Weber's Heidelberg circle through Emil Lask and to whom Weber dedicated the second volume of his *Gesammelte Aufsätze zur Religionssoziologie* 1920–1), and Else Jaffé (a former student of Weber's and to whom the third volume of the *Gesammelte Aufsätze zur Religionssoziologie* is dedicated). The exact details of these relations are not known, as the personal correspondence from Weber to Tobler and Jaffé has

been withheld from print. The resulting lack of insight into Weber's private life has led scholars to err on the side of caution on this matter. Dirk Käsler, for example, refuses to speculate on the nature of these relationships and their bearing on Weber's work without the evidence of personal correspondence. He states: 'The intention to publish Weber's eighty or so letters to Marianne, his hundred and twenty or so to Else Jaffé and his one hundred and twenty or so to Mina Tobler will no doubt throw light on the problems of this area on Weber's development' (Käsler, 1988, 218). Lawrence Scaff (1991) also takes this position, arguing that we 'must await publication of Weber's correspondence in the *Max Weber Gesamtausgabe* for fuller discussion' (p. 109). The recent decision, however, not to publish Weber's correspondence to Mina Tobler and Else Jaffé in the *Gesamtausgabe* leaves the autobiographical nature of the '*Zwischenbetrachtung*' open to interpretation, and clouds the exact nature of Weber's own attempt to escape modern rationalism through erotic activity. This said, a number of theorists have attempted to overcome this problem, by reading the changes made by Weber to the text of the '*Zwischenbetrachtung*' between 1911 and 1920 as reflecting the sexual consummation of his affair with Else Jaffé. This line of interpretation, which was originally suggested by Eduard Baumgarten, is advanced by Martin Green (1988), who argues that Weber's relationship with Jaffé 'is echoed in the amplifications of one chapter of the *Religionssoziologie* (Sociology of Religion) ... Weber wrote chapter 2 in 1911, rewrote it in 1916, giving it the title "Zwischenbetrachtung", and rewrote it again in 1920. Each time the sexual and aesthetic spheres of experience received more extensive and sympathetic treatment' (p. 171). The differences between the initial text of the '*Zwischenbetrachtung*' published in November 1915 in the *Archiv für Sozialwissenschaft und Sozialpolitik* and the 1920 revision (which is reproduced by Gerth and Mills in Weber, 1970, *From Max Weber*) have also been expounded and analysed by Sam Whimster. Whimster states that there are twelve additions to the text Weber revised from 1919 onwards, of which nine concern the erotic. These nine additions address the questions of love as destiny, sexual consummation of love and the 'fusion of souls'. On the basis of this Whimster (1995) draws the speculative conclusion that 'in 1916 Weber developed the theme of eroticism up to the point of its sexual consummation, whereas by 1920 there is no doubt that full sexual consummation is included in his analysis' (P. 458). See Whimster (1996–7) for a further elucidation of this point. This line of interpretation may also be supported by a consideration of the influence of Otto Gross on Weber's Heidelberg circle, and of Weber's visits to Ascona in 1913 and 1914. In 1907 Weber refused to publish an article by Gross, a pupil of Freud, in the *Archiv für Sozialwissenschaft und Sozialpolitik*. In spite of this, one may note the clear similarities between Weber's writing on the erotic sphere in the '*Zwischenbetrachtung*'and Gross's doctrine of 'sexual communism', which is described by Marianne Weber (1975) as follows: 'The life-enhancing value of eroticism is so great that it must remain free from extraneous considerations and laws, and, above all, from any integration into everyday life. If, for the time being, marriage continues to exist as a provision for women and children, love ought to celebrate its ecstasies outside its realm' (p. 374). On the experience of Weber in Ascona

Bibliography

Adair-Toteff, C. (1996) 'Wissenschaften Waffen: Contrasting Concepts of Epistemological Power in Kant and Weber'. Unpublished paper presented to the ISA Research Committee on the History of Sociology, Amsterdam, 17 May 1996.

Adorno, T. W. and Horkheimer, M. (1992) *Dialectic of Enlightenment*. London and New York: Verso.

Albrow, M. (1990) *Max Weber's Construction of Social Theory*. Basingstoke: Macmillan – now Palgrave.

Alexander, J. (1983) *Theoretical Logic in Sociology* ,vol. 3, *The Classical Attempt at Theoretical Synthesis: Max Weber*. Berkeley: University of California Press.

Antonio, R. and Glassman, R M. (eds) (1985) *A Weber–Marx Dialogue*. Lawrence: University of Kansas Press.

Arato, A. and Breines, P. (1979) *The Young Lukács and the Origins of Western Marxism*. London: Pluto.

Aristotle (1976) *Ethics: The Nicomachean Ethics*, trans. J.A.K. Thomson. Harmondsworth: Penguin Books.

Bataille, G. (1991) *The Accursed Share*,vol. 1, *Consumption*, trans. R. Hurley. New York: Zone Books.

Baudrillard, J. (1975) *The Mirror of Production*, trans. M. Poster. St Louis: Telos Press.

Baudrillard, J. (1981) *For a Critique of the Political Economy of the Sign*, trans. C. Levin. St Louis: Telos Press.

Baudrillard, J. (1987) *Forget Foucault*, trans. N. Dufresne. New York: Semiotext(e).

Baudrillard, J. (1990a) *Seduction*, trans. B. Singer. Basingstoke: Macmillan Education.

Baudrillard, J. (1990b) *Fatal Strategies*, trans. P. Beitchman and W.G.J. Nieluchowski. New York: Semiotext(e).

Baudrillard, J. (1990c) *Cool Memories*, trans. C. Turner. London and New York: Verso.

Baudrillard, J. (1993a) *Symbolic Exchange and Death*, trans. I.H. Grant. London: Sage.

Baudrillard, J. (1993b) *The Transparency of Evil: Essays on Extreme Phenomena*, trans. J. Benedict. London and New York: Verso.

Baudrillard, J. (1996a) *Cool Memories Two*, trans. C. Turner. Durham: Duke University Press.

Baudrillard, J. (1996b) *The System of Objects*, trans. J. Benedict. London and New York: Verso.

Baudrillard, J. (1996c) *The Perfect Crime*, trans. C. Turner. London: Verso.

Bauman, Z. (1987) *Legislators and Interpreters: On Modernity, Post-Modernity and Intellectuals*. Cambridge: Cambridge University Press.

Bauman, Z. (1989) *Modernity and the Holocaust*. Cambridge: Polity Press.

Bauman, Z. (1992) *Intimations of Postmodernity*. London and New York: Routledge.

Bauman, Z. (1997) *Postmodernity and its Discontents*. Cambridge: Polity Press.

Beck, U. (1994) 'Self-Dissolution and Self-Endangerment of Industrial Society: What Does This Mean?', in U. Beck, A. Giddens and S. Lash, *Reflexive Modernization: Politics, Tradition and Aesthetics in the Modern Sociology Order.* Cambridge: Polity Press.

Beetham, D. (1974) *Max Weber and the Theory of Modern Politics.* London: George Allen and Unwin.

Bellah, R. (1999) 'Max Weber and World-Denying Love: A Look at the Historical Sociology of Religion'. *Journal of the American Academy of Religion*, 67/2, 277–303.

Bendix, R. (1966) *Max Weber: An Intellectual Portrait.* London: Methuen.

Bendix, R. and Roth, G. (1971) *Scholarship and Partisanship: Essays on Max Weber.* Berkeley: University of California Press.

Benjamin, W. (1973) *Illuminations*, trans. H. Zohn. London: Fontana.

Bennington, G. (1988) *Lyotard: Writing the Event.* Manchester: Manchester University Press.

Berlin, I. (1967) 'Tolstoy and Enlightenment', in *Tolstoy: A Collection of Critical Essays*, ed. R. E. Matlaw. New Jersey: Prentice-Hall.

Bernstein, J. (1995) *Recovering Ethical Life: Jürgen Habermas and the Future of Critical Theory.* London and New York: Routledge.

Best, S. and Kellner, D. (1991) *Postmodern Theory.* New York: Guilford Press.

Bolough, R. (1990) *Love or Greatness.* London: Unwin Hyman.

Brubaker, R. (1984) *The Limits of Rationality: An Essay on the Social and Moral Thought of Max Weber.* Hemel Hempstead: George Allen and Unwin.

Bruun, H.H. (1972) *Science, Values and Politics in Max Weber's Methodology.* Copenhagen: Munksgaard.

Burger, T. (1976) *Max Weber's Theory of Concept Formation.* Durham: Duke University Press.

Callinicos, A. (1989) *Against Postmodernism: A Marxist Critique.* Cambridge: Polity Press.

Callinicos, A. (1991) *The Revenge of History: Marxism and the East European Revolutions.* Cambridge: Polity Press.

Carroll, D. (1987) *Paraesthetics: Foucault, Lyotard, Derrida.* London: Methuen.

Conroy, M. (1985) 'Review of the Postmodern Condition'. *Southern Humanities Review*, 19/4, 374–7.

da Vinci, L. (1989) *Leonardo on Painting*, trans. M. Kemp and M. Walker, ed. M. Kemp. New Haven and London: Yale University Press.

Dean, M. (1994) *Critical and Effective Histories: Foucault's Methods and Historical Sociology.* London: Routledge.

Deleuze, G. (1988) *Foucault*, trans. S. Hand. London: Athlone Press.

Derrida, J. (1977) *Writing and Difference*, trans. A. Bass. Chicago: University of Chicago Press.

Dews, P. (1987) *Logics of Disintegration: Post-Structuralist Thought and the Claims of Critical Theory.* London and New York: Verso.

Diggins, J. (1996) *Max Weber: Politics and the Spirit of Tragedy.* New York: Basic Books.

Drury, S. (1988) *The Political Ideas of Leo Strauss.* Basingstoke: Macmillan Press – now Palgrave.

Drysdale, J. (1996) 'How are Social-Scientific Concepts Formed? A Reconstruction of Max Weber's Theory of Concept Formation'. *Sociological Theory*, 14/1, March, 71–88.

Durkheim, E. (1973) 'Sociology in France in the Nineteenth Century', trans. M. Traugott, in *Emile Durkheim: On Morality and Society*, ed. R. N. Bellah. Chicago: University of Chicago Press.

Durkheim, R. (1982) *The Rules of Soicological Method*, trans. W. D. Halls. Basingstoke: Macmillan Press – now Palgrave.

Durkheim, E. (1984) *The Division of Labour in Society*, trans. W. D. Halls. Basingstoke: Macmillan Press – now Palgrave.

Durkheim, E. (1992) *Professional Ethics and Civic Morals*, trans. C. Brookfield. London and New York: Routledge.

Eden, R. (1983) *Political Leadership and Nihilism: A Study of Weber and Nietzsche*. Tampa: University of South Florida Press.

Eden, R. (1987) 'Weber and Nietzsche: Questioning the Liberation of Social Science from Historicism', in *Max Weber and His Contemporaries*, ed. W. Mommsen and J. Osterhammel. London: Unwin Hyman.

Elias, N. (1996) *The Germans: Power Struggles and the Development of Habitus in the Nineteenth and Twentieth Centuries*, trans. S. Mennell and E. Dunning. Cambridge: Polity Press.

Featherstone, M. (1995) *Undoing Culture: Globalization, Postmodernism and Identity*. London: Sage.

Foucault, M. (1967) *Madness and Civilization: A History of Insanity in the Age of Reason* (abridged), trans. R. Howard. London: Tavistock.

Foucault, M. (1970) *The Order of Things*, trans. anon. London: Routledge.

Foucault, M. (1971) 'Monstrosities in Criticism', trans. R. J. Matthews. *Diacritics*, Fall.

Foucault, M. (1977) *Language, Counter-Memory, Practice: Selected Essays and Interviews*, ed. D. F. Bouchard, trans. S. Simon and D. F. Bouchard. Ithaca: Cornell University Press.

Foucault, M. (1978) *I, Pierre Rivière, Having Slaughtered my Mother, my Sister, my Brother...: A Case of Parricide in the 19th Century*, trans. anon. London: Peregrine.

Foucault, M. (1980) *Power/Knowledge: Selected Interviews and Other Writings 1972–1977*, ed. C. Gordon, trans. C. Gordon. L. Marshall, J. Mepham and K. Soper. Hemel Hempstead: Harvester.

Foucault, M. (1986a) 'Kant on Enlightenment and Revolution', trans. C. Gordon. *Economy and Society*, 15/1, 88–96.

Foucault, M. (1986b) *The History of Sexuality*, vol. 2, *The Use of Pleasure*, trans. R. Hurley. Harmondsworth: Penguin Books.

Foucault, M. (1988) *The History of Sexuality*, vol. 3, *The Care of the Self*, trans. R. Hurley. Harmondsworth: Penguin.

Foucault, M. (1989a) *The Archaeology of Knowledge*, trans. A. M. Sheridan Smith. London and New York: Routledge.

Foucault, M. (1989b) *Foucault Live*, trans. L. Hochroth and J. Johnston. New York: Semiotext(e).

Foucault, M. (1990) *The History of Sexuality*, vol 1, *An Introduction*, trans. R. Hurley. Harmondsworth: Penguin Books.

Foucault, M. (1991a) *Remarks on Marx: Conversations with Duccio Trombadori*, trans. R. J. Goldstein and J. Cascaito. New York: Semiotext(e).

Foucault, M. (1991b) *Discipline and Punish: The Birth of the Prison*, trans. A.M. Sheridan Smith. Harmondsworth: Penguin Books.

Foucault, M. (1991c) 'What is Enlightenment?', trans. C. Porter, in *The Foucault Reader*, ed. P. Rabinow. Harmondsworth: Penguin Books.

Foucault, M. (1992) *The Foucault Effect: Studies in Governmentality*, ed. G. Burchell, C. Gordon and P. Miller, trans. C. Gordon. Hemel Hempstead: Harvester Wheatsheaf.

Freund, J. (1968) *The Sociology of Max Weber*, trans. M. Ilford. London: Allen Lane.

Gane, N. (1996) 'Review of Jon Simons's Foucault and the Political', *Sociology*, 30/2, May, 406–7.

Gane, N. (1997a) 'Review of Norbert Elias's The Germans'. *Acta Sociologica*, 40/3, 318–21.

Gane, N. (1997b) 'Max Weber on the Ethical Irrationality of Political Leadership'. *Sociology*, 31/3, August, 549–64.

Gane, N. (1998a) 'Review of Wolfgang Schluchter's Paradoxes of Modernity: Culture and Conduct in the Theory of Max Weber'. *Acta Sociologica*, 41/3, 285–7.

Gane, N. (1998b) 'Review of David Owen's Maturity and Modernity: Nietzsche, Weber, Foucault and the Ambivalence of Reason'. *Acta Sociologica*, 41/4, 389–91.

Gane, N. (2000) 'Max Weber Revisited'. *Sociology*, 34/4, November, 811–16.

Gellner, E. (1992) *Postmodernism, Reason and Religion*. London and New York: Routledge.

Genosko, G. (1994) *Baudrillard and Signs: Signification Ablaze*. London and New York: Routledge.

Giradin, J-C. (1974) 'Toward a Politics of the Sign: Reading Baudrillard'. *Telos*, 20, Summer, 127–37.

Gordon, C. (1987) 'The Soul of the Citizen: Max Weber and Michel Foucault on Rationality and Government', in *Max Weber, Rationality and Modernity*, ed. S. Whimster and S. Lash. London: Allen and Unwin.

Grant, I. H. (1993) 'Introduction', in J-F. Lyotard, *Libidinal Economy*. London: Athlone.

Green, M. (1986) *Mountain of Truth. The Counterculture Begins*. Hanover and London: New England University Press.

Green, M. (1988) The von Richthofen Sisters, The Tragic and Triumphant Modes of Love. Albuquerque: University of New Mexico Press.

Habermas, J. (1981) 'Modernity versus Postmodernity', trans. S. Ben-Habib. *New German Critique*, 22, 3–18.

Habermas, J. (1984) *The Theory of Communicative Action*, vol 1, *Reason and the Rationalization of Society*, trans. T. McCarthy. Cambridge: Polity Press.

Habermas, J. (1987) *The Philosophical Discourse of Modernity*, trans. F. Lawrence. Cambridge: Polity Press.

Hanke, E. (1999) 'Max Weber, Leo Tolstoy and the Mountain of Truth', in *Max Weber and the Culture of Anarchy*, ed. S. Whimster. Basingstoke: Macmillan Press – now Palgrave.

Hennis, W. (1988) *Max Weber, Essays in Reconstruction*, trans. K. Tribe. London: Allen and Unwin.

Hennis, W. (1994) 'The Meaning of "Wertfreiheit": On the Background and Motives of Max Weber's "Postulate"', trans. U. and R. Brisson. *Sociological Theory*, 12/2, 113–25.

Holton, R. and Turner, B. (1989) *Max Weber on Economy and Society*. London and New York: Routledge.

Honigsheim, P. (1950) 'Max Weber: His Religious and Ethical Background and Development'. *Church History*, 19, 219–39.

Honigsheim, P. (1968) *On Max Weber*, trans. J. Rytina. New York: The Free Press.
Horowitz, A. and Maley, T. (eds) (1994) *The Barbarism of Reason: Max Weber and the Twilight of Enlightenment*. Toronto: University of Toronto Press.
Jameson, F. (1991) *Postmodernism, or, The Cultural Logic of Late Capitalism*. London and New York: Verso.
Jaspers, K. (1965) *Leonardo, Descartes, Max Weber: Three Essays*, trans. R. Manheim. London: Routledge and Kegan Paul.
Jencks, C. (1996) *What is Postmodernism?*, 4th edn. London: Academy Editions.
Kant, I. (1952) *The Critique of Judgement*, trans. J. C. Meredith. Oxford: Oxford University Press.
Kant, I. (1991) *The Moral Law: Groundwork of the Metaphysic of Morals*, trans. H.J. Paton. London and New York: Routledge.
Kant, I. (1993) *Critique of Pure Reason*, trans. Meiklejohn. London: Everyman.
Karádi, E. (1987) 'Ernst Bloch and Georg Lukács in Max Weber's Heidelberg', in *Max Weber and His Contemporaries*, ed. W. Mommsen and J. Osterhammel. London: Unwin Hyman.
Käsler, D. (1988) *Max Weber: An Introduction to His Life and Work*, trans. P. Hurd. Cambridge: Polity Press.
Kemple, T. (1998) 'Toward a Rational Analytics of Power: Some Nietzschean Themes in Max Weber's Concept of Domination'. Unpublished paper presented at the ISA 14th World Congress of Sociology, Montreal, 27 July 1998.
Kent, S. (1983) 'Weber, Goethe, and the Nietzschean Allusion: Capturing the Source of the "Iron Cage" Metaphor'. *Sociological Analysis*, 44/4, 297–320.
Kierkegaard, S. (1992) *Either/Or: A Fragment of Life*, trans. A. Hannay. Harmondsworth: Penguin.
Kleist, H. von (1981) 'On the Marionette Theatre', in *Hand to Mouth and Other Essays*, ed. I. Parry. Manchester: Carcanet New Press.
Kronman, A. (1983) *Max Weber*. London: Arnold.
Kuhn, T. (1996) *The Structure of Scientific Revolutions*, 3rd edn. Chicago: University of Chicago Press.
Landshut, S. (1989) 'Max Weber's Significance for Intellectual History', trans. R.C. Speirs, in *Max Weber's 'Science as a Vocation'*, ed. P. Lassman and I. Velody. London: Unwin Hyman.
Lash, S. (1987) 'Modernity or Modernism? Weber and Contemporary Social Theory', in *Max Weber, Rationality and Modernity, ed*. S. Whimster and S. Lash. London: Allen and Unwin.
Lash, S. (1994) 'Reflexivity and Its Doubles: Structure, Aesthetics, Community', in U. Beck, A. Giddens and S. Lash, *Reflexive Modernization: Politics, Tradition and Aesthetics in the Modern Sociology Order*. Cambridge: Polity Press.
Lash, S. (1999) *Another Modernity, a Different Rationality*. Oxford: Blackwell.
Lassman, P. and Velody, I. (eds) (1989a) *Max Weber's 'Science as a Vocation'*. London: Unwin Hyman.
Lassman, P and Velody, I. (1989b) 'Max Weber on Science, Disenchantment and the Search For Meaning', in *Max Weber's 'Science as a Vocation'*, ed. P. Lassman and I. Velody. London: Unwin Hyman.
Lenhardt, C. (1994) 'Max Weber and the Legacy of Critical Idealism', in *The Barbarism of Reason: Max Weber and the Twilight of the Enlightenment*, ed. A. Horowitz and T. Maley. Toronto: University of Toronto Press.
Lepenies, W. (1988) *Between Literature and Science: The Rise of Sociology*, trans. R.J. Hollingdale. Cambridge: Cambridge University Press.

Lévi-Strauss, C. (1966) *The Savage Mind*, trans. anon. Chicago: University of Chicago Press.

Lewis, J. (1975) *Max Weber and Value-Free Sociology: A Marxist Critique*. London: Lawrence and Wishart.

Löwith, K. (1989) 'Max Weber's Position on Science', trans. E. Carter and C. Turner, in *Max Weber's 'Science as a Vocation'*, ed. P. Lassman and I. Velody. London: Unwin Hyman.

Löwith, K. (1993) *Max Weber and Karl Marx*, trans. H. Fantel (rev. T. Bottomore and W. Outhwaite). London: Routledge.

Lukács, G. (1974) 'Heidelberger Philosophie der Kunst (1912–1914)', in *Georg Lukács Werke*, vol. 16, *Frühe Schriften zur Ästhetik I*, ed. G. Márkus and F. Benseler. Darmstadt: Luchterhand.

Luther, M. (1961) 'Preface to Latin Writings', in *Martin Luther: Selections From His Writings*, ed. J. Dillenberger. New York: Anchor Books.

Lyotard, J-F. (1971) *Discours, Figure*. Paris: Klincksieck.

Lyotard, J-F. (1978) 'On the Strength of the Weak', trans. R. McKeon. *Semiotext(e)*, 3/2, 204–14.

Lyotard, J-F. (1981) 'Theory as Art: A Pragmatic Point of View', trans. R. Vollrath, in *Image and Code*, ed. W. Steiner. Michigan: Michigan University Press.

Lyotard, J-F. (1983a) 'Fiscourse, Digure: The Utopia Behind the Scenes of the Phantasy', trans. M. Lydon. *Theatre Journal*, 35/3, 333–57.

Lyotard, J-F. (1983b) 'Presentations', trans. K. McLaughlin, in *Philosophy in France Today*, ed. A. Montefiore. Cambridge: Cambridge University Press.

Lyotard, J-F. (1984a) *Driftworks*, ed. R. McKeon. New York: Semiotext(e).

Lyotard, J-F. (1984b) *The Postmodern Condition: A Report on Knowledge*, trans. G. Bennington and B. Massumi. Manchester: Manchester University Press.

Lyotard, J-F. (1988a) *Peregrinations: Law, Form, Event*. New York: Columbia University Press.

Lyotard, J-F. (1988b) *Heidegger and 'the Jews'*, trans. A. Michel and M. S. Roberts. Minneapolis: University of Minnesota Press.

Lyotard, J-F. (1988c) *The Differend: Phrases in Dispute*, trans. G. Van Den Abbeele. Manchester: Manchester University Press.

Lyotard, J-F. (1989) *The Lyotard Reader*, ed. A. Benjamin. Oxford: Basil Blackwell.

Lyotard, J-F. (1991) *The Inhuman: Reflections on Time*, trans. G. Bennington and R. Bowlby. Cambridge: Polity Press.

Lyotard, J-F. (1992) *The Postmodern Explained to Children: Correspondence 1982–1985*, trans. D. Barry, B. Maher, J. Pefanis, V. Spate and M. Thomas. Sydney: Power Institute of Fine Arts.

Lyotard, J-F. (1993a) *Libidinal Economy*, trans. I. H. Grant. London: Athlone.

Lyotard, J-F. (1993b) *Political Writings*, trans. B. Readings and K. P. Geiman. London: UCL Press.

Lyotard, J-F. (1994) *Lessons on the Analytic of the Sublime*, trans E. Rottenberg. Stanford: Stanford University Press.

Lyotard, J-F. (1997) *Postmodern Fables*, trans. G. Van Den Abbeele. Minneapolis: University of Minnesota Press.

Lyotard, J-F. and Thébaud, J-L. (1985) *Just Gaming*, trans. W. Godzich. Minneapolis: University of Minnesota Press.

Macey, D. (1998) 'Obituary: Jean-François Lyotard, 1924–1998'. *Radical Philosophy*, 91, September/October, 53–4.

Maffesoli, M. (1996) *The Time of the Tribes: The Decline of Individualism in Mass Society*, trans. D. Smith. London: Sage.

Mahon, M. (1992) *Foucault's Nietzschean Genealogy: Truth, Power and the Subject.* New York: State University of New York Press.

Marcuse, H. (1968) *Negations: Essays in Critical Theory*, trans. J. Shapiro. London: Allen Lane.

Marx, K. (1976) *Capital*, vol. 1, *A Critique of Political Economy*, trans. B. Fowkes. Harmondsworth: Penguin Books.

Marx, K. (1992) 'Excerpts from James Mill's Elements of Political Economy', trans. R. Livingstone and G. Benton, in *Karl Marx: Early Writings*, ed. L. Colletti. Harmondsworth: Penguin.

Mauss, M. (1966) *The Gift: Forms and Functions of Exchange in Archaic Societies*, trans. I. Cunnison. London: Cohen & West.

Mayer, J. P. (1950) *Max Weber and German Politics: A Study in Political Sociology.* London: Faber and Faber.

McCarthy, T. (1984) 'Translator's Introduction', in J. Habermas, *The Theory of Communicative Action*, vol. 1, *Reason and the Rationalization of Society.* Cambridge: Polity Press.

McKeon, R. (1984) 'Opening', in J-F. Lyotard, *Driftworks*. New York: Semiotext(e).

Miller, J. (1993) *The Passion of Michel Foucault.* London: Harper Collins.

Mitzman, A. (1971) *The Iron Cage: An Historical Interpretation of Max Weber.* New York: Grosset & Dunlap.

Mommsen, W. (1974) *The Age of Bureaucracy: Perspectives on the Political Sociology of Max Weber.* Oxford: Basil Blackwell.

Mommsen, W. (1984) *Max Weber and German Politics, 1890-1920*, trans. M. Steinberg. Chicago: University of Chicago Press.

Mommsen, W. (1989) *The Political and Social Theory of Max Weber.* Cambridge: Polity Press.

Mommsen, W. and Osterhammel, J. (eds) (1987) *Max Weber and His Contemporaries.* London: Allen and Unwin.

Münch, R. (1988) *Understanding Modernity: Toward a New Perspective Going Beyond Durkheim and Weber.* London and New York: Routledge.

Nietzsche, F. (1968) *The Will To Power*, trans. W. Kaufman and R. J. Hollingdale. New York: Vintage Books.

Nietzsche, F. (1969) *Thus Spoke Zarathustra: A Book for Everyone and No One*, trans. R. J. Hollingdale. Harmondsworth: Penguin Books.

Nietzsche, F. (1970) *Nietzsche Werke: Kritische Gesamtausgabe*, part 8, vol. 2, ed. G. Colli and M. Montinari. Berlin: Walter de Gruyter.

Nietzsche, F. (1974) *The Gay Science*, trans. W. Kaufman. New York: Vintage Books.

Nietzsche, F. (1983) *Untimely Meditations*, trans. R. J. Hollingdale. Cambridge: Cambridge University Press.

Nietzsche, F. (1990) *Twilight of the Idols/The Anti-Christ*, trans. R. J. Hollingdale. Harmondsworth: Penguin Books.

Nietzsche, F. (1994a) *Also sprach Zarathustra: Ein Buch für Alle und Keinen.* Stuttgart: Philipp Reclam jun.

Nietzsche, F. (1994b) *On the Genealogy of Morality*, trans. C. Diethe. Cambridge: Cambridge University Press.

Nietzsche, F. (1998) *On the Genealogy of Morality*, trans. M. Clark and A. Swensen. Indianapolis: Hackett.

Oakes, G. (1988) *Weber and Rickert: Concept Formation in the Cultural Sciences.* Cambridge: Cambridge University Press.

O'Neill, J. (1995) *The Poverty of Postmodernism.* London and New York: Routledge.

Owen, D. (1994) *Maturity and Modernity: Nietzsche, Weber, Foucault and the Ambivalence of Reason.* London and New York: Routledge.

Parsons, T. (1968) *The Structure of Social Action,* vol. 2, *A Study in Social Theory with Special Reference to a Group of Recent European Writers.* New York: The Free Press.

Pascal, B. (1961) *The Pensées,* trans. J. M. Cohen. Harmondsworth: Penguin.

Pefanis, J. (1991) *Heterology and the Postmodern: Bataille, Baudrillard, and Lyotard.* Durham: Duke University Press.

Pierson, A. T. (n.d.) *Many Infallible Proofs: The Evidences of Chrisitianity, or, The Written and Living Word of God.* Kilmarnock: John Ritchie.

Plato (1987) *The Republic,* trans. D. Lee. Harmondsworth: Penguin.

Rajchman, J. (1985) *Michel Foucault: The Freedom of Philosophy.* New York: Columbia University.

Readings, B. (1991) *Introducing Lyotard: Art and Politics.* London and New York: Routledge.

Rickert, H. (1989) 'Max Weber's View of Science', trans. R. C. Speirs, in *Max Weber's 'Science as a Vocation',* ed. P. Lassman and I. Velody. London: Unwin Hyman.

Ringer, F. (1998) *Max Weber's Methodology: The Unification of the Cultural and Social Sciences.* London: Harvard University Press.

Ritzer, G. (1996) *The McDonaldization of Society: An Investigation into the Changing Character of Contemporary Social Life.* Thousand Oaks: Pine Forge.

Ritzer, G. (1999) *Enchanting A Disenchanted Word: Revolutionising the Means of Consumption.* Thousand Oaks: Pine Forge.

Rose, G. (1981) *Hegel Contra Sociology.* London: Athlone Press.

Rose, M. (1991) *The Post-modern and the Post-industrial.* Cambridge: Cambridge University Press.

Rosenau, P. (1992) *Postmodernism and the Social Sciences: Insights, Inroads, and Intrusions.* Princeton: Princeton University Press.

Roth, G. and Schluchter, W. (1979) *Max Weber's Vision of History: Ethics and Methods.* Berkeley: University of California Press.

Said, E. (1988) 'Michel Foucault, 1926–1984', in *After Foucault: Humanistic Knowledge, Postmodern Challenges,* ed. J. Arac. New Brunswick: Rutgers University Press.

Saussure, F. de (1974) *Course in General Linguistics,* ed. C. Bally, A. Sechehaye and A. Reidlinger, trans. W. Baskin. Glasgow: Fontana.

Sayer, D. (1991) *Capitalism and Modernity: An Excursus on Marx and Weber.* London and New York: Routledge.

Scaff, L. (1989) 'Weber Before Weberian Sociology', in *Reading Weber,* ed. K. Tribe. London and New York: Routledge.

Scaff, L. (1991) *Fleeing the Iron Cage.* Berkeley: University of California Press.

Schluchter, W. (1981) *The Rise of Western Rationalism,* trans. G. Roth. Berkeley: University of California Press.

Schluchter, W. (1989) *Rationalism, Religion, and Domination.* Berkeley: University of California Press.

Schluchter, W. (1996) *Paradoxes of Modernity: Culture and Conduct in the Theory of Max Weber,* trans. N. Solomon. Stanford: Stanford University Press.

Schroeder, R. (1987) 'Nietzsche and Weber: Two "Prophets" of the Modern World', in *Max Weber, Rationality and Modernity*, ed. S. Whimster and S. Lash. London: Allen and Unwin.

Schroeder, R. (1992) *Max Weber and the Sociology of Culture*. London: Sage.

Schroeder, R. (ed.) (1998) *Max Weber, Democracy and Modernization*. Basingstoke: Macmillan Press – now Palgrave.

Schwentker, W. (1987) 'Passion as a Mode of Life: Max Weber, the Otto Gross Circle and Eroticism', trans. B. Selman, in *Max Weber and His Contemporaries*, ed. W. Mommsen and J. Osterhammel. London: Unwin Hyman.

Sim, S. (1996) *Jean-François Lyotard*. Hemel Hempstead: Harvester Wheatsheaf.

Simmel, G. (1997) *Simmel on Culture*, ed. D. Frisby and M. Featherstone. London: Sage.

Simons, J. (1995) *Foucault and the Political*. London and New York: Routledge.

Smart, B. (1993) *Postmodernity*. London and New York: Routledge.

Smart, B. (ed.) (1999) *Resisting McDonaldization*. Theory, Process and Critique', London: Sage.

Stauth, G. and Turner, B. (1988) *Nietzsche's Dance: Resentment, Reciprocity and Resistance in Social Life*. Oxford: Basil Blackwell.

Strauss, L. (1953) *Natural Right and History*. Chicago: The University of Chicago Press.

Swedberg, R. (1998) *Max Weber and the Idea of Economic Sociology*. Princeton: Princeton University Press.

Szakolczai, A. (1998) *Max Weber and Michel Foucault: Parallel Life-Works*. London and New York: Routledge.

Tenbruck, F. H. (1989) 'The Problem of Thematic Unity in the Works of Max Weber', trans. M. S. Whimster, in *Reading Weber*, ed. K. Tribe. London and New York: Routledge.

Tiryakian, E. A. (1966) 'A Problem for the Sociology of Knowledge: The Mutual Unawareness of Emile Durkheim and Max Weber'. *European Journal of Sociology*, 7/2, 330–6.

Tolstoy, L. (1934) *On Life and Essays on Religion*, trans. A. Maude. London: Oxford University Press.

Tolstoy, L. (1937) *Recollections and Essays*, trans. A. Maude. London: Oxford University Press.

Tolstoy, L. (1993) *War and Peace*. Ware: Wordsworth Classics.

Tönnies, F. (1955) *Community and Association*, trans. C. Loomis. London: Routledge and Kegan Paul.

Turner, B. (1996) *For Max Weber: Essays on the Sociology of Fate*, 2nd edn. London: Sage.

Turner, C. (1990) 'Lyotard and Weber: Postmodern Rules and Neo-Kantian Values', in *Theories of Modernity and Postmodernity*, ed. B. Turner. London: Sage.

Turner, C. (1992) *Modernity and Politics in the Work of Max Weber*. London: Routledge.

Turner, S. and Factor, R. (1984) *Max Weber and the Dispute Over Reason and Value: A Study in Philosophy, Ethics, and Politics*. London: Routledge and Kegan Paul.

Turner, S. and Factor, R. (1994) *Max Weber: The Lawyer as Social Thinker*. London and New York: Routledge.

Voegelin, E. (1925) 'Über Max Weber'. *Deutsche Vierteljahresschrift für Literaturwissenschaft und Geistesgeschichte*, 3, 177–93.

Waltzer, M. (1976) *The Revolution of the Saints: A Study in the Origins of Radical Politics.* New York: Atheneum.

Warren, M. (1994) 'Nietzsche and Weber: When Does Reason Become Power?', in *The Barbarism of Reason: Max Weber and the Twilight of the Enlightenment,* ed. A. Horowitz and T. Maley. Toronto: University of Toronto Press.

Watson, S. (1994) 'Applying Foucault', in *Reassessing Foucault: Power, Medicine and the Body,* ed. C. Jones and R. Porter. London and New York: Routledge.

Weber, Marianne (1975) *Max Weber: A Biography,* trans. H. Zohn. New York: John Wiley and Sons.

Weber, Max (1922) *Gesammelte Aufsätze zur Religionssoziologie, I.* Tübingen: J. C. B. Mohr.

Weber, Max (1923) *Gesammelte Aufsätze zur Religionssoziologie, II.* Tübingen: J. C. B. Mohr.

Weber, Max (1949) *The Methodology of the Social Sciences,* ed. and trans. E. A. Shils and H. A. Finch. New York: The Free Press.

Weber, Max (1951) *Gesammelte Aufsätze zur Wissenschaftslehre,* ed. J. Winckelmann. Tübingen: J. C. B. Mohr.

Weber, Max (1958a) *Gesammelte Politische Schriften.* Tübingen: J. C. B. Mohr.

Weber, Max (1958b) *The Rational and Social Foundations of Music,* trans. D. Martindale. Carbondale: Southern Illinois University Press.

Weber, Max (1967a) *Ancient Judaism,* trans. H. H. Gerth and D. Martindale. New York: Free Press.

Weber, Max (1967b) *The Religion of India,* trans. H. H. Gerth and D. Martindale. New York: Free Press.

Weber, Max (1968) *The Religion of China,* trans H. H. Gerth. New York: Free Press.

Weber, Max (1970) *From Max Weber,* ed. and trans. H. H. Gerth and C. Wright Mills. London: Routledge.

Weber, Max (1975) *Roscher and Knies: The Logical Problems of Historical Economics,* trans. G. Oakes. New York: Free Press.

Weber, Max (1976) *The Agrarian Sociology of Ancient Civilizations,* trans. R. I. Frank. London: New Left Books.

Weber, Max (1978a) *Economy and Society,* 2 vols, ed. G. Roth and C. Wittich, trans. E. Fischoff, H. Gerth, A. M. Henderson, F. Kolegar, C. Wright Mills, T. Parsons, M. Rheinstein, G. Roth, E. Shils and C. Wittich. Berkeley: University of California Press.

Weber, Max (1978b) *Weber: Selections in Translation,* ed. W. G. Runciman, trans. E. Matthews. Cambridge: Cambridge University Press.

Weber, Max (1978c) 'Anticritical Last Word on The Spirit of Capitalism', trans. W. M. Davis. *American Journal of Sociology,* 83, 1110–30.

Weber, M. (1981) *General Economic History,* trans. F. Knight. New Brunswick: Transaction Books.

Weber, Max (1989) 'The National State and Economic Policy (Inaugural Lecture, Freiburg, May 1895)', trans. B. Fowkes, in *Reading Weber,* ed. K. Tribe. London: Routledge.

Weber, Max (1992) *The Protestant Ethic and the Spirit of Capitalism,* trans. T. Parsons. London and New York: Routledge.

Weber, Max (1993) *Die protestantische Ethik und der 'Geist' des Kapitalismus.* Bodenheim: Athenäum Hain Hanstein.

Weber, Max (1994) *Weber: Political Writings,* ed. P. Lassman and R. Speirs. Cambridge: Cambridge University Press.

Weber, Max (1995) *The Russian Revolutions*, trans. and ed. G. C. Wells and P. Baehr. Cambridge: Polity Press.

Weiss, J. (1986) *Weber and the Marxist World*, trans. E. King-Utz and M. J. King. London and New York: Routledge and Kegan Paul.

Whimster, S. (1995) 'Max Weber on the Erotic and Some Comparisons with the Work of Foucault'. *International Sociology*, 10/4, December, 447–62.

Whimster, S. (1996–7) 'Max Weber, Rationality and Irrationality'. *Aldgate Papers in Social and Cultural Theory*, 1, 5–23.

Whimster, S. (ed.) (1999) *Max Weber and the Culture of Anarchy*. Basingstoke: Macmillan Press – now Palgrave.

Whimster, S. and Lash, S. (eds) (1987) *Max Weber, Rationality and Modernity*. London: Allen and Unwin.

Williams, J. (2000) *Lyotard and the Political*. London and New York: Routledge.

Wilson, H. T. (1976) 'Reading Max Weber: The Limits of Sociology'. *Sociology*, 10/2, May, 297–315.

Wolin, S. (1994) 'Legitimation, Method, and the Politics of Theory', in *The Barbarism of Reason: Max Weber and the Twilight of the Enlightenment*, ed. A. Horowitz and T. Maley. Toronto: University of Toronto Press.

Index

Adair-Toteff, C.   74
Adorno, T.   2, 50, 99, 157
affirmation   108
Albers, J.   107
Albrow, M.   3
Alexander, J.   158
Antonio, R.   157
Arato, A.   164
archaeology   114, 116
Aristotle   64, 73, 85
art *see* value-spheres (aesthetic)
authority *see* legitimacy, domination

Bacon, F.   50
Bataille, G.   3, 134, 158, 173,
    175
Baudrillard, J.   4, 10–11, 43, 60,
    83–4, 86–8, 100, 131–55, 158,
    169–70, 174, 176
Bauman, Z.   2, 37, 50, 61, 123, 167,
    171
Baumgarten, E.   177
Beck, U.   156, 178
Beetham, D.   164
Bellah, R.   162
Bendix, R.   5, 38, 165
Benjamin, W.   137
Bennington, G.   100, 171
Bernstein, J.   3
Best, S.   110, 167, 171–2
Blanchot, M.   173
Bloch, E.   31
Breines, P.   164
Brubaker, R.   5, 68–9, 76, 77
Bruun, H. H.   75
Burckhardt, J.   165
bureaucracy 24,   26–7, 94, 160–1
    see also domination (bureaucratic)
Burger, T.   157

calling   19
Callinicos, A.   157
Calvin, J.   19

capitalism   19–21, 24, 32, 102, 122,
    132, 151, 161
Carroll, D.   106, 167, 171–2
categorical imperative   76
catastrophe theory   94
charisma   73
    see also domination
childhood of thought   85
Clausewitz, K.   125
communism   1
community   29–30, 99
Comte, A.   62, 164
critical theory (Frankfurt School)   3
culture   1–2, 22–4, 29, 103, 111, 142
    consumer   104
    homogenization of   28, 43
    modern   7, 10, 15, 22, 28–9, 35,
        41–2, 48, 62, 78–9, 83–5, 87–8,
        95–6, 99–100, 113–15, 147,
        151, 153
    postmodern *see* postmodern,
        postmodernism, postmodernity
    sociology of   2
    Western   3–4, 8–9, 11, 15, 104–5,
        114, 139
    see also rationalization (cultural)
cultural differentiation   8, 10, 28–34,
    40, 42, 89, 95, 94–102, 139, 151,
    170
cultural theory   1–2

da Vinci, L.   50
Dean, M.   115, 173
de-differentiation   8, 41–4
Deleuze, G.   174
Derrida, J.   3, 125, 168
Descartes, R.   160
devaluation (*Entwerten*)   23, 27, 29,
    48, 52, 159
    see also disenchantment
Dews, P.   171–2
difference   10, 85–6, 98, 101, 103,
    116–17, 125, 138

différend 98–9, 109, 112, 153
Diggins, J. 3, 52, 71, 157
disenchantment (*Entzauberung*) 4,
   8–11, 15–46, 48–9, 51, 63–4, 78,
   83, 87–9, 104–5, 112, 120, 136,
   145–6, 149, 151, 155, 159
domination 2, 114, 119, 151–2
  bureaucratic (legal-rational) 8,
    24–5, 43, 141
  charismatic 8, 25–6, 52, 141
  traditional 8, 25–6
Dostoyevsky, L. 163
Drysdale, J. 157
Durkheim, E. 2, 36– 40, 47–9, 54,
   59, 62, 69, 158, 160, 164
duty 76

Eden, R. 3, 38, 166
Elias, N. 165
Enlightenment 2, 51–3, 61, 63, 92,
   118, 147
ethics 11, 37, 124–9
  of conviction (*Gesinnungsethik*) 9,
    64, 66–79, 165–6
  of responsibility (*Verantwortungsethik*)
    9, 64, 66–79, 165
  religious 22, 89
ethical irrationality 65, 78, 125
excess 109

Factor, R. 71, 157, 166
Featherstone, M. 43, 48
Fichte, J. G. 92, 126
figure 106–8
Foucault, M. 2–4, 10, 11, 43, 65,
   83–8, 100–1, 113–30, 131, 151–5,
   158, 167, 169–70, 172–5
fractal theory 94, 138
Fraser, N. 174
Freud, S. 85, 106–7, 168, 172
Freund, J. 5
future anterior 84, 86, 102
  identity 86, 115

Galileo 50
Gane, N. 2, 7, 52, 117, 121, 165
Gellner, E. 167
genealogy 11, 84, 86, 113–25,
   128–9, 139, 153, 173

Genosko, G. 175
George, S. 60
gerontocracy 25
Gerth, H. 74, 162, 165
gift exchange 134–5, 147
Giradin, J-C. 175
Glassman, R. 157
Godzich, W. 171
Gordon, C. 3, 113, 120
grand narratives *see* metanarratives
Grant, I. H. 172
Green, M. 177–8
Gross, O. 177–8

Habermas, J. 3, 5, 21, 24, 40, 117,
   121, 128, 161, 174
Hanke, E. 163
Hassan, I. 168
Hegel, G. 3, 84, 92, 169
Heidegger, M. 3
Hennis, W. 3, 4, 6, 122, 157
heteronomy 76–8
history of the present *see* genealogy
Hollingdale, R. J. 159, 164
Holton, R. 2, 3, 7–8, 28–9, 41–2, 88,
   158, 160
Honigsheim, P. 163
Horkheimer, M. 2, 50, 157
Horowitz, A. 157
humanness (*Menschentum*) 6–7, 25,
   121–2

ideal-types 30, 66, 121, 158
innovation 106
Itten, J. 107

Jaffé, E. 176–7
Jameson, F. 52, 157
Jaspers, K. 78, 166
Jencks, C. 168
Judaism 18, 160
judgement 73–5, 109, 115
jurisprudence 56–7

Kandinsky, W. 107
Kant, I. 3, 41, 56, 64, 76–7, 85,
   108–9, 168, 172–3
Karádi, E. 164
Käsler, D. 157, 177

Kaufman, W.   159
Kellner, D.   110, 167, 171
Kemple, T. M.   3, 52
Kent, S.   5, 164
Kierkegaard, S.   151
Klee, P.   107
Kleist, O.   148
Kronman, A.   71
Kuhn, T.   105

Lacan, J.   176
Landshut, S.   60
language games   95–6, 100–1,
    103
Lash, S.   114, 120, 156–7, 178
Lask, E.   176
Lassman, P.   3, 62, 74, 157, 169
law   40, 56–7, 163
    natural   35, 40–1
legitimacy   10, 21, 30, 35–6, 55–7,
    61, 91–2
Lenhardt, C.   77
Lenin, V.   157
Lepenies, W.   60, 155
Lévinas, E.   168
Lévi-Strauss, C.   176
Lewis, J.   157
life-orders (*Lebensordnungen*)   8, 28,
    31, 99, 161
Löwith, K.   5, 47, 50, 66, 157
Lukács, G.   31, 56, 164
Luther, M.   19, 165–6
Lyotard, J-F.   2, 4, 10–1, 62, 83–113,
    129, 131, 149, 151–6, 158,
    167–73, 175

Macey, D.   172
Maffesoli, M.   2
magic   16
Mahon, M   173
Maley, T.   157
Mandelbrot, B.   94
Marcuse, H.   61, 157
Marx, K.   1, 5, 37, 49, 62, 84, 107,
    132–3, 157, 169, 174–5
Mauss, M.   134, 175
Mayer, J. P.   70
McCarthy, T.   3
McKeon, R.   108

metanarratives   11, 84, 87, 92, 96,
    99, 101, 112, 129–30, 169
metaphysics   3, 56, 91
Miller, J.   173
Mills, C. W.   74, 162, 165
Mitzman, A.   75
modernity   2–3, 8, 11, 21, 24, 35, 44,
    63, 84–5, 88, 95, 97, 112, 119–23,
    132, 135, 149, 152–4, 167
Mommsen, W.   6, 43, 44, 74, 157,
    164–5
Münch, R.   158
mysticism   32–3
myth   15, 91

naturalism   16–17
natural right   35, 38–40
neo-Kantianism   31, 37, 58, 90,
    95–9, 112, 121, 123, 126
Nietzsche, F.   2, 3, 9, 15, 18, 21, 24,
    40–2, 45–6, 49–53, 61–4, 107,
    115, 121–3, 157–8, 160, 163, 165,
    172
nihilism   2, 4, 8, 15, 21, 26, 38,
    40–2, 45, 52, 88, 107
normalization   119–20

Oakes, G.   157, 164
otherness   10
O'Neill, J.   3, 50, 120
Osterhammel, J.   6, 157
Owen, D.   2–3, 15, 18, 73, 113,
    121–2, 157

paralogy   85, 92, 106, 110, 153
    see also science (postmodern)
Parsons, T.   5, 158, 164
Pascal, B.   45
pathology   36
patriarchalism   25
patrimonialism   25
Pefanis, J.   175
Plato 49,   163
Plessner, H.   155
political leadership   65–79, 124–6
polytheism   29
positivism   35
postmodern
    definition of   83–5, 167–8

theory 3–4, 7, 83, 87, 154–5
postmodernism 3, 96, 169
postmodernity 3, 97, 101
power 69, 74, 93, 119, 124, 139
  bio-power 114, 119–20
  power/knowledge 113–15, 117–18
predestination 19
Protestantism 18–21, 32, 160, 163

Rajchman, J. 117
rationality 5–7, 21–22
  value (*Wertrationalität*) 2, 8–10,
      26, 59, 71, 96, 98–9, 103, 105,
      158
  instrumental (*Zweckrationalität*) 2,
      10, 63, 71, 93, 105, 113–14,
      118, 143, 157–8
  see also social action
rationalization 2, 4–11, 15–46, 49,
      51, 55, 59, 63–4, 77–9, 83, 87–9,
      91, 95, 98–106, 111–12, 116, 120,
      123, 130–1, 135, 140, 142, 145,
      147–55
  cultural 20, 23–4, 89, 102,
      113–14, 152
  reversal of 86, 140
  societal 23–6
Readings, B. 106, 167, 171
reason 38, 109, 145, 147
  instrumental 2, 8–9, 26, 44, 46,
      59, 61, 77, 87, 98–9, 102, 112,
      151–4
  scientific 37, 39–40, 50, 63
  subject-centred 3
re-enchantment 11, 41, 87, 131–50
religion 29, 104, 142–3
  primitive 8
  universal 8, 15, 17–18
responsibility *see* ethics
Rickert, H. 31, 53, 98, 121, 163–4
Ringer, F. 157
Ritzer, G. 2, 87, 170, 176
Rose, G. 164, 170
Rosenau, P. 167
Roth, G. 38, 67, 165

Said, E. 173
Saussure, F. 133, 176
Sayer, D. 157

Scaff, L. 2–3, 6, 31, 43, 122, 157,
      161–2, 164, 177
Schluchter, W. 2, 5, 7, 52, 53, 67,
      70, 157, 159, 160, 162, 165–6
Schroeder, R. 2–3, 5, 15, 18, 24, 159,
      164
Schumpeter, J. 166
Schwab, F. 53
Schwentker, W. 178
science 2, 21, 23, 26, 35–9, 45–63,
      70, 105, 112, 127, 140–1
  cultural 113, 120–4
  fate of 46–7
  postmodern 10, 89–94, 148
  presuppositions of 55–59
  specialization of 46
  supervision of 61–2
  value of 49–53, 55, 57, 59–62
seduction 11, 86, 131, 142–50, 155
semiotics 107, 152
sign 132–7, 175–6
Sim, S. 172
Simmel, G. 47–8, 60
Simons, J. 117
simulation 137–9
simulcra
  orders of 135–9, 145
Smart, B. 87, 158, 170
social action 5, 26, 68, 123, 155
  instrumentally rational 25, 65–6,
      70, 75
  value-rational 25, 27, 65–7, 75
social theory 2, 3
Socrates 49
Spiers, R. 74
Stalin, J. 157
Stauth, G. 3
Strauss, L. 38–40, 49, 162
sublime 108–9
  modern and postmodern
      approaches to 110–11
sultanism 25
Swedberg, R. 159, 163
symbolic exchange 11, 84, 87,
      132–5, 139–40, 143, 145, 147,
      175
symbolic order 11, 54, 86–7, 131,
      135, 141, 152, 154
symbolism 17

Szakolczai, A.   3, 158, 172

Tenbruck, F.   5, 158–9
Thom, R.   94
time   83–4, 97, 167
Tiryakian, E.   158
Tobler, M.   176–7
Tolstoy, L.   9, 45–6, 48, 53–5, 57, 63, 163
Tönnies, F.   60
transgression   117, 120, 122
Turner, B.   2–3, 7–8, 28, 29, 41–2, 88, 158, 160
Turner, C.   3, 29–31, 38, 89, 95–100, 162, 165–6
Turner, S.   71, 157, 166

ultimate values   9–10, 20–1, 23, 25–6, 29–30, 38, 48, 51–2, 61, 64, 70, 77–8, 124
utilitarianism   51

value   132–5, 139–40, 144
value-freedom (*Wertfreiheit*)   37, 39, 59, 61, 74, 120, 123, 127
value-incommensurability   38, 58–9, 71, 97
value-judgements   9, 37, 54, 58, 70, 127, 154
value-philosophy *see* neo-Kantianism
value-relevance (*Wertbeziehung*)   58
value-spheres (*Wertsphären*)   8, 35, 40–1, 43, 56, 96, 99–100, 104, 138, 140, 161–2
    aesthetic   10, 43, 88, 103–12, 141, 148
    economic   32–3, 42

erotic   11, 43, 88, 131, 142–6
intellectual   33–4, 42
political   33, 42, 88, 113–130
relgious   31
Velody, I.   3, 62, 157, 169
vocation (*Beruf*)   32, 44–79
Voegelin, E.   66

Waltzer, M.   163
war   125
Warren, M.   3
Watson, S.   174
Weber, Marianne   31, 131, 165, 177
Weber, Max
    Economy and Society   75
    Gesammelte Aufsätze zur Religionssoziologie   30–1
    'Intermediate Reflection'   (the '*Zwischenbetrachtung*')   8, 30–4, 111, 140, 143, 162
    personal life   176–7
    'Politics as a Vocation'   64–79, 122
    'Science as a Vocation'   9, 45–63, 111, 122, 149
    The Agrarian Sociology of Ancient Civilizations   122
    The Protestant Ethic and the Spirit of Capitalism   6, 24, 51, 122
    The Religion of India   122
Weiss, J.   157
Whimster, S.   2–3, 157, 159, 177–8
Williams, J.   172
Wilson, H. T.   3
Windelband, W.   31
Wittgenstein, L.   85
Wolin, S.   163, 165